I-DEALS:

Idiosyncratic

Deals Employees

Bargain for

Themselves

Denise M. Rousseau

I-DEALS:

Idiosyncratic Deals Employees Bargain for Themselves

M.E.Sharpe
Armonk, New York
London, England

Library of Congress Cataloging-in-Publication Data

Rousseau, Denise M.
 I-deals, idiosyncratic deals employees bargain for themselves / by Denise
M. Rousseau.
    p. cm.
 Includes bibliographical references and index.
 ISBN 0-7656-1042-6 (cloth : alk. paper) — ISBN 0-7656-1043-4 (pbk. : alk. paper)
 1. Industrial relations. 2. Negotiation. 3. Deals. I. Title: I-deals.
 II. Title.

HD6971.R69 2005
650.1—dc22   2004026588

To my husband,
Paul S. Goodman—scholar, educator, film maker and sailor

Contents

Preface and Acknowledgments

My motives in writing this book are both professional and personal. Professionally, as an organizational psychologist who has spent many years in field settings, I have witnessed an amazing array of employment arrangements among individuals working for the same employer, ostensibly doing the same job. In my fieldwork, I find ample evidence of intra–work group differences in the psychological contracts and on-the-job behaviors of workers, from staff nurses to research scientists.[1] These differences hold true even for people doing similar work for the same boss. I have come to believe that idiosyncratic deals individual workers have negotiated for themselves are important contributors to this variation.

A wit might say that this book's subject is tailorism, since it calls attention to the ways employees shape their own employment, in contrast to top-down, employer-driven arrangements, the Taylorism conventionally implemented via scientific management.[2] The tailorism that idiosyncratic deals reflect can be a means for all of us as individual workers to have *who we are* taken into account in our organizational roles and employment relations. Idiosyncratic deals also can contribute to the well-being of the firm and its collective workforce by making it easier to improvise and adapt to a changing environment. A passage from Mike Arthur, Kerr Inkson, and Judith Pringle's book on individualized careers captures the kind of worker and work situation on which this book focuses:

> Priscilla's identity is a cross between "loyal company servant" and "enterprising business professional." She identifies strongly with the company, and prides herself on excellence at every job in the office. Yet the list of acquired skills that she reels off, and the client base she has built, are not necessarily company-

specific. She has become an accomplished designer and business person with transferable skills and a portable network. She is married and would like to have children and hopes the company will negotiate to let her work part-time, at least temporarily. When the moment for that negotiation comes, one can imagine the company needing her more than she needs the company.[3]

Like Priscilla, the workers described in this book are valued by their employer and as a result have bargaining power in shaping the conditions of their employment. It is important to note that, like Priscilla, they, too, have chosen *not* to work as freelancers or independent contractors. The people described in this book are employees working within firms, among colleagues and coworkers with whom they interact day to day—where their productivity depends to some extent on the sustained cooperation and goodwill of their fellow workers.

Very little attention has been given to how to make individualized treatment fair for people who must work together. Justice research typically maintains that standardization is the key to fairness.[4] Yet workers as individuals don't always want the same things. Moreover, it is often impractical for employers to offer the same things to everyone. For instance, a few workers going from full- to part-time employment might be fine, but having everybody do so could create chaos. Nonetheless, in a world where new services and products are created every day, individuals can easily come to value things for which employers have no set policies—from traveling to France from the Netherlands each Thursday night to attend a weekend executive program to the opportunity for an employer to spin off part of a firm's training function into a profit-generating subsidiary. Employer responses to such requests aren't readily standardized. The saying "separate but equal never is" underscores the problem of how to treat people fairly when they value different kinds of flexibility—more still when what they value is subject to change.

Workers have long desired greater say in the terms of their employment.[5] Little scholarly attention has been given to how individual employees can genuinely participate, influencing the employment relations to which they contribute so much of their lives. Individual negotiation is itself a form of participation. Of course, all workers aren't in a position to negotiate. An employer who engages the services of many workers may care little about the services of any particular one. While the latter condition characterizes marginally skilled workers, others can and do bargain for themselves when they recognize that they are valued and valuable.

Conventional industrial relations generates only standardized solutions to employee demands for participation. Collective bargaining and high-performance work teams limit their focus to the common bread-and-butter needs workers in general hold or to the interests of the average worker. Insofar as standard solutions leave many worker needs and interests to fall through the cracks, idiosyncratic deals provide an alternative. Complicating the picture is the evidence that standardized responses to employee demands for participation are being eroded, particularly in the United States. The decline of collective bargaining parallels a reduction in the standard benefits both unionized and nonunionized employers offer as conditions of regular employment. More is left to individual workers to seek out for themselves.[6]

The desire for a voice in matters in which one's interests are affected is particularly high in the United States, where private employers have more influence over employee well-being than do employers in other industrialized countries. Where workers are valued and mobile, they are in a position to demand more varied and expanded choices in employment arrangements. In particular, knowledge workers with skills more portable than those possessed by past generations comprise a growing portion of the contemporary labor force, making it likely that individual bargaining will increasingly be the norm in employment relations.[7] These issues raise important concerns for organizational scholars, workers, and managers seeking to understand and navigate the changing nature of employment.

My other motives in writing this book are more personal. Growing up in a blue-collar family, I was raised with the inevitable assumption that "you don't bargain with the company." The union bargained, and we waited for the negotiations—and sometimes the strike—to be settled. Though individualized arrangements were the mainstay in employment arrangements up until the early twentieth century, these types of arrangements are unfamiliar territory in unionized settings. The long-standing assumption of trade unionism maintains that individual workers cannot bargain effectively.[8] It presumes that workers have no money in reserve, must sell their labor immediately or risk someone else taking their job, have no market knowledge, and possess no bargaining skills. With only his or her own labor to sell, the worker is disadvantaged. This belief—often this reality—that a person cannot bargain on his or her own can take a toll on an individual's sense of mastery, membership, and meaning at work and potentially in other parts of life as well. The ability to assert one's interests is a basic requirement of human dignity, reflecting the need to have influence over matters affecting important aspects of one's life.

I have been fortunate to learn as an adult that there are other possibilities. When my daughters were young, I faced the typical working-mother challenges of trying to juggle caring for them, a full-time academic job, and the need to make ends meet as a single parent. A consulting firm called to ask whether I would help design a survey for a client. In thinking it over, I realized that while I wanted the work, the very thought of having to put on a professional demeanor and a business suit to visit the firm and get up to speed on this project made me weary. On impulse, I said, "I'll do it if I don't have to come to your office all dressed up." The principal I spoke to on the phone was a woman who also had been a single parent. Without skipping a beat, she said, "No problem." Two days later I went to her office in sweats, just to be sure she meant it. I am happy to report that I worked for this firm for several years. The flexibility it provided and the friendships I developed there form the basis of a story I have told my daughters over the years while encouraging them to test the waters for themselves. If an idiosyncratic deal can be made around consulting in sweats, the possibilities are endless.

Since I married my husband, Paul Goodman, I have acquired a whole new perspective on negotiation and flexibility. Some of Paul's talents in this regard surely stem from his father. My father-in-law, Morris Goodman, an accountant and adviser for many privately held businesses in New England from the 1930s to the 1960s, didn't set a billing rate in advance of performing his services for long-standing clients. He would put together deals, handle taxes, perform audits, identify prospects, develop business plans, and help arrange financing. Clients visited his house and he vacationed in their summer homes. When it came time to bill for his services, he told clients how much his services had saved them and then said, "Pay me what you think my services are worth." Not surprisingly, he retired a fairly wealthy man. In Morris's case, the confidence and high regard his clients vested in him brought a satisfying outcome from these idiosyncratic terms.

Many employees seek the same opportunity to shape the quality of their working conditions in ways that benefit themselves and their employer. However, working as an employee is a far cry from being a freelance consultant or business adviser. Employees whose performance depends at least in part on the goodwill and support of coworkers face particular challenges in creating customized arrangements. Those who bargain for themselves can be stars or deviants, trendsetters or precedent violators, privileged or vulnerable. This book explores the phenomenon of employee bargaining for idiosyncratic arrangements, its benefits, and its risks, to deepen appreciation of the influence individual workers wield in the contemporary and future workplace.

Acknowledgments

Many friends and colleagues have contributed to the development of ideas on which this book is based, including Soon Ang, Linda Babcock, Wai

Fong Boh, Barbara Brewton, Vivien Clark, Ruth Currier, Guillermo Dabos, Bill Glick, Jerry Greenberg, Severin Hornung, Violet Ho, Mark Kamlet, David Kaufer, Tai Gyu Kim, Matt Kraatz, Laurie Levesque, Roger Malek, Steve Miller, Michael Moch, Brenda Peyser, Pradeep U.N., Don Prentiss, Sandra Robinson, Tom Rousseau, Zipi Shperling, Herb Simon, Lowell Taylor, Laurie Weingart, and Mark Wessel. Alvaro Cristiani and Jason Merante provided invaluable research assistance, tracking down stray facts and intriguing details. Alvaro Cristiani and Jessica Cooke helped design the artwork included in this book. Cathy Senderling again proved a marvelous, clear-headed copy editor. Finally, as she has for the past ten years, Carole McCoy, aka "the General," did her usual superb job word processing text and figures, while managing the array of details associated with getting a manuscript in shape. Harry Briggs, my editor on this and other projects, showed amazing patience and reassuring enthusiasm. Thanks are also due to Elizabeth Granda and Amy Odum at M.E. Sharpe for managing the publication process. My husband, Paul Goodman, to whom this book is dedicated, read its numerous iterations, providing both critical feedback and sustaining faith in the project. Thank you all so very much.

Denise M. Rousseau
Pittsburgh

I-deals: Idiosyncratic Deals Employees Bargain for Themselves

Introduction

The subject of this book is how employees negotiate individualized conditions of employment. Negotiability is part and parcel of the free-agent employment pursued by independent contractors and freelancers. But regular employees also seek out and bargain for working conditions they particularly care about. Unlike free agents, however, typical employees depend on people with whom they work for their success on the job and the quality of their day-to-day work experiences. Workplace relationships with peers and colleagues make negotiating individual employment conditions far more complicated for employees than for free agents. The deals these employees make with their managers and sometimes their coworkers are the focus of this book.

Idiosyncratic deals, i-deals for short, typically manifest themselves in the quiet, informal ways in which workers and employers figure out how to make work arrangements flexible enough to meet each other's needs. These arrangements bring experimentation and innovation into human resource practices and work structures, driving adaptation to changing demands valued workers make in competitive business environments. Insofar as workers and employers benefit from idiosyncratic deals, more negative effects often befall coworkers. Injustice is the downside of individualized deals, in the form of widely unequal pay and rewards and the resultant erosion of trust between employer and employees. Moreover, while intended to benefit employee and employer, individual arrangements can put the workers who negotiated them in a vulnerable position as circumstances and managers change. Employers, too, risk creating precedents that are difficult to manage and can find it tough to create appropriate policies for dealing with exceptions.

Research on i-deals is relatively recent. Yet, the examples presented in this book are real, obtained from news reports, case studies, and research conducted in a variety of firms across many countries. With a few exceptions, the names used are pseudonyms. I supplement recent research on i-deals with findings in related areas to reveal an understudied aspect of employment, the active role employees play in shaping their own employment. By examining idiosyncratic deals from the diverse perspectives provided by related research on employment relations, leadership, work-family balance, negotiation, and justice, this book's goal is to advance understanding of how idiosyncratic deals can operate to the benefit of their three essential parties: the individual worker who bargains, the employer who grants the deal, and the coworkers who as a result are treated differently.

As the first book to focus upon idiosyncratic deals, it starts by taking the reader through the basics, describing what i-deals are, what they aren't, and how recognition of their existence has been foreshadowed in organizational research. It then drills down into the specific i-deals employees negotiate and how they do so. Next, it details the roles employers and coworkers play in creating and maintaining i-deals. Lastly, it turns to big-picture issues, addressing cross-national influences and the future promise i-deals offer as a source of innovation and flexibility for both organizations and workers. The book's layout, with brief chapter summaries, is as follows:

Defining idiosyncratic deals. Idiosyncratic deals aren't just a rare exception made for rock superstars or CEOs. Regular employees bargain for distinctive deals, too. Idiosyncratic deals result when individual employees successfully bargain for employment terms different from their coworkers', where employee and employer can both benefit.

Everyday idiosyncrasies. Individualized work arrangements arise from the inherent incompleteness of employment contracts and the flexibility that some work settings offer workers to customize their employment relationship. Inherent latitude in employment relations can permit either worker or employer to introduce changes, often without any negotiation at all. The workplace is full of idiosyncrasies workers have introduced on their own—without negotiation. Workers pursue i-deals when the idiosyncrasies they seek are difficult to introduce without the employer's approval.

Shady deals and how they differ from idiosyncratic deals. Preferential treatment and unauthorized or illicit deals—two dysfunctional arrangements sometimes confused with idiosyncratic deals—are shady deals. In contrast to idiosyncratic deals, shady deals harm the organization, undermining trust between an employer and its workforce. This chapter examines how i-deals can be kept from looking like their shady, dysfunctional counterparts.

The invisible presence of idiosyncratic deals in organizational research. Idiosyncratic deals have gone largely unrecognized in organizational research until now. Nonetheless, their occurrence coincides with phenomena observed for years in scholarly research across widely ranging areas—from work-family balance, idiosyncratic jobs, role creation, and change, to leader-member exchange, boundaryless careers, and psychological contracts.

The types of idiosyncratic deals employees negotiate. The six types of i-deals are identified by the conditions under which they occur (recruiting, performance-based rewards, or retention) and by whom they are initiated (the worker or the employer). Their psychological consequences for employees depend on the particular way a deal arose and what resources the employee obtained from it.

The processes workers use to negotiate. How workers go about negotiating an i-deal affects their likelihood of success and the deal's sustainability. Certain tactics give employees leverage in bargaining with their employer. Three critical stages and their respective tactics are explored, from the initial steps taken to prepare to bargain, through actual negotiations, to the management of the i-deal's aftermath.

How coworkers are affected. Where coworkers are concerned, the conventional wisdom regarding negotiation falls short: idiosyncratic deals may be win–win for worker and employer, but coworkers often believe themselves to be losers when a deal is struck. The ultimate effectiveness of idiosyncratic deals rests on whether they can be made "win–win–win" (or, at minimum, "win–win–no loss") from the perspective of all their parties: worker, employer, and coworkers alike.

Organizational factors shaping idiosyncratic deals. Employer interests in i-deals are shaped by the firm's human resource strategy and practices, managerial style and actions, and corporate culture. Managers play the central role in enacting the firm's human resource practices, and in this brokering role, they shape the frequency, content, and sustainability of i-deals.

Cross-national perspectives. How individual workers approach bargaining depends in part on societal factors. Societies differ in whether workers can directly ask for what they want, whether it is acceptable to be different from peers, and whether their preferences are socially permitted.

Lessons. Idiosyncratic deals call attention to the collective as well as individual nature of justice. Making i-deals work in a win–win–win fashion requires development and learning on the part of both workers and firms, including a deeper appreciation of justice and an enhanced capacity to experiment and learn.

Idiosyncratic deals lead workers and employers on a course fraught with unpredictability, novelty, inconsistency, and precedent setting. They challenge the conventions of standardization and consistency that dominate ideologies espoused in management practice. The reader will decide whether they are dangerous exceptions or normal day-to-day experiences—or both. Idiosyncratic deals may be the kind of phenomenon Elbert Hubbard had in mind when he said, "An idea that is not dangerous is unworthy of being called at idea at all."

— 1 —

What Is an Idiosyncratic Deal?

"Educational leave" for two Corning engineers to
spend a year doing underwater photography.[1]

Access to corporate planes, apartment, cars, for
20 years. Financial planning with $8,000 limit in
reimbursable expenses annually, home security services . . .
— From IBM CEO Louis V. Gerstner Jr.'s retirement package.[2]

I-deals are special conditions of employment negotiated between an individual worker and his or her employer.[3] An i-deal can alter a single feature of a worker's relationship with an employer, as in the case of a trusted worker who seeks to work on a special project while enjoying the same compensation, title, hours, and work setting as his or her coworkers. Or, an i-deal can render every aspect of a worker's employment unique and customized, a circumstance enjoyed by a former chief executive who stays on as an adviser long after formally retiring, with special duties, compensation, perks, and recognition.[4]

I-deals are common in the workplace, yet their precise makeup is often invisible. Like the greater part of an iceberg, many aspects of i-deals lie below the waterline of public awareness. I-deals constitute the more private aspect of a highly personal experience: the customized arrangements, special conditions, or accommodations a worker obtains from an employer. Our focus is the nature of these arrangements, their consequences (positive and negative), and the processes whereby i-deals arise—in particular, the often secret negotiations between one worker and his or her employer.

This chapter sets the stage for this book. It defines i-deals, describes their distinctive features, and illustrates the kinds of i-deals workers negotiate. Finally, it highlights some of the dilemmas i-deals raise that must be addressed for them to benefit all the parties involved.

Defining I-deals

Idiosyncratic deals are voluntary, personalized agreements of a nonstandard nature that individual employees negotiate with their employers regarding terms that benefit them both. These individualized employment arrangements differ in some fashion from those received by others in the organization employed to do similar work. Several distinct features characterize i-deals and differentiate them from more dysfunctional and generally unfair forms of person-specific employment arrangements (e.g., cronyism or favoritism).[5] Specifically, i-deals are

- individually negotiated by a worker;
- different from the employment conditions experienced by others in that worker's work group or unit, even among those who have negotiated their own i-deals;
- beneficial to both the worker and the employer; and
- varying in scope from a single feature to the entire employment relationship.

Individually Negotiated Deals

An i-deal arises when a worker negotiates a customized arrangement with an employer. The market power of certain workers, or the value their employer places on them, or both, puts them in a position to demand significantly greater perquisites than their less-advantaged coworkers receive. These conditions also make workers more willing to negotiate rather than merely accept what an employer offers.[6]

A central feature of i-deals is that the employee directly negotiates with the employer regarding some aspect of his or her employment. The concept of an individual worker bargaining with an employer flies in the face of traditional notions of labor relations.[7] The conventional labor-management relationship, in which the firm sets the price and work conditions and the worker accepts or rejects the offer, is predicated on a view of individual workers as powerless in comparison to the firm. It presumes workers have no money in reserve, must sell their labor immediately or else another will readily take their place, have no market knowledge, and possess no talent for bargaining. Contemporary firms, however, do increasingly depend on worker skills and organization-specific knowledge, which in themselves can provide sustainable competitive advantage.[8] Under such conditions, individual workers can have considerable bargaining power.

Our focus is on workers who recognize that they have power—knowledge workers and others with scarce and highly valued skills—who can behave in ways often unimaginable to those who see themselves as having less power. The notion of individual workers having power was to a great extent unimaginable at the turn of the twentieth century in industrialized nations, on the heels of twenty years of violently squashed strikes in the dominant industries of the day, such as coal and steel.[9] The dominant industries of the twenty-first century have a different balance of power. Insofar as their employer gains competitive advantage through its workforce, individual workers are more likely to assert their preferences and be accommodated by employers when they possess valued resources and can control their use. Valued resources include worker skills, knowledge, and relationships (with coworkers, customers, or suppliers) that increase productivity. Employees are positioned to exert control over their efforts when the work they do is not highly standardized or easily monitored. Unlike assembly-line work, for example, knowledge work allows employees to control their own work processes and output. This control extends from shaping the information and analyses used to solve a design problem or write a policy report to the quality of the relationships built with customers and clients.

Mobility makes it possible for a worker to decide when, how, and for whom to be productive. Workers cannot bargain effectively where they can be easily laid off, replaced, or forced into retirement. In contrast, many workers have alternatives to joining or remaining with a particular firm. They may go to work for another employer for whom their skills have value. Some have the opportunity to become productive not only with an employer, but also by going it alone as independent contractors or as entrepreneurs who become employers themselves. In a survey of high-technology employers in Pittsburgh, the vast majority of employers indicated that at least some of their employees were capable of successfully founding their own businesses.[10] This mix of roles and identities creates blurry boundaries between the notions of the individual as a worker, self-manager, and entrepreneur owner or contractor.[11] Yet the essence of the traditional trade unionist's assumption still holds: To bargain advantageously, a worker needs to be in a powerful position, and this means having three things: control over the exercise of his or her labor or use of scarce knowledge, possession

9

of market information relevant to both labor and the employing organization itself, and some skill in negotiating. When these conditions come together, the individual worker who recognizes the power of his or her position can effectively negotiate terms of employment. Nonetheless, not all idiosyncrasies need to be bargained for. As we shall see, in many instances workers have the means to customize certain features of their own jobs without employer approval. It is when they lack the opportunity or authority to do so that negotiation enters the picture.

I-deals can arise at the worker's initiative, as, for instance, when a banker requests paid leave to attend an international executive program overseas. Alternatively, a worker can negotiate an i-deal after the company initiates a change, as, for instance, in the case of the engineer who bargains for special pay and career opportunities when asked to accept a transfer. In either case, to negotiate an i-deal a worker must believe he or she has the power to do so.

Heterogeneity: Differences Among Coworkers

I-deals grant a worker certain conditions of employment that differ from those of other employees in similar positions or in the same work group. The result is intra-workgroup heterogeneity in some aspects of the rewards and benefits employees receive.[12] This variation is a potential motivator as well as a source of perceived inequity and injustice.

Our focus is on regular employees. We are *not* talking about the kind of work variation Dan Pink describes in his fascinating book *Free Agent Nation*.[13] The workers I have in mind are not the independent contractor cum permalancer, hired gun, guru, lone worker, or 1099er (Form 1099 is the tax form received by self-employed American workers) that Pink describes, though they may desire many of the same things. Rather, we are dealing with the full-time office worker in a corporate headquarters, valued marketing manager in a high-tech company, creative designer in a start-up firm, corporate accountant in a petrochemical plant, veteran steelworker in a small Pennsylvania factory, and tenured college professor or her administrative assistant, among many others, each of whom has bargained successfully for some condition of employment that their coworkers doing the same work do not have. This book brings a different perspective to the study of employment by investigating the conditions under which individual *employees* enjoy unique flexibility, special training, unusually challenging projects, more resources, and other working conditions that differ from those of their coworkers in the same jobs.

Being able to garner idiosyncratic conditions in one's employment is a sign of one's acceptance as a valuable contributor to the organization—someone worthy of special treatment, a situation akin to the phenomenon of *idiosyncrasy credits* accorded to high-status group members.[14] In circumstances where the distinctive qualities of high-status members create tolerance of their special treatment or unusual behavior on the part of others in the group, the concept of idiosyncrasy credits explains how exceptions come to be acceptable in work groups, as with this example from a Pennsylvania steel mill:

> One guy who kind of got special treatment worked on the paint line. He was probably the most senior guy in the mill, although he was only around 40 or 45. This guy did the same thing every day. He hung beams on the paint line, all day long. I did this job before, and consider it physically the most difficult in the mill. But this guy loved it, and he was amazing at it. He was like a machine in his ability to work constantly, or at whatever the pace of the paint line was. Everyone in the mill liked and respected this guy. When he wanted to take a break, we did so, even if the boss was coming around. It was understood that when he was on the job, the work would get done. Management and the workers did what they could to accommodate this guy.[15]

I-deals originate from some of the same processes as the idiosyncratic arrangement the steelworker enjoyed: the idiosyncrasy credits accorded a person of high contribution or distinctive value to the employer.[16] The bargaining leverage these credits afford can be used to obtain special visibility and recognition, along with more concrete rewards, such as money and perks. In one case, an outside offer given to a high-status employee caused his coworkers to storm the office of the president asking that the firm counter it in order to retain the colleague they saw as a star. Implicit in the use of idiosyncrasy credits is the existence of a differentiated perception of an individual and his or her contributions on the part of fellow group members. In the case of i-deals, this differentiated perception regarding an individual worker is extended to the employer. A worker's capacity to negotiate an i-deal is based on beliefs on the part of the employer (or the managers representing it) that that worker differs from peers with respect to his or her past, present, or future contribution to the firm. This is to say that the individual worker who successfully negotiates an i-deal is seen as a valued contributor, in good standing with the firm, and possibly more valuable to the firm than his or her fellow workers. This differentiated regard promotes the granting of an i-deal because employers can be expected to be reluctant to create exceptional arrangements for one worker unless there is a good reason to do so. Whether employer and coworkers share the same high regard for the would-be i-dealer is an important factor in determining whether an i-deal an employer grants one worker is viewed as fair by his or her colleagues.

Differential treatment among work-group members can mean different things to the employer, the individual worker, and the worker's coworkers. From the perspective of an employer who allocates opportunities for flexibility differentially among a set of workers, this heterogeneity reflects the practice of rewarding high performers.[17] To a worker negotiating an i-deal, it can signal the special value an employer places on him or her. To coworkers, differences among themselves in the nature of such opportunities can signal their own relative standing in the eyes of the employer (whether higher or lower), as well as their employer's supportiveness, fairness, or trustworthiness, depending on the information they possess, the comparisons they make, and the nature of their own relationship with the employer.[18]

It is important to note that workers experience i-deals differently depending upon whether they are its principals or third parties. A consultant who has negotiated an assignment to special projects that will further develop her own valuable technical skills may believe her employer is very supportive. Her coworkers, unaware of why certain projects are allocated to only one person, may see the employer playing favorites while neglecting the rest. Despite the potential within-group friction, idiosyncratic arrangements can be seen as fair by third parties, *if* steps are taken to appropriately differentiate i-deals from other arrangements that are patently unjust and self-serving. Differentiating i-deals from favoritism and illicit arrangements is important to protect coworkers, the employer, and the i-dealer from the potentially negative consequences that poorly implemented i-deals can have.

Benefits for Both Employee and Employer

I-deals are intended to serve both the worker's interests and those of the employer. Workers do not initiate an i-deal unless they value its terms; employers do not agree unless they value what the worker offers them. Other unjust and self-serving arrangements such as favoritism have clear negative consequences for the firm and are not even intended to benefit it directly, as in the case in which the nephew of a senior executive is automatically given fewer job demands and more flexible hours—in effect, lowering the quality of one worker's contributions to the firm.[19] I-deals, in contrast, can aid both workers and employers by providing an effective means of attracting, motivating, or retaining the services of a valued contributor. Interestingly from the perspective of broader research on employment, i-deals have played an important but often invisible role in many aspects of the employment relationship, from work-family accommodation to supportive leader relations with workers. Viewing this research through the lens of i-deals reveals the widespread but heretofore largely invisible role i-deals have played in employment.

Individual workers who effectively negotiate i-deals with their employer recognize not only a deal's value to themselves but also how the employer benefits. Negotiation strategies workers use often leverage the i-deal's value for the employer, too, as a reward for a high performer or as a crucial source of innovation and adaptation to workforce changes.

Variations in Scope

I-deals vary in their scope, constituting anywhere from 1 percent to 100 percent of the employment relationship. They can consist of a single idiosyncratic element in a larger standardized employment package or an entirely idiosyncratic employment arrangement. For example, a worker enrolled in an evening MBA program might negotiate fewer travel demands than required of her peers but otherwise share the same pay, job duties, and other conditions of employment. In contrast, another worker with uncommon skills might have a unique arrangement in which almost all his terms of employment are specially negotiated, from pay and hours to duties and title. Both of these individuals have idiosyncratic features in their employment arrangements, although the relative proportion of idiosyncratic to standardized conditions is greater for the second worker.

I-deals occur in the context of a broader set of compensation and human resource practices characterizing an individual's employment, and are tied to the employer's broader human resource strategy. What else is included in the worker's conditions of employment shapes the meaning he or she gives to the i-deal. These other conditions can include standardized employment terms workers receive by virtue of membership in the firm (e.g., health-care benefits provided to all regular employees) as well as the more narrowly applied employment terms associated with particular positions or jobs (e.g., the flexibly scheduled vacation time often accorded a firm's professional staff but not its production workers). Although standardizing employment conditions through wage structures, bonuses, or benefit plans is a means of promoting cooperation and trust,[20] employers also face increasing pressure to attract especially highly valued workers by offering them attractive but less commonly available employment conditions. The result is that more idiosyncratic elements are included in certain individuals' employment arrangements. The standard and position-based conditions of employment can influence what the i-deal means to the worker who negotiated it and to his or her coworkers. Having to negotiate every condition of one's employment tends to make workers highly sensitive to their treatment relative to others. If, however, the bulk of one's compensation and other conditions of employment are based on a generous set of standard practices, the i-deal tends to be seen in a different light, a sign of flexibility on the part of an already highly supportive employer.[21]

Recognizing Idiosyncratic Deals

Consider the following scenarios:

- A talented designer seeking employment with an office-furniture manufacturer announced during his recruitment that his child-care responsibilities made it impossible for him to come to the office every day. Despite the fact that all existing employees did their work in the company's offices, the designer asked for a different arrangement, which the design department's manager worked out for this exceptionally talented young man. She offered to let the designer have flexible hours and work at home several days a week if he agreed to join the company.
- An attorney at an East Coast law firm needed to make several visits to Los Angeles over the course of a few months to check into some personal business investments. Because this travel schedule stood to interfere with her legal practice and caseload, she asked her firm's managing partner whether she could be assigned new cases requiring her presence in California. Although this was not how work assignments were normally made at the firm, the attorney's request was granted. This arrangement precluded the need for her to take a time off, which would have burdened the firm.

Despite their obvious differences, these scenarios illustrate a common theme: In both cases, a deal was struck between an employee (or prospective employee) and a company official that enabled both the employee and the firm to benefit. By giving the designer the flexible working conditions he needed and by granting the attorney a geographically desirable work assignment, company officials were able to attract or retain the services of valued workers. Moreover, in both cases the particular arrangements fell outside the firms' usual terms of employment. The manufacturer did not normally offer such flexibility and the law firm did not typically assign cases on the basis of geographic preference. In effect, established employment conditions were augmented or superseded for the mutual good of the firms and the particular employees in question.

We refer to these individually negotiated idiosyncratic employment arrangements as idiosyncratic deals (i-deals). These are unique employment terms individual workers negotiate for themselves to satisfy their personal needs and desires. More than a play on words, use of the term "i-deals" intends both to abbreviate "idiosyncratic deals" and to highlight the fact that such arrangements are intended to be "ideal" in some way for each party. Indeed, both the employers and employees in these examples benefited by the arrangements that were made.

I-deals as the Rare Exception: Only Stars Need Apply

I-deals are commonly recognized as the bailiwick of rock stars, CEOs, and other "high fliers." The prominence of distinctive, sometimes extreme, personal arrangements can affect the way i-deals are thought of in popular culture, making some people reluctant to propose an i-deal for themselves out of concern that they will appear overly demanding. The superstars and winners who get special treatment often are thought of as both heroes and villains. The title of Robert Frank and Philip Cook's book conveys this well: *Winner Take All: How More and More Americans Compete for Fewer and Bigger Prizes, Encouraging Economic Waste, Income Inequality, and an Impoverished Cultural Life.*[22]

Accounts of a few exceptional individuals—"superstars" or "winners" capable of negotiating distinctive employment conditions—are not new. Idiosyncratic arrangements can take the form of perks for high-status people, whose exotic lifestyles and distinctive work settings make them fodder for gossip by ordinary folk and targets for the paparazzi. For example, the Smoking Gun Web site documents the renowned contracts of rock stars and other entertainers, and receives thousands of hits a day, attesting to the intense interest generated by celebrity i-deals (Table 1.1).[23] Over the years, scholars have noted that such individuals capitalize on their uniqueness by differentiating themselves in subtle and not-so-subtle ways from their more ordinary colleagues.[24] Famous movie stars who demand lavish working conditions to match their lavish salaries immediately come to mind. So, too, do stories of rock band members whose contracts specify that all the brown M&Ms be removed from the requisite candy bowl in their dressing rooms. Generally, however, these individuals are seen as the exceptions to the rule, and the nature of their requests seems to underscore their personal uniqueness.

The connotation of extreme special treatment these practices raise can make some workers and their managers reluctant to ask for or agree to i-deals, even when the benefits of doing so are great for both parties. Still, ordinary folks can and do negotiate i-deals.

Table 1.1

Idiosyncratic Deals for the Stars

Dressing Room

Jennifer Lopez	White room (including white roses and lilies); white candles, drapes, and chairs
Neil Diamond	Fabric-covered couches and chairs (no vinyl)
Luciano Pavarotti	No flowers or odors near artist; all sofas set on six-inch (twenty-centimeter) risers

Entertainment

Guns n' Roses	Assortment of "adult" magazines (e.g., *Playboy*)
Cher	TV and VCR with cable hookup (including Turner Classic Movies)
Rolling Stones	One full-size snooker table—not a pool table—with a full set of cues, bridges, chalks, and racks (tour provides snooker balls)

Catering

Dionne Warwick	Hot hors d'oeuvres (no seafood, shellfish, or mushrooms) including barbecued ribs, little franks, meatballs, and egg rolls
Busta Rhymes	No pork or beef in food or vicinity of dressing room; six bottles of Moet champagne; twenty-four-piece Boston Market or Kentucky Fried Chicken meal
Joe Cocker	Beer to be iced at 6 p.m., re-iced at 8 p.m., and re-iced again at 10:45 p.m.

Transportation

Dionne Warwick	New dark-colored limousine (never white), furnished with telephone, television, minibar, and chauffeur
Rolling Stones	Quality town car (must not be a limousine) in a color other than white, with dark-tinted windows and driver
Christina Aguilera	Police escorts for band vehicles, empowered to route vehicles through traffic (under no circumstances must vehicles encounter traffic delays)

Source: Smoking Gun, http://www.thesmokinggun.com (accessed October 15, 2003).

I-deals Are for Regular People, Too

Not just superstars get special treatment. Changing conditions in the labor market have expanded the opportunities for a broader array of workers to seek and receive i-deals.[25] A survey of an entering class of international MBA students found that over 30 percent had negotiated i-deals with their employers. About 25 percent of the health-care workers in a small American hospital indicated that they had i-deals.[26] A survey of teleworkers em-

Table 1.2

Idiosyncratic Deals Workers Make

Advancement

Career development	Taking off work two hours early each Friday to attend advanced-degree program
	Shifting from technical sales to marketing to learn new competencies
Visibility	Junior employee gets to present key report to corporate executives

Job Content

Workload	Reduced work volume to help worker cope with job stress
Interesting work	Working on one large project rather than many small ones
	Focusing on activities in which worker is particularly interested
Travel	International assignments with perks
	Younger employee given opportunity to deal with clients where travel is required
	Parents of young children given opportunity to deal with clients where travel is not required

Time

Flexible work hours	Shift from full-time to part-time work
	Flexible start and end of workday
	Permission to bank hours for flexibility in the future
Leave of absence	Unpaid time off to pursue personal hobby
	Permitting worker to join another company in the hope that he or she will return to current employer

Pay

	Expanded work hours to increase worker take-home pay
	Raise in response to comparative information provided by worker

ployed by the government of Bavaria indicated that more than 35 percent had some idiosyncratic features of employment that they had negotiated individually.[27] Table 1.2 illustrates the array of i-deals reported by workers in these and other studies. These are far from being isolated cases. In fact, the growth of i-deals highlights the changing nature of traditional paradigms for recruiting, motivating, and retaining valuable workers. As importantly, i-deals call attention to the flexibilities that firms and some workers have long enjoyed, though not necessarily acknowledged.

I-deals represent one outgrowth of employer responses to market pressures and to workers' heightened expectations for greater say in their experiences on the job.[28] Together, these forces promote greater customization in aspects of employment. As such, i-deals represent a dimension of shifting assumptions regarding the employment relationship. Although human resource management textbooks assume homogeneity in employment arrangements for workers in similar positions, real organizations don't work this way.[29] Idiosyncratic arrangements are endemic in the workplace, existing in traditional work settings even prior to the emergence of the postindustrial economy, globalization, and knowledge work. People often assume that more workplace standardization exists than really does. Idiosyncratic work arrangements are becoming more commonplace, but greater understanding is needed to realize the potential benefits that i-deals offer to workers and employers. People often assume that there should be *more* standardization, based on the belief that standardization is "fair." We will drill down into the processes of implementing i-deals to understand how standardization and fairness relate to flexibility when individual workers have different needs, interests, and contributions to make to the firm.

Dilemmas

Despite their potential benefits, i-deals pose some dilemmas. The concept of differential treatment at work raises an almost knee-jerk negative reaction. Sensitivity to inequity and connotations of politics and favoritism take center stage. These concerns are morally and socially appropriate. Nonetheless, not all special treatment is unfair. One person's special treatment can be a source of innovation for the company and can lead to more flexible treatment of workers firmwide. Some differential treatment may be essential to human fulfillment, self-expression, and general well-being. In effect, the concept of idiosyncrasy is complicated and warrants more careful consideration than it has received. This consideration is particularly important since forces are at work that can increase the incidence of i-deals.

Several forces endemic to contemporary firms promote i-deals. Workers whose career plans or personal goals set them along a course different from that of their peers need not be superstars to create an idiosyncratic deal, if their employer values them nonetheless. Employer demand for knowledge workers with distinctive competencies in a hypercompetitive marketplace means that many workers have greater power to negotiate employment conditions that suit their tastes and preferences.[30] A few individuals working in the same unit may each have their own distinct i-deals. The weakening, if not demise, of the job-security-based model of organizational careers, once supported by unionism, legal requirements, or both, leads to fewer standardized conditions of employment in nearly every sector of the economy, particularly in the United States.[31] Moreover, the expanded choices that consumers have in the marketplace have led to ever-greater diversified products and services, creating rising expectations for customization that extend from the retail market to the workplace.[32] Although we note that employment arrangements can still be very standardized in some workplaces (e.g., government employment) and in some countries (particularly non-English-speaking nations), the trend toward greater flexibility and customization is evident worldwide to some degree.[33] The greater number of women in the workforce has challenged norms that firms developed when their employees were predominately male. One impact of the feminization of the workplace has been the questioning of norms regarding career paths and requisite criteria for advancement (e.g., shifting to results in place of long hours).[34] While these forces at work in the American economy make it particularly ripe for i-deals, we will examine the cross-national factors that influence the role of i-deals worldwide.

Increasing instances of idiosyncratic work arrangements are consistent with the expanded choices people have in the marketplace. Mass customization lets computer users order the particular system that fits their business or personal needs.[35] The old McDonald's slogan "We do it all for you" has given way to Burger King's "Have it your way"—not just in fast food, but in many other market segments as well. Expanded choices and the democratization of personal taste create new, more varied approaches to marketing and product development. Yet where the workforce is concerned, it is not that simple.

Idiosyncratic deals have both positive and negative consequences for third parties who aren't involved in the initial decision to grant an i-deal. Costs and benefits to others not involved in making a particular decision are referred to as externalities. An externality occurs when decision makers do not bear all of the costs or reap all of the benefits from their actions. A negative externality is an external cost borne by third parties, which in the case of i-deals might be the extra work that coworkers must perform when a colleague negotiates reduced hours. A positive externality is an external benefit enjoyed by third parties, which might take the form of the increased opportunities for flexibility coworkers enjoy because one worker talked the employer into letting her be the first staff member to work from home.[36] I-deals can be a source of inefficiency and conflict among coworkers unless negative externalities are addressed. They can also be a source of innovation and healthy adaptation to change when their potential positive externalities are realized. As we shall see, the spillover effects i-deals have on third parties are largely shaped by the circumstances under which i-deals arise and the ways in which they are implemented.

Although those with more individualistic proclivities might approve of "different strokes for different folks," cooperation among a firm's workforce can be undermined by wide variations in worker inducements and contributions. Idiosyncratic arrangements are a source of flexibility and signal employer responsiveness to the needs and preferences of individual workers. Yet, unless attention is paid to how i-deals are effectively created, managed, and implemented, a proliferation of special treatment will undermine trust and cooperation at work. Where workers are highly interdependent, the success of their efforts depends on their willingness to cooperate. Highly divergent employment arrangements among interdependent workers can impede cooperation by creating the perception of inequity and unfairness among the workforce and reducing workers' willingness to trust either one another or their employer.

Standardization and consistency have been the watchwords of employment practice for the past fifty years. For much of the latter half of the twentieth century, the trend was to reduce the wage gap within firms, particularly between white-collar and blue-collar workers, consistent with increasing intrafirm interdependence among work units and the concomitant need to enhance trust and collaboration.[37] (Note that the ongoing gap between CEO and worker pay in some American firms is actually made more salient by the aforementioned trend.) It is a stylized fact of modern management theory that inequitable compensation and inconsistent treatment can reduce trust among workers and between workers and their employer.[38] When an organization lacks open and consistent procedures for determining conditions of employment (a defining feature of procedural justice), a climate of injustice results.

Idiosyncratic arrangements that are implemented in a preferential or haphazard fashion give rise to dysfunctional practices such as

- pay secrecy—when firms threaten to fire employees (or give them no more special deals) if they reveal their salary to coworkers. This practice can perpetrate persistent feelings of pay inequity.
- discrimination based on demographic factors—where personal characteristics unrelated to work give some workers unintended advantages over others. For example, the solidarity managers feel with workers whose backgrounds are similar to their own can make it easier for them to form trusting relationships with these subordinates than with their dissimilar coworkers—and to grant i-deals to those subordinates with whom the managers are personally comfortable.
- mistrust of the firm's human resource and related procedural justice systems—where a plethora of person-specific arrangements and side deals erode interpersonal trust. For example, the dominance of cronyism and politics characteristic of firms in the former Soviet bloc made it

difficult for those firms to implement modern management systems that would align employee and employer interests.

Finally, because idiosyncratic arrangements can become dysfunctional, it is important to be vigilant about the processes through which they are created and the roles they play in the broader fabric of the employment relationship. Given our focus on i-deals in the context of employees working inside an organization, the employment relationship on which we focus has three interested parties: the individual worker, the employer (and the managers who act as its agents), and the individual worker's coworkers. The effectiveness of an i-deal is thus to be gauged in relation to its impact on all three parties. One of the goals of this book is to reveal the often conflicting demands that i-deals raise where flexibility and fairness are both valued. In doing so, this book strives to represent the balancing act an effective i-deal necessitates among the interests of the individual worker who seeks it, the employer who grants it, and the coworkers whose own employment arrangements may be impacted by that bargain. Since none of these parties is monolithic, the specific circumstances of each shape what is required to join fairness with flexibility. The dilemmas an i-deal raises are resolved or exacerbated depending on how the interests of the i-deal's three parties are addressed in its creation and implementation, at its inception and over time.

Conclusion

I-deals are distinctive arrangements that individual workers negotiate to satisfy their needs as well as those of their employers. Although such arrangements might be expected among workers who hold unique positions (e.g., rock stars, high-powered executives), they are also found among valued employees whose coworkers often perform ostensibly the same work and hold the same job. It is in the latter situation where the dilemmas surrounding i-deals arise, in the differential treatment that otherwise similar coworkers experience. Thus, i-deals have the potential for both positive and negative externalities, for flexibility and for injustice. Their place on the employment menu calls attention to important contemporary challenges: achieving both individual flexibility and collective fairness, and fulfilling unique personal needs while promoting mutuality and cooperation at work. Because idiosyncratic arrangements can become dysfunctional, it is important to be vigilant about the basis on which they are created and the roles they play in the broader fabric of the employment relationship. We go forth to explore idiosyncrasy in employment and the conditions that motivate individual workers to negotiate on their own.

— 2 —

Everyday Idiosyncrasy and Its Many Forms

The employment relation is dense, rich, and particular.
—Richard Freeman and Joel Rogers[1]

We cannot seek or attain health, wealth, learning, justice or kindness in general. Action is always specific, concrete, individualized, unique.
—John Dewey[2]

On a given day in virtually any organization, one individual employee or another is taking the initiative to individualize some aspect of his or her employment relationship. Idiosyncrasy in employment is found wherever individual workers change their job titles, draft their own job descriptions, revise the ones they started with, or otherwise customize their duties, work hours, and other conditions of work. Employees modify old roles and break in new ones to reflect their personal values, interests, and capabilities. In their day-to-day dealings with their employer, employees shape the conditions of their employment through the expectations they convey and the contributions they make. The idiosyncrasies we focus on in this chapter abound in organizations, though not all of them are i-deals that a worker has negotiated. This chapter's key point is that the phenomenon of everyday idiosyncrasy sets the stage for why and when individual workers do negotiate.

This chapter describes how opportunities for idiosyncrasy arise in employment, whether negotiated or not. It depicts the role that incompleteness, a characteristic of the vast majority of employment arrangements, plays in creating idiosyncrasy. This chapter then maps the forms idiosyncrasy takes and the conditions that determine whether worker and employer must negotiate it or can create it informally.

Incompleteness: A Source of Idiosyncrasy in Employment

Idiosyncratic arrangements take many forms, planned and negotiated or spontaneous and impromptu. They arise out of the dynamic characteristics of work settings, roles, and workers, particularly for those individuals who differentiate themselves by their contributions, demands, or tenure. The term "idiosyncrasy" is often used as a synonym for "eccentricity," indicating something strange or odd. Though an eccentricity is a deviation from an established pattern or norm (according to the dictionary, it also can be "a mild mental aberration"!), idiosyncrasy also "stresses the following of one's particular bent or temperament and connotes strong individuality and independence of action," a more positive definition that corresponds to the potential value i-deals offer to workers and employers.[3] To understand when and how individual workers negotiate with their employer, we first need to appreciate the myriad ways, mundane or eccentric, negotiated or not, whereby workers can come to differ from peers in their conditions of employment.

To make a point about how widespread idiosyncrasy really is, I often ask my MBA students whether they have ever changed their job title without asking for permission to do so. Typically around a third of them say they have. Some do this on their resume to make themselves more marketable by embellishing their past work experience. More often students say they did it on the job because their role had changed, and retitling their job clarified the changes for their coworkers. The students had initiated many of these changes on their own; renaming their job helped legitimate the changes. This was the case for Timothy, a software designer in a start-up firm who took over the training of new hires after the rocky start he experienced upon joining the company. Before long Timothy had retitled his job, becoming his firm's first trainer. As Timothy's actions and those of my job-retitling students suggest, contemporary workplaces are replete with individual workers who modify old roles, break in new ones, and otherwise shape the conditions of their employment.

This is not to say that workers get it all their own way. There are also forces against flexibility, particularly in terms of ever-increasing employer demands. To illustrate this point, I also ask my students whether they

23

actually are able to use all the vacation time their employer officially provides them. Nearly half indicate that, while they would prefer to, they don't use all the vacation allocated to them. Their reasons for taking less time off include both fear that they will be judged negatively if they are away too long and anxiety over the amount of work they would face upon their return.[4]

My essential point is that the formal contract is only part of the story in understanding employment arrangements. The actual exchange between worker and employer is shaped by informal norms affecting the behavior of organizational members, such as pressure to minimize time away from the job. It is also shaped by the idiosyncrasies a worker accumulates over the course of an employment relationship.

One virtually inevitable feature of regular employment drives idiosyncrasy: *incompleteness.* I use the word "inevitable" because original employment arrangements commonly are incomplete: At the time of hire neither worker nor employer typically can anticipate or communicate all the demands each may ultimately make of the other. From the most hidebound bureaucracy to the most loosely structured start-up, incompleteness is endemic to employment. The complex dynamics of organizations and human life make the future uncertain.[5] Incompleteness also results from human cognitive limits that make it impossible to recall or effectively convey at the time of hire all relevant conditions likely to arise in employment.[6]

The Nobel Prize winner Herbert Simon underscored the inherent incompleteness of regular employment arrangements by differentiating them from sales contracts.[7] Sales contracts involve discretely specified commodity or labor agreements (e.g., an order for fifty T-shirts to have a company logo stenciled on them by Wednesday, at twelve dollars apiece; the temporary worker hired through an agency such as Kelly or Manpower to perform a well-specified task such as moving palletized containers using a forklift for three days at eleven dollars per hour). The typical sales contract is effectively complete, providing explicit detail regarding how goods or services are to be exchanged for money. By contrast, regular employment contracts are inherently incomplete because their terms cannot be fully detailed up front and are subject to change (e.g., hiring a director for a start-up project, where uncertainty and changing demands are the norm). The latter contracts involve unforeseeable complexity and unexpected exceptions. In the case of the director hired for a start-up project, whether the work requires ten hours a day or sixteen, or permits support staff to be hired in two months or a year, cannot be known in advance. Over time, the director's actual experiences with this start up will fill in at least some of the blanks regarding this employment arrangement's particular terms. Simon used the metaphor of a blank check to describe what workers agree to, because no detailed job posting could eliminate the inherent incompleteness of the employment agreement. He maintained that management would typically resolve this incompleteness unilaterally by filling in the blanks as it saw fit with the view that employment is a hierarchical, asymmetrical relationship where only one party is in charge.[8] However, Simon also recognized that authority in the workplace could operate in several other directions, too:

> Authority, in the sense here defined, can operate "upward" and "sidewise" as well as "downward" in the organization. If an executive delegates to his secretary a decision about file cabinets and accepts her recommendation without reexamination of its merits, he is accepting her authority.[9]

Extrahierarchical authority takes the form of employee expertise and competence as well as the informal influence trusted employees exert. Informal mechanisms such as worker initiative and peer pressure influence how workers serve customers, manage work-family conflict, and otherwise conduct themselves in performing their jobs. In the day-to-day work world, these informal, sideways, and upward manifestations of authority help flesh out the otherwise incomplete employment arrangement. As a result, hierarchical, top-down authority tends to be reserved for resolving those disputes not settled through nonhierarchical means.[10]

Incompleteness can also be deliberate. Both worker and employer can be motivated to create contracts that are incomplete out of the desire to protect their freedom of action. Incompleteness arises from the interest of both worker and employer in preserving their own autonomy even while they seek to form a workable relationship. Employment is by definition a voluntary agreement, unlike slavery or involuntary servitude, that gives the employer some authority over the worker to dictate the performance of certain duties and execution of organizational directives.[11] This transfer of power from individual to employer can evoke abuse, or at the very least fear of it, creating rebelliousness and effort on the part of workers to protect their autonomy. Insofar as individual workers are ambivalent toward authority, they can be expected to guard their freedom of action.[12] Workers may be reluctant to tell an employer that they intend to start a family within a year or plan to go back to graduate school part-time. Keeping back such information reduces its potential adverse impact on the decisions employers make regarding workers. Similarly, employers can create incompleteness to protect their own freedom of action. They may be reluctant to disclose an upcoming restructuring or planned change for fear of demotivating workers or scaring them off.

Information can also be kept back until the conditions are more opportune to negotiate an accommodation. Once employee and employer have come to rely on each other and trust each other more readily, requests for flexibility that would have been rejected earlier are more likely to be granted.[13] Employers who refuse to grant a new hire's request for flextime or the opportunity to work at home may be more than willing to grant such a request later, once that employee has proved competent and trustworthy. Similarly, a recently hired worker who refuses to accept a burdensome work schedule out of fear of being taken advantage of can become more willing to accept a sudden increase in hours after coming to feel committed to the company.

While employers conduct their business and employees go about their jobs, idiosyncratic arrangements arise as certain performance demands, duties, or working conditions are added and others downplayed. Consider the case of Jerry Schaeffer, a deeply religious retired businessman hired to help launch a university's masters of manufacturing program, a partnership between its business and engineering schools. Since neither school had ever partnered with another unit on campus, relations between them needed to be built from scratch. A former manufacturing executive, Jerry saw his role as providing support (he used the basketball term "assists") to help faculty and administrators create an educational innovation while strengthening ties across the university community. Jerry articulated a highly personalized concept of his role: "My job is to help others succeed." During his first two months on the job, Jerry fleshed out a role for himself, seeking approval when special resources were required, and otherwise improvising how best to help establish the new program. When a faculty head suggested that Jerry take over part of his job, Jerry declined to accept responsibility for day-to-day administration of program activities. Instead, he met with all faculty members involved in administering the program to find ways of coaching them be more effective. Two months into the job, he proposed a series of events and activities, soon implemented, to help the two schools' faculty and staff work together better. In short order, Jerry became invaluable to the university, beyond the program he initially helped to launch, receiving uncommonly wide latitude and visibility through the activities he initiated. In the process of fleshing out his role in the university, Jerry filled in many blanks in his otherwise incomplete employment contract.

As in Jerry Schaeffer's case, an employee's distinctive employment arrangements arise in response to new and emerging job demands, as well that person's preferences, habits, and proclivities. Employees can alter or add improvised or spontaneous arrangements (e.g., downplaying administrative duties while focusing instead on assisting others). Alternatively, they

26

can seek formal approval where they lack the authority to make the desired changes themselves (e.g., creating special events). This chapter's treatment of idiosyncrasy in employment arrangements is based on two core ideas:

1. Many idiosyncratic arrangements employees enjoy occur without negotiation. Employees on their own can individualize some employment conditions without formal authorization.
2. Negotiation is a way to obtain formal approval for individualized arrangements an employee cannot create on his or her own. Employer approval to create idiosyncrasies is often forthcoming in cases in which employees cannot introduce the change by themselves.

Idiosyncrasies allow firms and workers to adapt to changing circumstances as well as to express their needs for freedom and control. Understanding idiosyncrasy alerts us to the circumstances in which workers need to negotiate to get their needs met and those in which they don't.

Idiosyncrasy Is Normal

Workplaces are full of idiosyncrasies. Idiosyncrasies can involve virtually any resource exchanged by workers and employers, from concrete items—money, equipment, hours, and specific duties—to intangibles such as interpersonal support and external visibility in one's profession. Two people may be paid differently while doing the same work, because they were hired under different market conditions or because one bargained harder than the other. Idiosyncrasies also involve more intangible differences; for example, an employer might display extraordinary support to an exceptionally valued employee who is experiencing problems at home but need not extend the same consideration to less-valued colleagues. In these cases, the extraordinary support provided to certain workers and not others reflects idiosyncratic treatment authorized by the employer.

When an employee initiates a change that is within his or her authority to carry out, an idiosyncrasy may be introduced. A custodian mopping hospital floors may personally define her housekeeping duties to include patient care and service, by offering support to a patient's bereaved family or by sensitively cleaning up after a patient has an embarrassing accident with the family present. Such worker-initiated informal job customization, referred to as "job crafting," adds both contributions to the employer (and patients', or customers', families) and personal meaning to the worker beyond formal job specifications.[14] As long as the individual worker performs those duties required by the employer in an acceptable manner, personally crafted jobs can be sustained without employer approval.

High performers have ample opportunity to initiate changes in their working conditions without seeking authorization. Indeed, a benefit of being a high contributor can be the enjoyment of more individualized employment arrangements. A proactive high performer can subtly, gradually create differences between him- or herself and coworkers by displaying more confidence in making decisions and exercising greater job latitude than do peers.[15] In time, coworkers, managers, and customers can come to expect different behavior from this proactive high performer than they expect or even would accept from lower-performing peers. As a result, high performers are sought out regularly for advice, solve more problems, and otherwise make singular contributions on the job. By virtue of the caliber of their contributions, high performers can come to expect more in return, from tangible rewards and recognition to intangibles such as greater support, consideration, and status.[16] The idiosyncratic arrangements that in effect reward high performers are one reason why workers in a firm who have been stars for a long time are less likely to leave than are workers newly designated as stars.[17] Importantly for retention, accumulated idiosyncrasies can be hard to replicate with a new employer. It's difficult to imagine that even the most valuable star could successfully approach a new employer with the demand "Do you promise to always appreciate me, hold me in higher esteem than my peers, and ensure that all my colleagues honor and respect me?" Some resources can only be exchanged in the context of strong, existing relationships.

Renate Miller, a private banker in a firm that managed large trusts, was one such high performer. The respect she garnered from her superiors and peers allowed her to spend virtually every day from noon to 2 p.m. in her office managing her own financial and real estate investments. She declined meetings during these hours and took no bank-related phone calls. Her strong track record over the years in serving her clients coupled with her sensitive handling of family issues associated with the trusts assigned to her made her highly respected by both management and her peers—a sign of the intangible but valuable support high performers can merit. Such an arrangement might be difficult to demand especially at the time of hire but can emerge over time as the employment relationship develops.

The pervasiveness of idiosyncrasy may well underlie many human resource processes; promotions are a case in point. Though strikingly little is known about the process by which firms fill higher-level jobs, most personnel actions workers call promotions involve no change in position or duties. Instead, many so-called promotions are simply an upgrade of a worker's current position. In a national sample of American workers, Permagit and Veum found that more than 50 percent received a promotion *at* their current job, which can mean continuing to perform the same duties as before but receiving a new title with more pay, or having one's existing position upgraded.[18] A smaller portion of the sample involved the conventional understanding of a promotion: filling a higher-level position or taking over one's supervisor's job. Not all promotions entail the competitive tournaments they connote.[19] According to Permagit and Veum, one-third of all promotions occur without any competition.[20] These position upgrades also were more systematically related to wage increases than were other types of promotions. Some of these noncompetitive promotions are likely to effectively formalize informal accommodations to the skills, preferences, and aspirations of individual job incumbents. Employee efforts to get more from their employer (e.g., status, wages, recognition) while doing much the same work constitute an idiosyncratic component of many promotions.

Standard job analysis methodologies recognize the prevalence of idiosyncrasies in the workplace. Conducted to systematically assess job requirements, job analyses acknowledge that individual workers do their jobs differently by relying on sampling criteria. Job analysis data usually are gathered from several incumbents having different educational and career backgrounds and lengths of time on the job to obtain a representative sampling of the job's skill requirements, duties, and interdependencies with others. This sampling approach takes into account how different people in ostensibly the same job perform their duties. Thus, for example, Sidney Gael, a job analysis expert, suggested that "if information is needed about all possible variations in the way work is performed then every [job] incumbent should complete a . . . questionnaire."[21] In effect, job analysis methodologies recognize how commonplace idiosyncrasy is.

Job analysis commonly reveals that people with the same title, formally responsible for the same performance deliverables and ostensibly in the same job, actually perform very different duties. When I worked at Pacific Gas and Electric (PG&E) as an industrial psychologist, my job involved interpreting job analyses conducted on line and repair crews. One of the first things I learned was not to rely on the job analysis data from workers who had spent twenty years or more on the job. These veterans tended to have widely varied combinations of activities. Some did relatively little strenuous physical activity, working more with a clipboard and seldom climbing up a pole or down a manhole. Other veterans did a good deal of physical work but left any required paperwork to a coworker.

The counterpoint to this variation found among veterans was those workers who had been on the job five to ten years. These more junior yet experienced workers tended to perform a relatively fixed, standard set of tasks combining physical activity and paperwork. As evidence of a peculiar form of "veterans preference," PG&E veterans did those tasks they liked or were good at, while those with shorter tenures performed a more standard set of duties. Evident variation in job duties over time suggests that idiosyncrasies accumulate over the course of a worker's tenure in the organization.

Differences in the way a dozen people in a work group enact their work roles can look random—but that is not necessarily the case. Idiosyncrasies have a finely patterned structure when viewed in relation to the particular circumstances in which they have arisen. We now turn our attention to the processes that underlie these idiosyncrasies.

Four Ways to Create Idiosyncratic Arrangements

In the evolution of their work roles, individual workers experience four processes that make their employment in some respect idiosyncratic in relation to that of coworkers ostensibly doing the same job. These four avenues to idiosyncrasy vary in their subtlety and explicitness, but each can be a means of creating workplace flexibility and responsiveness to change. They exemplify the "dense, rich, and particular" qualities of an individual worker's relationship with an employer.[22]

Given our focus on how individual workers negotiate on their own behalf, it is important to note that these processes for creating idiosyncratic work arrangements are foreshadowed in the meanings the *Oxford English Dictionary* offers for the term "negotiation": (1) a business transaction, (2) a treaty with another to obtain some result, (3) the act of coming to terms with others, and (4) the action of getting over or around something by skillful maneuvering.[23] Two themes underlie these definitions. The first is the act of accomplishing an intended result through mutual agreement, a characteristic of idiosyncratic arrangements arising from negotiations. The second theme is based on overcoming some obstacle through dexterity and skill, and characterizes an informal and sometimes covert process where an actor on one side of the employment relationship initiates a change and the other side acquiesces to the new conditions.

The processes leading to idiosyncratic arrangements are differentiated in terms of two dimensions: (1) whether they are created via acquiescence or negotiation and (2) whether they are initiated by a worker or by his or her employer (Table 2.1).

Table 2.1

Idiosyncratic Arrangements for Individual Workers

	One-Sided Acquiescence	Two-Sided Negotiation *(The basis of i-deals)*
Worker-Initiated	Acquiescence (e.g., job crafting)	*The Classic I-deal*
	Informal accommodation Worker initiates idiosyncrasy and employer acquiesces	Worker proposes idiosyncrasy and then negotiates with employer
	Exemplar: Programmer takes over training for new employees without discussing with employer	*Exemplar:* Marketing manager negotiates time off and financial support to complete an evening MBA program
Employer-Initiated	Authority-Acceptance (e.g., job creep)	*A Potential I-deal* (i.e., if worker feels free to negotiate)
	Employer initiates idiosyncrasy and worker acquiesces	Employer proposes idiosyncrasy and then negotiates with worker
	Exemplar: New client requires out-of-state travel for an employee who never traveled before; employee accepts new demand without comment	*Exemplar:* Company asks manager to accept a transfer, and they bargain over the salary, benefits, and responsibilities the new position would entail

Acquiescence

Acquiescence means passive assent or compliance. It arises when either the employer or the employee initiates a change in employment conditions without asking the approval of the other—and the other party accepts these new conditions. Employers can direct workers to perform duties that were not previously part of the employment arrangement—when a secretary who has never traveled on the job is asked to accompany her boss on a business trip, for example, or the supervisor of a clerk who works from nine to five expects him to stay late when work is behind schedule. Employees can also initiate acquiescence, as in the case of the upstanding employee who does his evening class's homework at his desk during the day when the office isn't busy, with no adverse reaction on the part of his employer.

Seminal writers on behavior in organizations Chester Barnard and Herbert

31

Simon link acquiescence to the way supervisors exercise authority over their subordinates.[24] When workers accept that their managers have the prerogative to determine conditions of work, they acknowledge management's legitimate authority. Indeed, employers initiate a substantial portion of changes that occur in work conditions, such as shifts in performance goals, redesign of task environments (e.g., equipment used, work sequences followed, quality standards adhered to), or changes in service providers (e.g., United Parcel Service instead of Federal Express). Managers introduce such changes under the general assumption that they have the authority to do so, with the expectation that workers will accept these changes as legitimate and appropriate. In many cases workers are expected to be indifferent to the change; being told to send overnight mail via UPS rather than FedEx probably raises no particular concern among most staff members if their employer prefers one over another. Nonetheless, whether workers are simply indifferent to an employer-initiated change or passively accept directives they might otherwise prefer not to follow, their behavior is a response to authority. According to Simon,

> . . . the arbitrary element in authority is limited to the "area of acceptance" of the subordinate. The magnitude of the area of acceptance depends upon the sanctions which authority has available to enforce its commands. At least as important as the negative sanctions—physical and economic force—are community of purpose, social acceptance, and personality.[25]

Simon defined authority in terms of the behaviors that subordinates demonstrate in response to managerial directives. These behaviors are not a simple outgrowth of the controls that superiors may wield. Rather, the subordinate's acquiescence—his or her acceptance of the dictates of the superior—depends not only on the clout a superior exercises but also on the subordinate's commitment to both the superior and the organization as a whole.[26] Simon used the term "acceptance" based on the belief that a worker's expected response is to follow the dictates of authority "without deliberation on his own part on the expediency of those premises."[27]

I will use the terms "acquiescence" and "acceptance" interchangeably, with one qualifier. In contrast to Simon, I believe that acquiescence at times involves deliberation on the part of the worker or employer who ultimately accepts a change initiated by the other. Acquiescence need not only be a blank check or blind faith but can also reflect the parties' acceptance of ongoing learning over the course of their relationship. This learning entails an updating of beliefs regarding what employment conditions are legitimate. This updating occurs based on knowledge the worker and employer acquire over time regarding each other's interests and preferences, as well as in recognition of changing circumstances. In response to these conditions, employer and worker can implicitly revise their understandings, according acceptance a broad and dynamic role in shaping the employment relationship.

Idiosyncrasy arising through employee actions but without formal managerial approval suggests that the zone of acceptance functions in both a bottom-up as well as a top-down fashion. The zone of acceptance applies not only to worker responses to management dictates but also to how an organization and its management respond to changes workers themselves initiate. Moreover, coworkers can endorse the idiosyncrasies fellow workers introduce, as in the case of colleagues who respect the privacy and time required for a nursing mother to tend to her child at work, extending acceptance and legitimacy to a worker-initiated change. Such behavior reflects a sideways exertion of authority where peers convey approval of an exceptional employment arrangement. Implicit accommodations employers, workers, and coworkers make to one another can substitute for or supplement more explicitly negotiated arrangements, or do both.

Employee-Initiated Acquiescence

These idiosyncratic arrangements emerge from an informal process whereby a worker initiates change and his or her supervisor goes along with that change after learning about the worker's altered behavior. Jessica, a chemist who repeatedly stays late when needed to get the job done, starts showing up to work on her own preferred time schedule. Her boss and coworkers go along with this change because they appreciate how much Jessica contributes. This passive acceptance of worker-initiated employment arrangements is closer in its dynamics to "the skillful maneuvering" aspect of negotiation, since workers can create their own job-related flexibility by reworking the zone of acceptance surrounding their work role.[28]

Workers can informally initiate a change in the conditions of work and employment without seeking permission. Spontaneous role-making behavior is characteristic of loosely managed work settings such as those found in start-up firms. This role making also arises when a worker enjoys substantial autonomy due to her impressive track record or because it is her supervisor's style to give workers leeway. In either case, she may be well positioned to initiate informal accommodations. The same can also be true for workers whose performance demands are lower than their true abilities can accommodate. Workers with capabilities exceeding their job requirements can carry out activities they personally prefer while still completing their work. An employer learning of such changes may not consider objecting as long as the worker continues to make valued contributions.

Job crafting is recognized as a form of employee-initiated acquiescence. As identified by Amy Wrzeniewski and Jane Dutton, job crafting occurs when workers enhance their work roles by adding elements that they personally enjoy or find meaningful.[29] Job crafting provides an example of a one-party accommodation in which changes occur without negotiation. Such one-sided—but potentially mutually beneficial—accommodations can fall within the zone of acceptance, where the employer is unconcerned about what new, different, or extra things the worker does as long as the basic job requirements are met.[30]

A corollary to our discussion of employer acquiescence to employee-initiated changes is the difference in employer reactions to special, peculiar, or unusual employment conditions *before* they are introduced, as opposed to after, when they are a *fait accompli*. A worker who asks to bring his young child to the office when he cannot get day care on Wednesday may well meet with a different response if he makes this request Tuesday afternoon as opposed to doing so Wednesday morning with his young child in tow. One reason that workers may initiate changes without asking is in effect to test the waters or stymie resistance, exemplifying the truth behind the adage "It is often easier to seek forgiveness than permission."

Employer-Initiated Acquiescence

Employer-initiated acquiescence occurs when employees accept conditions of employment, including duties, performance levels, and hours, that differ from formal job requirements.[31] Often these changes take the form of job creep, described by Van Dyne and Ellis as the gradual expansion of employee duties:

> Job creep changes the fundamental nature of the employment relationship by causing supervisors and work group peers to assume that a specific employee will take responsibility for certain tasks or activities, even though this is not part of the job and they get no formal tangible or intangible recognition.[32]

Job creep causes workers to make contributions over and above their established job requirements. Highly conscientious workers may be particularly responsive to such pressures. In the aftermath of downsizing, job creep arises when remaining workers must take on the additional responsibilities terminated workers once performed. If survivors have few job options, their employer can readily demand more from them.[33]

One-sided accommodations are endemic among postdownsizing survivors, who often do the work of several of their erstwhile peers without any explicit negotiation between the worker and employer. Employer-induced accommodations can occur where workers have limited choices and believe themselves to be unable to simply refuse or negotiate more favorable arrangements. Such cases may be indicative of coercion rather than acceptance.

Formal organizational changes also can create employer-initiated acquiescence on the part of workers. The success of planned organizational changes often depends on workers proactively stepping up to alter their roles, reconceptualizing the contributions required of them.[34] Planned changes alter workers' roles by forcing a departure from the traditional duties and contributions job descriptions specify, sometimes making such specifications obsolete. Ella Fong, a research scientist hired as an individual contributor, found that she was expected to act like a team player. Though she generally bought into this shift in roles, neither her manager nor the change consultants the company hired to promote teamwork could tell Ella exactly what it meant to be a team player in the lab in which she worked. Ella had to figure out many of the particulars on her own (e.g., what priority to place on her own projects, her colleagues' projects, and their joint work). Her willing acceptance of this change in role is likely to be affected by the quality of her relationship with the employer.[35]

Many management texts stress the importance of enhancing organizational success by continuing to demand more from employees, with the expectation that they typically will comply.[36] This is not to say, though, that employers always get what they ask for. They do often get more than is explicitly negotiated with workers, however. Whether via job creep or planned organizational change, employers more readily initiate changes under conditions predisposing workers to accept those changes. Acceptance is greater where workers trust management, view the reasons for the change as legitimate, and incur few costs or losses as a result of the change. Under these circumstances, workers asked to work longer hours, perform more complex tasks, or achieve more challenging goals may do so without even thinking of objecting. In contrast, even a potentially positive change, such as more flexible work roles, may generate resistance where the quality of the employment relationship is poor.[37]

Although employer-initiated changes are commonplace, there is little research on their impact on the jobs and employment conditions *individual* workers experience. Instead, the focus has been on broader interventions such as restructurings, where attention is given to the effects on work groups and the organization resulting from large-scale employer-induced change.[38] Research on large-scale change indicates that workers respond positively under conditions where changes are expected to be short-term, when changes are introduced gradually to allow adjustment and learning, where trust and the quality of the employment relationship are high, and where workers have sufficient autonomy to rebalance existing performance demands in response to the changes the employer initiates.[39] It is not yet known how generalizable these group-level effects are to changes an employer introduces into the job of an individual worker. However, trust and the quality of the employment relationship are likely to be as important to individually targeted change as they are to organization-wide interventions.

Negotiation

Negotiation is the strategy of choice when employee or employer cannot effectively create or alter a condition of employment without the other's consent. It is used when the would-be initiator lacks the authority to impose an idiosyncrasy—as in the case where changes to already agreed-upon employment conditions are sought. Negotiation also occurs when agreed-upon features are very general and need to be explicated so as to be implemented—as in the case where the employer had promised to be supportive if and when a worker went back to school, but the details of this agreement couldn't be worked out until the worker was actually ready to enroll.

Day-to-day management and human resource practices require managers and workers to negotiate, particularly regarding personnel actions whose details cannot be worked out until the situation requires it.[40] Bargaining arises when employer and employee need to work out deliverables, time frames, resources, and supports to be deployed in performing a job, as well as when the inducements to be offered for accepting a task or assignment must be determined. Basic organizational features such as authority and responsibility can themselves be products of employer-employee bargaining. By implication, workers and managers must negotiate from time to time as they put the workplace's informal structures, systems, and practices to use. Agreement on what employee and employer owe each other is at the heart of all functional formal and informal arrangements between an individual and his or her employer.[41] Creating agreement regarding personnel actions or management directives can require workers to interact with a company's managers or human resource staff—and many of these interactions involve negotiation. Lax and Sebenius express it well: "If our premise is right, that superiors inevitably negotiate with subordinates, then the reverse must also be true."[42]

Negotiations can occur throughout the employment relationship, from the time of hire to the day the relationship comes to a close, which may follow the termination of regular employment, as in the case of retirees who stay on in specially created job categories. Not surprisingly, then, the longer the duration of the employment relationship, the more likely the accumulation of negotiated idiosyncrasies as well as informally initiated ones. Either the worker or the employer may initiate a negotiation that results in an i-deal, as long as the worker is able to effectively influence the bargain struck on his or her own behalf. Although employers might suggest idiosyncratic arrangements without workers having to initiate them (e.g., to motivate a worker to accept a transfer or new assignment), the dynamics of worker-initiated i-deals differ from the dynamics of those the employer initiates. Employer-initiated negotiations are more likely to involve asymmetrical power that can limit the worker's influence or authentic participation. Workers who are "asked" to accept a transfer, an assignment with more extensive travel, or a demanding project may feel compelled to accept without raising an objection—or an alternative plan. In other cases, workers can use a transfer or opportunity for promotion to bargain for an i-deal. The essential feature of an i-deal is a balance of power in the employment relationship such that the worker has sufficient influence to shape his or her conditions of employment via negotiation. The i-deals on which we focus entail worker-employer negotiations, where individual workers actively bargain for terms of their employment, regardless of who initiates the process.

Worker-Initiated Negotiation

A worker can seek a change in employment terms by negotiating for an employer's approval and support. The particular person or persons who represent the employer in these instances depend on the situation. This negotiation can occur locally, between a worker and his or her immediate supervisor, if the idiosyncratic arrangements can be implemented without affecting clients or other employees. Brian Washington, a scientist who wanted to serve on his professional association's governing board, negotiated with his research and development manager for revised due dates on several projects to allow time for this professional service. No others needed to approve Brian's arrangement since his manager directly controlled project deadlines. At other times, worker-initiated negotiations can involve multiple parties in a process of bargaining and joint problem-solving if the arrangements cannot be implemented without affecting others. Violet Gagnon, a talented engineer who enjoyed international travel, sought out re-assignment to London from Chicago. This worker-initiated arrangement involved explicit negotiation between the worker and several representatives of the employer (in Violet's case, her immediate manager, the manager's boss, and a human resource manager specializing in expatriate assignments). Indeed, it would be difficult to bargain for some i-deals without the explicit involvement of multiple parties.

I-deals arise from a broad array of personal motives, from the need to adapt to changing family or health conditions to the desire to know that one is valued and appreciated. Idiosyncratic arrangements give certain workers opportunities that employers do not provide across the board. Such deals can go beyond the limitations of the firm's formal human resource development, compensation, and performance management practices. They make it possible for organizations to offer flexibilities that formal policies do not anticipate. Moreover, as the examples we have used suggest, trusted veterans, stars, high performers, and otherwise valued workers are in the best position to negotiate with employers.

Employer-Initiated Negotiation

Employers themselves can initiate idiosyncratic arrangements, though not all of these can be considered i-deals unless the workers involved actually influence the arrangement's terms. Employer-initiated idiosyncratic arrangements are created to help the company meet its own needs and sometimes those of the employee too. Consider a case in which a supportive employer used special accommodations to motivate, develop, or retain a particular worker: Carl Jordan, a retail clerk who is very good with customers, is regularly tardy. To get to work on time using the public transportation on which he relies would require him to leave home before he can see his son off to school. Trying to retain Carl rather than terminate his employment, the store's owner offers him the opportunity to work only the store's busiest hours (from 10 a.m. until 4 p.m.) Carl asks if he might then come in an extra day a week to earn a full-time paycheck. By agreeing to shorter daily hours and a longer workweek, the store gains a worker at a vital time of day and permits a valued worker to keep his job. In Carl's case, the store owner's motive in creating this idiosyncratic arrangement is to solve a problem for a worker who is struggling to keep his job and for a company that needs good, reliable job performers. Employer-initiated idiosyncrasies can serve important functions, from creating remedies for employee problems at work to providing special incentives for valued workers.

Although employers can have employees' best interest at heart in proposing i-deals, not all employer-initiated negotiations yield clear benefits to workers. Inherent differences in the power between the worker and his or her employer can lead to the worker's involuntary involvement in employer-initiated negotiations. Cait Maclean, a manager in a Canadian petrochemical firm, was asked to accept a transfer to her company's Pennsylvania office. Although she preferred to stay in her present location, she feared that declining the transfer would hurt her subsequent chances for promotion. Reluctant to say that she didn't want to relocate, she told the company that the transfer would make it difficult for her to finish the executive MBA program she had recently begun at a local Canadian university. In response, her employer offered to let her fly back on weekends to continue the program. Under these conditions, Cait believed that her career would stall if she didn't accept the transfer. Employer-initiated idiosyncratic arrangements give rise to different dynamics for workers than do deals they initiate themselves. If Cait had heard of the transfer opportunity and volunteered for the job under the same conditions, the arrangement would be something completely different: a mutual agreement that reflects Cait's value to the company and her willingness to help her employer. As an employer-initiated arrangement, however, there is an element of coercion to Cait's transfer agreement. Indeed, this sense of coercion can also occur in employee-initiated negotiations when managers believe themselves to have little choice after a valued worker threatens to quit unless an i-deal is approved.

Some Situations Are More Flexible than Others

Work settings differ in the access workers have to individualized conditions of work. The degrees of flexibility inherent in work settings determine whether the worker needs to negotiate to create individualized conditions of employment—or can bring these about on his or her own (see Table 2.2). The highest levels of flexibility are to be found in *innovative settings*, which operate with few rules or structures constraining employment arrangements and where the culture is pro-innovation and supportive of workers.[43] IKEA, the houseware and furniture retailer, offered such flexibility in an advertisement circulated in the Netherlands:[44]

> Time has gone that "the boss" decides how your workday is organized. Everybody chooses the job that fits him or her. Even better: Compose your job yourself. We make individual arrangements over working hours (varying from 6 to 36 hours, different parts of the day, evenings, weekends), career development, job-content, education, etc. We offer options at every level, in different areas, inside and outside the subsidiary, inside and outside the Netherlands.

Other such settings include start-up firms, newly created units in a larger firm, and organizations in which the demands of creative work necessitate support for the individual proclivities of a creative workforce (such as the California design firm whose dress code is "You must!"). Local pockets of

Figure 2.2 **Idiosyncrasy Across Settings**

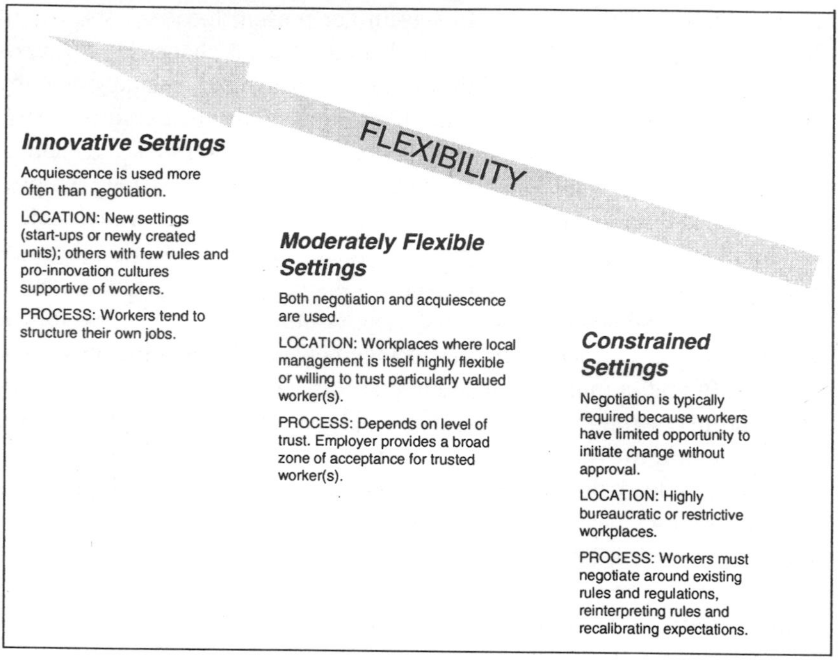

Innovative Settings

Acquiescence is used more often than negotiation.

LOCATION: New settings (start-ups or newly created units); others with few rules and pro-innovation cultures supportive of workers.

PROCESS: Workers tend to structure their own jobs.

FLEXIBILITY

Moderately Flexible Settings

Both negotiation and acquiescence are used.

LOCATION: Workplaces where local management is itself highly flexible or willing to trust particularly valued worker(s).

PROCESS: Depends on level of trust. Employer provides a broad zone of acceptance for trusted worker(s).

Constrained Settings

Negotiation is typically required because workers have limited opportunity to initiate change without approval.

LOCATION: Highly bureaucratic or restrictive workplaces.

PROCESS: Workers must negotiate around existing rules and regulations, reinterpreting rules and recalibrating expectations.

innovation exist in departments and work groups even in relatively traditional firms, and workers seeking special accommodations often pursue assignments there.

High flexibility is found in parts of organizations that are new, pursuing novel business strategies, or simply more informal and loosely organized, with norms promoting offbeat or experimental arrangements. Similarly, a brand-new firm or a start-up unit in a larger organization may constitute one big innovation pocket, whose mode of organizing can shock people who are used to more structured roles.[45] As Theodore, the human resource director of a rapidly expanding Web-based software start-up,[46] says:

> What a lot of people don't realize in a start-up company, if you are making a transition from an older or small company or any type of company, when you get into a start-up company, it's you. It's you and a piece of paper. It's a white piece of paper.

Local management in an otherwise less-than-innovative firm can create pockets of innovation, as in the case of a manager whose open and trusting style permits her employees to craft their own work arrangements as long as they get their work done. Innovation pockets can contain a myriad of alternative employment practices (from sabbaticals to special project assignments), illustrating what one's employer has already found acceptable. Individuals working in innovative settings can readily shape their employment conditions on their own, without the need for negotiation. In highly flexible work settings, idiosyncrasies are not really exceptional if customized employment conditions are the norm.

Moderate flexibility exists in situations with more established structures and standardized work practices, where local conditions expand the opportunity for idiosyncratic arrangements for some individual workers. Some individuals, by virtue of their distinctive skills, high contributions, or long-standing service, can find themselves more trusted than others in their work group. Trusted employees are supervised less closely and enjoy greater autonomy.[47] This may be the case particularly in situations in which these workers are in a position to perform their duties relatively independently of coworkers. In these settings, such workers can enjoy greater tolerance for deviant behavior as long as their high contributions are sustained. In situations of moderate flexibility, accommodation is achieved both by negotiation and via changes workers introduce on their own.

An enlarged zone of acceptance selectively bestowed by an employer permits certain employees to individualize their work role and other employment conditions without having to get permission. It can also make them more comfortable in asking for further accommodations. Especially skilled or motivated workers may capitalize on gaps in existing in duties, tasks, and organizational activities to create a new role whose focus hasn't previously existed in the firm. This gap filling may involve solving a problem the employer doesn't know it has. Idiosyncratic arrangements based on gap filling not only are satisfying to workers but can help the employer become more adaptive. Though veteran workers are often the ones to spot gaps, relatively new hires also can capitalize on the gaps they see, as in the case of the programmer who received no training at all when he joined the firm and thus decided to take responsibility for training subsequent new hires.

Employees can test the waters to identify what constitutes acceptable behavior, which enables them to initiate their own preferred arrangements or formulate their requests for an i-deal so as to make them appear less deviant. Careful attention to the dynamics of the particular setting can reveal whether there really is an enforced rule or binding precedent to oppose the particular arrangement a worker seeks.[48] Tom Schultz, a manager in a pharmaceutical firm, was elected to the council of the small township in which he lived. This part-time public service role was performed mostly in the evenings and on weekends. But it required Tom sometimes to field phone calls from the township office while at work. Since his firm's code of ethics stressed public service and many of its senior leadership were visibly involved in community activities, Tom felt comfortable doing some township business during the workday, without asking for permission.

Decoupling is another way to create individualized arrangements in moderately flexible settings, redefining existing work by creating a new job category to legitimate an exception. This process requires negotiation because job categories are typically an important part of a firm's established structure. Decoupling can break up existing roles or duties into new job categories to the advantage of the worker seeking a special arrangement. It can involve redefining the entire role of a worker whose request for accommodation would otherwise create conflicts or burdens for coworkers. The classic examples are early retirees who become technical advisers and other valued workers who shift from regular employment to independent contractor status with the same firm. These workers continue to provide the employer with valuable knowledge but often do not have direct responsibilities. In these cases, decoupling can result in workers having special titles in job categories that signal unique or distinctive status (e.g., "consultant," or "special assistant").

Finally, workers have less freedom to initiate change in *constrained settings* with limited flexibility, for instance in situations where they might be closely supervised or serve several demanding constituents. Informal flexibility is limited when the demands of managers, colleagues, or customers constrain how a worker does the job. Working from home rather than in the office, starting and stopping work at different times throughout the week, and other manifestations of personal preference may be impossible for a person whose work is highly interdependent with that of others, unless the worker obtains approval to do so. In such circumstances, the zone of acceptance characterizing the job is narrow, and workers have difficulty initiating idiosyncratic arrangements unless they explicitly negotiate them with their manager and any affected coworkers or clients.

In settings characterized by many established rules and complicated approval processes to legitimate exceptions, work-arounds represent ways of reinterpreting existing rules to make them more flexible.[49] Work-arounds can bend (or sometimes technically break) rules but are accomplished with formal authorization. For example, opportunities for flexibility can result from liberal interpretations of existing policy. A manager who grants an educational leave to a worker who wants to spend a year traveling the globe, in the hope that she will return to the company, can capitalize on the fact that the firm has no hard-and-fast rules regarding what sort of education a "leave" might entail. In settings with limited flexibility, most idiosyncrasies require negotiation because work roles tend to be narrow and inelastic. Idiosyncrasies in less-flexible situations tend to be exceptional both in the process through which they arise and in their content.

In highly bureaucratic settings, idiosyncrasies can be difficult to sustain due to forces for consistency and standardization. Because they require approval, often from several layers of management, and can be difficult to sustain over time, work-arounds are the least flexible sources of innovation. Nonetheless, workers and managers in bureaucratic settings can use work-arounds to shift the meanings ascribed to employer policies. Continued use of this ploy can, however, undermine the legitimacy of the firm's existing procedures.

Conclusion

Idiosyncrasy is an inevitable response to the complexity of human and organizational life. It arises out of the inherent incompleteness in employment arrangements. While incompleteness is a by-product of the uncertain and dynamic circumstances employers and workers face, it is also motivated by each party's desire to retain their autonomy and freedom. Idiosyncrasy arises via four processes: employer-initiated acquiescence (e.g., job creep), worker-initiated acquiescence (e.g., job crafting), employer-initiated negotiation (which may or many not constitute an i-deal depending on the degree of worker influence over the arrangement), and worker-initiated i-deals. Work settings differ in their opportunities for flexibility. Highly innovative work settings permit idiosyncrasy to emerge via acquiescence. Less-flexible settings require more negotiation since workers in these environments tend to lack the authority to introduce idiosyncrasies on their own. Nonetheless, idiosyncrasy is a normal feature of employment where veteran, star, and other highly valued workers are concerned because the opportunity to individualize one's employment arrangement is a common reward for exceptional contributors.

Insofar as some employees have sufficient authority to create idiosyncratic conditions on their own without formal authorization, they need to negotiate only when they cannot institute particular arrangements on their own. In effect, workers pursue i-deals when they believe they need approval to make an individualized arrangement legitimate.

— 3 —

Shady Deals:
What I-deals Are *Not*

A fav'rite has no friend!
—*Thomas Gray*[1]

Crime, like virtue, has its degrees.
—*Jean Racine*[2]

Commitment moves us from the mirror trap of
the self absorbed with the self to the freedom
of a community of shared values.
—*Michael Lewis*[3]

Workers and employers get the most benefit from those i-deals that are kept from looking like their dysfunctional counterparts, or what I refer to as "shady deals." Shady deals lack the "win–win" quality of i-deals, where both worker and employer benefit (Table 3.1). It is important to note that these arrangements are deficient because of their inability to be legitimated in the eyes of third parties. When viewed from the perspective of coworkers and other organizational constituents (e.g., stockholders), shady deals impair their participants' moral standing and reputation. Though i-deals ostensibly arise under legitimate conditions, third parties may think differently. Coworkers don't necessarily share the same information or vantage point as the i-deal's principals. In consequence, i-deals can resemble shady deals in the eyes of coworkers, unless efforts are made to distinguish i-deals from

44

Table 3.1

Facets of Person-Specific Arrangements

	Arrangements		
	Preferential	Unauthorized	Idiosyncratic
Exemplar	The owner's cousin takes longer lunch breaks than workers are allowed. The supervisor scolds all other workers if they don't return from their lunch break in an hour. Trying to curry favor with this influential cousin, the supervisor says nothing when the cousin shows up two hours late from lunch.	A department store salesperson sets aside an expensive swimsuit, waiting until the price is marked down after the season before buying it herself.	An auditor whose career goal is to become a tax consultant negotiates with his boss to work with a tax partner's clients in order to learn that business.
Process	Favoritism, Politics	Usurped	Negotiation
Basis	Relationship	Rule breaking	Value to firm
Beneficiary	Worker and boss	Worker	Worker and employing firm

their illegitimate and dysfunctional counterparts. The distinction between i-deals and shady deals rests in the dynamics of workplace justice and the legitimacy of organizational action.

Dysfunctional Employment Arrangements

I-deals have two dysfunctional counterparts: preferential treatment and unauthorized taking.

Preferential treatment occurs when a worker receives favored treatment from an agent of the firm, usually the immediate manager or supervisor, to strengthen their personal relationship or to reinforce the manager's political ties, as in the case of lowered performance standards for a worker who is a friend of the boss. Though extending special treatment to individual workers is part of the legitimate authority managers exercise, preferential treatment undermines this authority. Preferential treatment is self-aggrandizing behavior on the part of the individual manager or agent of the firm. It can entail accommodations to a favored worker with whom that manager has a personal relationship, or it can take the form of providing special favors to workers—not based on their performance or value to the firm but due to their personal or political ties.

45

Unauthorized taking occurs when a worker confiscates his or her employer's resources without authorization, as in the case of employee theft or misrepresentation. Unauthorized taking involves breaking formal rules or violating formal or implied organizational policies. It is self-serving and unauthorized use of the firm's resources, outside the legitimate authority of the individual worker, for example, taking money out of petty cash for personal expenses or doing one's personal business on company time.

I-deals are negotiated around the interests of both worker and firm, unlike preferential or unauthorized arrangements. While i-deals can benefit both firm and worker and strengthen their relationship, preferential treatment and unauthorized practices have adverse consequences for the firm in particular, eroding trust, undermining cooperation within the firm, and challenging the legitimacy of the firm's practices.[4]

Preferential Treatment

Preferential treatment arises when managers and other agents of a firm favor certain workers over others because of their personal relations or political ties. Such an arrangement takes the form of favoritism or cronyism whose primary basis is a personal relationship between the individuals involved (i.e., relatives, friends, or powerful third parties). Such arrangements strengthen the bond between worker and manager, permitting them to meet each other's needs at the expense of coworkers, colleagues, or the larger firm.

In traditional bureaucratic organizations, preferential treatment creates political benefits for managers, expanding their base of power beyond the firm's formal systems. As a union-busting strategy, for example, local managers may attempt to defeat organizing efforts by offering financial payoffs and special favors to influential workers to keep them from supporting the union. During the organizing of a local of the United Automobile Workers in Detroit during the 1930s,

> the foreman, under instructions from the management, called the workers into their offices one at a time and confidentially told each one that he was getting a five-cent raise for his loyalty to the company. An effort was made to create the impression that only he or a few like him were so favored. [5]

Having an in with management can be a reward in itself, conveying the status and other benefits of being part of an in-group. Along these lines, the cronyism seen in developing countries has counterparts in Western business culture, including the General Motors of the 1960s and 1970s. John DeLorean, in the book *On a Clear Day You Can See General Motors*, describes the politicking behind General Motors' practice of "non-obvious promotion."[6] Here, a senior executive (typically male) would promote a junior employee several levels down in the company hierarchy to be his immediate subordinate. In bypassing more senior and experienced people, the executive ensured that the new subordinate became indebted to him because of this unearned promotion. The loyalty this self-interested behavior created served the political interests of the General Motors executive but did nothing to enhance the overall competence of the company's management. Preferential treatment as such serves the political needs of a few powerful people while reducing cooperation and trust within the firm.[7]

Preferential treatment is relational and political in nature. It undermines the broader firm's legitimacy while advancing the personal interests of a few.[8] It might be argued that playing favorites benefits the firm, by giving it a lackey willing to do the employer's bidding. When the employer pays off influential workers to reduce a union's ability to organize, such an arrangement might seem win–win to the employer and those influential workers. Nonetheless, such payoffs undermine the overall relationship between the employer and its workforce. Predicated on relationships and political connections, preferential treatment is not based on those worker capabilities that add value to the firm.[9] For the firm, preferential treatment's net consequences are negative.

Unlike self-aggrandizing political acts, i-deals are legitimate because the interests of workers and the firm are reflected in their negotiation. One striking feature of the rise in idiosyncratic deals through worker power is that they seem to be less biased by traditional sources of corporate political power such as gender and race.[10] Along these same lines, in their systematic and detailed survey of participation and influence on the part of the U.S. workforce, Freeman and Rogers found that gender and race were far less important in shaping individual clout and opportunities for negotiation on the job than was a person's occupation.[11]

While i-deals, by definition, are not preferential treatment, the secrecy that often accompanies them can create the appearance of preferential treatment to coworkers. Coworkers discovering that a colleague has a "special" deal can resent its under-the-table nature. Moreover, coworkers are likely to possess different information than the i-deal's principals do and thus will probably not fully understand the deal's particulars, a condition exacerbating the appearance of preferential treatment. A former department head once told me:

> I had agreed to cut the teaching load of a faculty member in exchange for a reduction in his pay. Another professor came in a few days later and demanded that his teaching load be cut too. He was taken aback when I told him he also

would have to accept a reduction in pay. Somehow, that part of the arrangement hadn't come to his attention.

Although they differ from preferential treatment, i-deals often do represent private, local arrangements between workers and managers. As exemplified in many cases of pay secrecy, the idiosyncratic deal can arise out of a legitimate need to recruit, motivate, and retain good workers in a competitive marketplace. Yet making these deals risks creating a sense of inequity among those receiving fewer rewards or merely different ones. With ever-greater pressures toward customization, companies need to become savvier in creating flexible employment arrangements that don't look like illegitimate preferential treatment. To accomplish this, i-deals must be implemented in ways that are functional to the firm and its workers, rather than the result of who you know or even which boss you work for.

Demographic Diversity Complicates Use of I-deals

The pressure on employers to be flexible in ways that do not signal preferential treatment intensifies as the workforce becomes more demographically diverse. Information selectively transmitted to traditionally dominant groups of workers, from high-status white males to those workers with the same career-advantaging pedigrees, can permit these workers to develop political acumen to use the firm's formal and informal systems to their advantage.[12] Since demographically diverse workers often possess different information, otherwise justifiable special treatment for one worker may seem like an unfair advantage to that person's coworkers. When the employee with the i-deal and his or her peers come from different backgrounds, it is more likely that these coworkers will attribute the special treatment to that background, rather than to such legitimating conditions as merit or need.

Demographically diverse workers often disagree in their interpretations regarding ostensibly the same organizational practice.[13] In the doctoral program I teach in, senior PhD students with good track records in the program and success as teaching assistants are eligible, with the dean's consent, to serve as instructors in charge of their own course. Several years ago, senior women doctoral students noted that while they typically worked as teaching assistants to a professor, their male counterparts tended to work as instructors. Since instructors are paid more and get valuable experience that helps in getting a good job after graduation, this disparity was upsetting for both the women and the dean. When confronted with this fact, the dean realized that the male students knew who to ask to become an instructor, while the female students either didn't ask or didn't ask the right person. So that this career-enhancing opportunity didn't look like preferential treatment, the playing field between male and female doctoral students had to be leveled. To accomplish this, the dean began advertising both broadly and to each incoming class of PhD students the criteria that made senior doctoral students eligible to serve as instructors—and whom to ask about getting these assignments.

Accounting for I-deals Through Credible Reasons

When an i-deal is under discussion, the reasons that motivate an employer to grant it are critical to its legitimacy. Unless a clear and credible premise for the i-deal is conveyed to organization members, the i-deal is not likely to be construed as legitimate. Note that the criteria for "clear and credible" are gauged from the perspective of third parties, such as coworkers. Criteria judged acceptable in the eyes of the beholder are more likely if a shared set of values exist within the organization regarding the way in which the employer relates to workers, allocates rewards, and makes its other personnel decisions. This shared set of values can be thought of as a meta-contract, that is, agreed-upon conditions guiding employment-related decisions in the firm and promoting their legitimacy in the eyes of organization members.[14]

A classic example of such a meta-contract is the Common Bond, a widely relied upon statement of commitments shared between AT&T and its employees.[15] Encouraging accountability and teamwork to satisfy customers while supporting personal growth and learning, such values, when shared, can underpin a meta-contract, making it easier to determine whether a potential i-deal is appropriate to the interests of employer and individual employees (worker and coworkers alike).[16] A proposed i-deal that interfered with customer service or burdened coworkers might be judged as inconsistent with the meta-contract. In contrast, an i-deal that provided a worker with an opportunity to work in a more personally satisfying fashion while supporting both customers and coworkers would be consistent with this meta-contract.

Effective implementation of an i-deal reinforces the relationship between an employer and its workforce. Poor implementation weakens it. The signal indicator of poor i-deal implementation is the absence of explanation or discussion. Consider the case of Barbara Cruz, an immigrant to the United States from Latin America, who relied on public transportation to get to her day job. An otherwise hardworking and dedicated employee, she sometimes arrived half an hour past her scheduled work time and still left promptly at 5 p.m. to catch the bus home. Her sympathetic supervisor accepted the irregularity of Barbara's arrival times, consistent with the relational support this organization extended to its workforce. Yet that supervisor was less sanguine about tardiness on the part of other workers with cars, unless they had a reason he deemed acceptable. Barbara's coworkers who drove to work each day resented what seemed to be a different standard for her.

In Barbara's case, her supervisor needed to explain to other employees why this special arrangement was being made, and why being late when one has a car might differ from being dependent on public transportation—if indeed the difference is a meaningful one. He also would have been wise to require Barbara to ensure that her irregular start times did not in any way burden her colleagues, even if it required her to stay later or to take work home. In Barbara's organization, the meta-contract resided in its relational approach to its workforce. The employer tended to extend support when workers in good standing had a legitimate need for accommodation. What was lacking in Barbara's situation was agreement on and discussion of what "legitimate need" meant.

As these examples show, there is a slippery slope between an i-deal and preferential treatment, based on coworkers' understanding of the legitimacy of the conditions on which the i-deal is based. Since coworkers do not have complete information regarding the negotiation of an i-deal, especially when it is negotiated in secret, the way the deal arises can be taken as a sign that it lacks legitimacy.

Unauthorized Taking

Unauthorized arrangements arise when a worker takes resources for which he or she has no authorized claim or approval from the employer. Making personal use of company resources without permission can range from overt activities such as theft (e.g., embezzlement, misappropriation of company equipment and supplies) to more subtle behavior such as misrepresenting one's relationship with the firm for personal gain (e.g., making false claims about one's position).[17] Illicit acts take many forms. Employee theft is one way a worker can appropriate an employer's resources without authorization. Other examples include accepting bribes or stealing time to do unapproved personal business on the job.

Unauthorized arrangements typically occur without the knowledge or involvement of the employer and its agents (e.g., supervisors). Getting a haircut and doing personal shopping while out of the office to call on customers are examples of the unauthorized employment conditions a worker can initiate. A phone company employee, in a job he found boring, went out on cases of "trouble" to repair phone lines, but sometimes took the long way to the location, stopping to visit friends in the vicinity of the repair. Such activities reflect unauthorized use of employer resources—in this instance, time—activities the employer would probably not support if it knew about them. At times, these arrangements can be on the borderline of ethicality, particularly when there appear to be no clear negative consequences for the employer. Nonetheless, the intrajection of non-work-related activities into the work role can challenge the authority of the employer in specifying performance requirements and employment conditions and make it difficult to enforce credible performance standards.

Collusion between worker and manager can be involved when unauthorized behavior combines with preferential treatment. Individual supervisors can look the other way in a fashion that benefits both the worker and themselves while harming the broader organization. A case in point is the convenience-store manager who makes it more attractive to work the hard-to-cover late hours by letting night-shift workers take groceries without paying for them.[18] Practices such as theft of company property or misuse of company time can form part of a technically illegal, but sometimes normative, invisible wage structure in which managers and coworkers look the other way or perform illegal acts themselves.[19]

Unauthorized taking has numerous consequences. It reduces the authority of the formal organization by institutionalizing rule breaking. Deviance sometimes starts out as a way of restoring equity when pay is low or working conditions are otherwise unfair. Nonetheless, a worker's belief that deviance is a payback for poor employer treatment can spill over to his or her coworkers and give rise to norms that promote illicit acts. Should the employer later seek to pay its workers more equitably and restore its authority and trustworthiness, workers can be reluctant to give up the deviant behavior they have come to enjoy. Attempts to realign the interests of workers and employers can meet with wide resistance, while formal systems are viewed with suspicion and under-the-table practices continue.[20] Unauthorized arrangements, where deviance is the norm, complicate attempts to create a more open and trust-based employment system.

Gray Areas

At times, the boundaries between i-deals and their dysfunctional counterparts are ambiguous (Figure 3.1). Both unauthorized and idiosyncratic arrangements can come about under conditions in which a worker has a special relationship with his or her immediate manager. It is not uncommon for people with close ties to senior management to have unique employment roles. "Special assistants," "advisers," and long-standing "consultants" who serve at the discretion of a powerful manager commonly have personal ties as well as their own distinctive competencies to thank for the roles they

Figure 3.1 **Blurry Boundaries Between Person-specific Employment Practices**

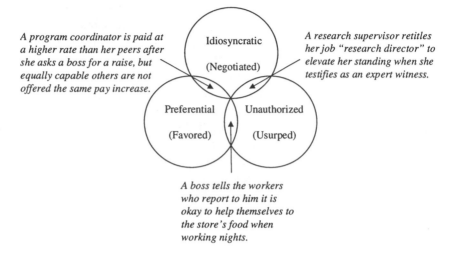

A program coordinator is paid at a higher rate than her peers after she asks a boss for a raise, but equally capable others are not offered the same pay increase.

Idiosyncratic

(Negotiated)

A research supervisor retitles her job "research director" to elevate her standing when she testifies as an expert witness.

Preferential

(Favored)

Unauthorized

(Usurped)

A boss tells the workers who report to him it is okay to help themselves to the store's food when working nights.

play. Similarly, preferential treatment sometimes borders on the illicit. Consider the driver for a highly successful entrepreneur on Chicago's South Side. The driver—who had been a boyhood friend of his boss—took bills out of the company cash box as "walking around money" to show off to his friends. Seldom spending it, he usually put it back in the cash box at the end of the week. The entrepreneur knew about his friend's behavior and looked the other way. Whether this situation is illicit or preferential depends on the perspective you take, pointing to the tension between the perceptions of the involved parties, the arrangement's actual features, and how third parties interpret the situation.

The slippery slope to the dark side of person-specific employment arrangements is the confusion of idiosyncratic arrangements with their dysfunctional counterparts. Although treating individuals with respect according to their needs and individual interests is valuable for the person and the firm, how this differential treatment is handled conveys important information to coworkers. The process involved in creating an i-deal spells the difference between being seen as acting in good faith and being seen as acting unjustly in the eyes of third parties. Since they typically are negotiated with the immediate manager, i-deals flirt with the dark side more often in their resemblance to preferential treatment. Even workers who believe they have negotiated an i-deal can become aware that it looks like unwarranted special treatment to others. In the words of a former restaurant manager describing his own i-deal,

From my first year working with the restaurant my employer provided "special perks" to keep me satisfied. I was paid more than my peers. I interpreted this to mean they found me valuable and wanted me to stay. . . . It's sad to say, but this restaurant was very political. . . . I never realized how much more I was on the "inside" than some others. I guess I took much for granted. It was in talking to people who were frustrated by the politics that I realized how strong an element it was with this company.

This restaurant, like many small businesses, had little in the way of formal performance appraisal or systematic employee development—and thus was ripe for the predominance of preferential treatment over i-deals, at least from the perspective of coworkers. Absence of such supports for performance-based personnel decisions makes it tough to keep legitimate i-deals distinct from favoritism. Similarly, if one worker receives more latitude in choosing assignments because he or she is highly trusted by management, whether this is an i-deal or preferential treatment is ambiguous. If in consequence of this special arrangement the worker's skills develop more rapidly than those of his or her colleagues, it is not surprising that this worker is then chosen for promotion over less-favored peers. Nonetheless, without clear standards for evaluating performance, this worker's promotion is unlikely to be understood as legitimate (i.e., based on shared values, in this case regarding high performance as a basis for special recognition) rather than politically motivated or otherwise preferential.

The illicit also can become a legitimated idiosyncrasy, if the employer acquiesces to a worker's rule violation. Joanna Jannsens, an organizational psychologist, thought that her formal job title (personnel research supervisor) was low in status compared to those of her professional peers. She printed up business cards and gave herself the title of personnel research *director* to make it easier for her to obtain expert witness opportunities. Eventually, her manager learned about this embellishment. Worrying that the false title might surface when Joanna was scheduled to testify before the state legislature on the company's behalf, the manager quickly changed the psychologist's title to personnel research director. This is an example of acquiescence, when the employer accepts the terms the worker has usurped.[21]

In our discussion of shady deals, the dysfunctional counterparts of the i-deal, we have identified a challenge, that is, how to resolve the difficulties that arise when individual workers, as i-deal recipients, and their colleagues seek to be treated fairly, equally, *and* differently at the same time. Equal treatment need not mean the *same* treatment, but to understand how such might be the case we need to address simultaneously the three parties impacted by the typical employment relationship: the employer, the worker, and his or her coworkers. We have established that an arrangement that is an i-deal to the worker and employer who negotiated it can nonetheless look like preferential treatment or unauthorized taking to coworkers. At the heart of this difference in perspective are the impact of the i-deal on the relative standing of coworkers and its related implications for justice issues in the organization.

The Dilemma of Relative Standing

Status in local hierarchies can have considerable value. While negative consequences arise from being at the bottom, being higher in the hierarchy brings with it valued resources that are often in limited supply (e.g., money, interesting assignments, career opportunities).[22] Robert Frank has argued that paying people based upon that portion of the firm's overall productivity directly attributable to them, the economists ideal, seldom occurs in reality, as people at the top of a hierarchy receive special returns from their position in addition to pay, while those at the bottom incur special costs. High-status members get nonmonetary payouts, such as recognition and deference, which put pressure on employers to reduce variations in pay. (Indeed, paying higher performers based exactly on what they contribute would be perceived as an unfair wage structure if these high performers were also accorded more respect and recognition than their lower-performing peers.) In effect, a "fair" wage compensates people for where they stand in their respective earning hierarchies.[23]

Relative standing among people in a work group is a powerful motivator of worker attitude and behavior, and in particular it can influence their beliefs regarding the employer's fairness and respect for them as individuals. I-deals can alter the relative standing of members in a work group by advantaging some over others in ways that can be unforeseen at the time of the i-deals' creation. The designer who proposes an i-deal to undertake a special project, thereby acquiring unique skills, may be better positioned to argue for a raise later if the employer comes to depend on the designer's new skills. On the other hand, the nonconformity of i-deals, from reduced hours to performing duties unlike those of peers, can diminish an i-dealer's status over time, in particular through lower subsequent performance ratings compared to those of their counterparts whose jobs are still in compliance with the firm's conventions. The lawyer whose i-deal lets him work part-time may well be evaluated less favorably over time than his full-time peers if performance criteria are based on absolute number of billable hours. Thus, i-deals can enhance or diminish the status of i-dealers over time, depending on how the organization gauges the individual i-dealer's contribution and value.

Concomitantly, the relative standing of third parties can also be affected by i-deals. The potential effects start with the way an i-deal is created. If coworkers learn of a deal made in secret, it suggests not only that it might be unfair, but that those coworkers are not considered worthy of being informed. In contrast, involving coworkers in the process of creating an i-deal, depending on how it is done, can convey respect, concern, or even deference. The potential effects i-deals can have on third parties continue with their implementation. When competitive resources are involved (from pay to promotion opportunities), third parties, in particular coworkers, may either gain or lose standing commensurate with the deal's impact on the relative status of the i-deal's recipient. If the i-dealer's opportunities for promotion or pay raises are improved by the i-deal, coworkers can lose standing. If these opportunities are subsequently reduced, coworkers can gain. In settings where workers monitor intensely how they are treated compared to peers, special treatment for one person can derive its meaning simply from the fact that that person receives something that others don't. In myriad ways i-deals can throw the internal equities within the organization out of kilter—unless the processes whereby they are created and implemented take the issue of relative standing among workers into account.

The sensitive issue of social standing is largely an intragroup process. As Robert Frank suggests, "Our 'needs' depend very strongly on those with whom we *choose* to associate closely."[24] A utility function for individual status needs could be operationalized as "feel bad whenever you are less well provided for than your peers."[25] Consider millionaire baseball players feeling cheated because even higher salaries are offered to their peers:

> To be 50 or 60 on the pay scale doesn't sit well in my stomach. . . . I signed a contract, but now, I'm not happy with it anymore because baseball is business just like any other job. There are A players, B players and C players. I have been an A player for a long time.[26]

Shifts in workers' standing in relation to one another is part and parcel of i-deals made by employees. Unlike the idiosyncratic arrangements independent contractors make, i-deals are made by employees embedded in work settings where their performance and employment conditions are inextricably tied to those of their fellow workers.[27] When i-deals alter the relative standing of workers in an organization (or appear to), issues of justice arise.

Justice

What makes i-deals special from a justice perspective is the presence of coworkers who are ostensibly doing the same or comparable jobs for the same employer. Having agreed to the i-deal in the first place, worker and

Table 3.2

I-deals and Organizational Justice Issues

Construct	Key Actors	Process	Resources	Constituencies
I-deals	Individual worker Employer Third parties, principally coworkers	Negotiation	Broad, ranging from socioemotional support to money	• Worker and employer are principals actively negotiating an i-deal. • Coworkers minimally are evaluators, but potentially also are participants in the process of creating an i-deal.
Distributive justice	Employer	Allocation	Typically, narrowly focused on money and monetizable resources.	• Employer allocates resources. • Worker receives resources. • Coworkers are evaluators.
	I-deals involve direct worker efforts to influence resources he or she receives.	*Multiple parties may influence decision regarding i-deal.*	*I-deals involve nonmonetary resources such as status, support, and information.*	*Employer, worker, and coworkers may each influence decision regarding i-deal.*
Procedural justice	Employer, typically with support of human resources and legal professionals	Rule following	Procedures followed in allocating money and monetizable resources (e.g., promotion) and information sharing (e.g., voice).	• Employer creates procedures • Worker may participate in procedures to varying degrees, and evaluates their fairness. • Coworkers are witnesses.

56

| Interactional justice | Employer, typically represented by managers interacting with employee

Focus in i-deals shifts to interactional justice experienced by third parties, including coworkers. | Relationship

Particularistic (quality of interpersonal treatment) | *I-deals may follow rules or arise in an ad hoc fashion, with no established procedures.*

I-deals involve nonmonetary resources for which proceduralization is difficult | • Employer is actor.
• Worker is recipient.
• Coworkers are witnesses.

Coworkers are recipients of interactional justice. I-deals create relational issues with coworkers for both the employer and the worker-recipient of an i-deal. | *Workers and coworkers may each actively participate in procedures surrounding creation of i-deal.* |

Note: Text in italics charactering how i-deals relate to each justice issue.

employer are predisposed to view it as fair. Yet, the very existence of an i-deal means that coworkers are treated differently from the i-dealer. Because multiple parties are affected by i-deals, issues of fairness must be addressed from three perspectives: that of the employer, that of the focal employee, and that of his or her coworkers. In attending to the i-deal's three parties we can understand how the benefits of i-deals can be optimized while distancing them from their dysfunctional dark side.

Procedural Justice

Procedural justice pertains to beliefs regarding the fairness of processes governing decisions. Originally conceptualized in terms of formal procedures, procedural justice also extends to informal ways people in power make decisions.[28] When procedural justice exists, workers express greater overall satisfaction with their employer's informal as well as formal personnel decisions. In general, procedural justice gives affected parties an opportunity to exercise their voice, that is, to express their points of view and to influence proceedings that affect them.[29] I-deals in themselves are a form of voice that individuals exercise over their own employment arrangements, at least in the case of the worker who negotiates the i-deal.

Though voice is a central feature of procedural justice, many workers have little say in the workplace decisions that affect them. We noted earlier that Freeman and Rogers, in a national survey of American workers, found that those workers with higher occupational status were more likely to avail themselves of an employer's open-door policy.[30] This aspect of the process relates to our discussion of relative standing: workers may need to believe that they have status in the firm before they are willing to speak up. If workers' opportunity to have their voices heard is not equally available—or equally exercised—the likelihood increases that people of different status in the organization will view its procedural justice systems differently. In the context of i-deals, voice pertains not only to the worker who speaks up to demand an i-deal, but also to his or her coworkers whose interests that i-deal impacts.

Voice, though important, is only one facet of procedural justice. Conditions for procedural justice include accurate information that is free of bias and consistent implementation of procedures across workers.[31] These conditions may be even more difficult to achieve when i-deals are concerned. I-deals arising from a negotiation between a worker and an employer may reflect only the information possessed by those two parties. Both have their own frame of reference and inevitably some degree of self-serving bias. Coworkers possess other information, regarding the consequences of the i-deal for customer service and their own job performance and the i-deal's future implications for their own career options. Such information can be critical to creating i-deals that benefit all parties involved.

Consistency, another feature of procedural justice, can be difficult to achieve in creating i-deals because so many of these arrangements arise from novel situations for which the firm has no precedent. The employer and its human resource director typically have no policy to rely on when dealing with the first-ever expatriate who refuses to accept a new assignment unless the firm moves her grand piano, or the pioneering manager who wants to go part-time. Employers are challenged to apply procedural justice principles in personnel decisions that involve novel or exceptional circumstances. Procedural justice generally involves the standardized implementation of personnel actions (e.g., terminations, layoffs, introduction of no-smoking policies).[32] Organizations are likely to require a base of experience in order to create standard procedures and then implement them consistently and effectively.[33] Not surprisingly, standardizing idiosyncratic arrangements is difficult because they often are a response to special demands or needs. (As one worker commented on this challenge, "Don't get rigid about flexibility."[34]) For example, when professional-service firms such as law and accounting firms began affirmative action programs to recruit and promote women, they had little experience and fewer policies regarding pregnant professionals or nursing mothers. These firms witnessed the introduction of breast-feeding at work, mommy tracks, and new challenges to traditional promotion systems based on working long hours. Coworkers, particularly males and women without children, sometimes view such changes as inconsistent and based on preferential treatment.[35]

The diversity of interests in the labor force also makes complete standardization of practices difficult. Cafeteria-type benefit arrangements are an exemplar of the standardization of flexibility.[36] Nonetheless, some departure from standard procedures is necessary in the face of environmental changes. In the early phases of adapting to such major changes in human resource practice, inconsistency is inevitable. Not surprisingly, this inconsistency can appear to be preferential treatment or a violation of the firm's own rules or precedents, particularly when the decisions behind it are made with little public deliberation or communication. In general, the conditions that promote procedural justice are absent in many instances where i-deals arise.

Procedural justice research to date has provided little guidance on how to experiment fairly in nonroutine, novel circumstances that arise in organizations. Moreover, it has little to say about the procedures associated with allocating nonmonetary resources (e.g., challenging work, support with work-family balance), which frequently are bargained for by workers pursuing i-deals.

Distributive Justice

Distributive justice refers to individuals' beliefs regarding the fair allocation of outcomes they and others receive. Individuals can have various standards of comparison for evaluating distributive justice (e.g., the external market, worker contributions to the firm, comparisons to other workers). The choice of comparison depends on the distribution or allocation rule used (e.g., equal pay for equal work, preexisting agreement, need-based pay). Distributive justice is, to a great extent, a function of social comparison, particularly when scarce and valued resources are involved.[37] Recall the millionaire baseball player described above who felt cheated by the even higher salaries offered to his peers.

Because an i-deal creates special treatment for one worker, it challenges the conventions of distributive fairness. Distributive justice typically focuses on up-front establishment of rules for determining how to allocate outcomes (e.g., rewards, punishments, and decisions at odds with employee interests, such as layoffs). Implementing such rules requires establishing criteria, for example, based on salary surveys, industry benchmarks, or incentives tied to performance targets. In contrast, the decision to grant an i-deal often is based on ad hoc criteria created in response to unusual circumstances.

Distributive fairness is particularly complicated when current employees use outside offers to bargain for an i-deal. An employer might decide to give a worker with an outside offer more money, on the notion that the offer indicates he or she is currently underpaid. However, that offer has implications for the potential market value of the i-dealer's colleagues, too. Nonetheless, few employers are likely to update their appraisal of the market value of the i-dealer's *peers*—even if the evidence suggests that their market value is comparable. To this i-dealer's coworkers, the way they are paid relative to their peers may now be distributively unfair, since the worker with the outside offer is seldom asked to contribute more in order to merit the raise. Because coworker adverse reactions are anticipated, the distributive unfairness of this i-deal is managed via pay secrecy, making it difficult for coworkers to know exactly what the i-dealer gained by brandishing an outside offer.

I-deals are often associated with obfuscation, that is to say, practices that limit the ability of coworkers to make comparisons to one another. Pay-secrecy policies are the exemplar of comparison-reducing practices, as an attempt to suppress communication between coworkers regarding compensation.[38] Informal practices used when i-deals are negotiated can also discourage comparison by suppressing information ("Don't tell anyone") or by making the deal difficult to verify ("Don't put it in writing"). These practices often backfire as i-deals made in this fashion can wind up having the same dysfunctional consequences as their less legitimate counterparts. This is particularly the case when coworkers learn about secret deals that have altered their standing with regard to competitively allocated resources such as pay.

Complicating the picture further, some i-deals are created in *response* to distributive injustice. Would-be i-dealers can demand special treatment in compensation for what they see as unfair or inequitable treatment. Past injustice can be used as a bargaining chip when workers seek i-deals as redress. Budget cuts that halt a promised promotion, raise, or educational opportunity can cause an affected worker to bargain with the boss for alternatives that remedy the situation. Remedial action takes the form of an idiosyncratic arrangement—such as a special assignment—that substitutes for a promised promotion or other reward that failed to materialize.[39] Special accommodations to rectify one injustice can raise new concerns regarding equitable treatment among observant coworkers, unless an appropriate justification is forthcoming. Unfortunately the circumstances behind such remedial actions can be embarrassing to the parties involved, leading to suppression of the facts. Insofar as coworker sentiments are a concern, the employer might need to acknowledge its failure to deliver on a promise, or the worker might have to own up that he or she was not promoted at the expected time. Nonetheless, worker and employer tend to downplay i-deals made as remedies for injustice, depriving coworkers of information relevant to their own employment relationship.

Distributive justice research is somewhat limited in the information it provides regarding i-deals and other idiosyncrasies in employment. To date, it has largely ignored the offsets workers seek on their own to make organizational practices more distributively fair, if only for themselves personally. It has also ignored the less-monetizable intrinsic and social rewards that workers derive from employment (e.g., visibility, recognition), which workers may attempt to negotiate when such rewards aren't otherwise forthcoming. Idiosyncratic arrangements commonly involve negotiations for employment terms other than money,[40] suggesting that justice research may be poorly informed regarding the broader array of noneconomic exchanges arising in employment. Lastly, in its focus on employer allocations to workers, distributive justice research has paid little attention to negotiated exchanges such as i-deals.

Interactional Justice

Interactional justice refers to the quality of interpersonal treatment received during the execution of an organizational decision or personal process.[41] Organizational decisions treating affected employees in a dignified and respectful fashion enhance interactional justice by maintaining their standing in their work group and in the organization broadly. Employees generally look to the person carrying out the procedure, such as a manager or human resource staff member, to provide interactional justice, in contrast to procedural justice, which tends to be attributed to the entity whose procedures are involved (e.g., the firm as a whole). As a result, interactional justice influences how workers view their supervisors, while procedural justice shapes their view of the organization.[42] The typical focus of interactional justice is whether recipients feel that they have been treated respectfully. The worker-recipient of the i-deal, having found his or her employer willing to grant a special request, is likely to have an enhanced sense of interactional justice. In contrast, i-deals can call attention to the lack of respect shown toward third parties such as coworkers. Respect in this context refers to consideration given to the implications an i-deal has for third parties and the means by which this consideration is conveyed.

A key influence on coworker perspectives is any communication the employer or i-dealer directs toward them regarding the reasons for making an i-deal. The explanations that are offered, referred to as social accounts, affect the beliefs third parties hold regarding interactional justice. Because these explanations are attempts to influence how third parties interpret an i-deal, such accounts can alter beliefs regarding the deal's legitimacy, the motives behind the deal, or the extent of the deal's favorability to third parties.[43] Third-party reactions regarding a deal's legitimacy and acceptability are complicated. Because worker and employer must agree in creating an i-deal, these two principals are disposed to see it as legitimate. Whether coworkers are informed regarding the i-deal, and at what point in the process, has implications for the credibility of the reasons given for the i-deal, as does the quality of treatment coworkers experience at the hands of both the employer and their i-dealing colleague.

I-deals can be made with full disclosure to all relevant third parties, in total secrecy, or somewhere in between. Social accounts that explain the basis for an i-deal can enhance its legitimacy, but doing so requires public disclosure of the arrangement (at least its existence if not all its terms). Secrecy exists where the idiosyncratic arrangement is not publicized, and thus no social account can be offered to explain it—unless it leaks out. Although secrecy can be a means of protecting recipients from an embarrassing disclosure (e.g., a medical condition precipitating some accommodation), more often it is employed to keep coworkers from feeling inequitably treated or making a similar request for themselves. Because open and honest communication conveys the respect that forms the basis of interactional justice, secrecy is expected to be negatively related to interactional justice.[44] In contrast, a social account conveying why an accommodation is legitimate can enhance feelings of interactional justice by signaling the organization's respect for its workers and their potential concerns regarding the i-deal.

Legitimacy Is the Essential Difference

Legitimacy is the essential distinction between i-deals and shady deals (i.e., preferential treatment and unauthorized taking). It arises when the bases for the difference between one worker's employment arrangement and another's are consistent with broadly held principles. It is fundamentally a collective process rather than a matter of private individual opinion. Legitimate i-deals reward exceptional performance, support workers in need, or otherwise promote widely shared organizational values. An idiosyncratic arrangement is legitimate when individuals believe that the specific practice is valid, such that he or she is obligated to accept it, even if he or she doesn't personally approve of it. The legitimacy of i-deals closely parallels the legitimacy of rules in the ways that people respond to them. The conservative who scrupulously pays taxes despite being vehemently opposed to big government comes to mind as someone who accepts the validity of a rule or practice without personally consenting to it. Similarly, i-deals seen as legitimate engender acceptance regardless of one's personal feelings about a specific i-deal.

The acid test of an i-deal's legitimacy is when work group members believe it is normative and appropriate for a particular coworker to enjoy arrangements different from their own. The support from others enhances the validity of idiosyncratic arrangements. When people in higher positions view the practice as normative, by virtue of the authority vested in their roles they provide authorization for i-deals. Similarly, support from workers of equal or lower status reflects endorsement of an i-deal. Authorization and endorsement are evidence of collective support, or in other words, a sign of an i-deal's legitimacy.[45]

The normative consistency of an i-deal is a judgment call on the part of its three parties. Employers and workers who negotiate i-deals tend to view them as legitimate since their values have shaped the negotiation. But these parties can possess different information than do coworkers and other third parties. As the saying goes, "We judge ourselves by our intentions, while others judge us by our behaviors." Given the limits of available information and the bounded rationality of human judgment, coworkers are not necessarily privy to all the facts and motives that lead to the creation of an i-deal.[46] Such conditions increase the likelihood that coworkers will respond negatively to the i-deals they know about. Instead, they must rely on whatever cues they might glean. To some extent this entails reading between the lines of organizational actions and the behavior of one's manager and peers.

Legitimacy exists where the motives coworkers associate with an i-deal are representative of values organization members share. In a firm where members generally believe that market factors set the standard for fair allocation of rewards, it may be normative to raise the pay of a worker who produces an outside offer promising a substantial boost in pay. In contrast, members of another firm may see such behavior as unacceptable if their own organization's norms emphasize loyalty and teamwork and downplay market-based reward allocations.

The process whereby the deal is created also affects its legitimacy by signaling whether the principals have behaved in ways consistent with broadly held values. I-deals made in secret and without the involvement of affected parties are more likely to look like shady deals, lacking a basis in appropriate values, than are those deals made in a more public fashion. How coworkers and their interests are treated throughout the creation and implementation of an i-deal is another signal regarding its validity, in that i-deals made in ways that protect the coworkers' status and relationship with the employer are more likely to be endorsed by them. In consequence, an i-deal's legitimacy is tightly intertwined with judgments regarding its fairness: whether its basis is distributively just, the processes creating it procedurally fair, and the regard shown third parties respectful throughout the deal's creation and execution. Creating i-deals in a just fashion promotes their endorsement by third parties, legitimizing these often exceptional, nonroutine, and otherwise distinct employment arrangements.

Conclusions

Special accommodations that individual workers bargain for can be a source of valuable flexibility and individual self-expression, *if* they can be effectively differentiated from shady deals. To reinforce the legitimate bases for i-deals, they must be distinguished from their patently dysfunctional counterparts. Even when ostensibly legitimate, however, i-deals can look like dysfunctional employment practices, at least to the i-dealers' coworkers, because of the secretive way i-deals often are implemented. The distinction between i-deals and shady deals resides in the conditions that give i-deals legitimacy. This legitimacy is accomplished through processes that promote three forms of justice in organizations: procedural, distributive, and interactive. The legitimacy of i-deals, in particular from the perspective of coworkers, is a consequence of the conditions that give rise to them, the motives of the parties involved, and how these factors are communicated to and understood by coworkers and other third parties.

— 4 —

Signs of I-deals in
Organizational Research

You don't see something until you have the
right metaphor to let you perceive it.
—*Robert Shaw*[1]

Signs of i-deals and other idiosyncratic arrangements can be found in organizational research over many years, yet these signs have gone largely unrecognized. Though not explicitly studied, i-deals have left traces in several
research domains. This chapter highlights organizational research that has
implicitly addressed idiosyncratic arrangements while ostensibly studying
something else. To paraphrase what Ebbinghaus said of psychology, i-deals
have a short history but a long past. We focus on what can be learned about
i-deals from research in areas as varied as work-family balance, idiosyncratic jobs, role theory, leader-member exchange, boundaryless careers, and
psychological contracts. The conceptualization of idiosyncratic deals this
book develops builds and expands on this prior work. This review highlights core processes by which workers can shape the employment relationship and who the parties involved in this process are (Table 4.1).

Work-Family Balance

Juggling work responsibilities with family life often involves special accommodations providing individual workers more flexibility in hours and
options about whether they work at home or in a corporate office. Ethno-

Table 4.1

Organizational Research Implications for I-deals

Research Domains	Core Processes	Focal Parties	Implications for I-deals
Work-family balance	Formal or informal	Worker-family, employer or agent, coworkers	Reduced work-family conflict; fairness tied to coworker access to comparable opportunities
Idiosyncratic jobs	Worker- or firm-initiated	Worker, employer	Greater opportunities for first incumbent; in new firms or other "weak" settings; reduced over time due to increased standardization
Role theory	Worker- or firm-initiated Negotiated with constituents	Role's constituents (e.g., worker, manager, coworkers, customers, clients)	Roles shape i-deals and vice versa; same contextual factors likely to influence both roles and i-deals
Leader-member exchange (LMX)	Negotiated based on trust	Worker, manager	LMX can create i-deals or preferential treatment; basis of LMX (performance or personal ties) determines which
Boundaryless careers	Negotiated based on contribution	Worker, employer	Contributions to firm give workers leverage; negotiations focus on development, enhanced contribution, employability
Psychological contracts	Negotiated exchange, shaped also by informal accommodations and social cues	Worker, employer or agent, work group, customers	I-deals shape the psychological contract, accounting for some differences in psychological contracts among work group members

graphic studies of workplace flexibility and work-family balance have described individualized arrangements that are essentially i-deals, without quite identifying them as such. For example, Hochschild's book *Time Bind* relates how workers at Amerco, a Fortune 500 American manufacturing firm, juggle work and home life—often in ways that are at odds with formal company policy.[2] One Amerco manager, Vicky King, struggles to find ways to create her own work-family balance and looks around Amerco for exemplars of how to do it. She discovers some "half-hidden" practices:

> Two "high-potential" men had asked their supervisor for a year off to travel around the world and do underwater photography of coral reefs. "I want them back," their supervisor had explained sheepishly, "so we gave them an 'educational' leave."[3]

This discovery leads King to collect other exceptions to the common rules of the Amerco workplace, which she refers to as "coral reefs." She turns up another worker who clears his calendar from 11 a.m. until 1 p.m. daily to broker real estate deals, without asking for permission. This employee's boss knows, but doesn't complain because of the volume of work this employee accomplishes during the remainder of the day. As the list of exceptions grows, King positions herself, as Hochschild describes, to begin negotiating more flexibility in the work schedules to which she and other Amerco staff adhere. But we note that at Amerco, lower-status employees often were unsuccessful in their attempts to negotiate flexibility. A secretary who attempted to negotiate was more likely to be told no than a professional who did so.

Similarly, Perlow, in her book *Finding Time*, notes several examples where professionals negotiated flexible schedules in the high-pressure software design firm Ditto.[4] In each case, however, the arrangement led to the worker being devalued by the firm, as in the case of Kate:

> Kate . . . tried to create an alternative way of working which would permit her to limit her hours and still meet her work demands. She decided to work at home one day a week. Within a year she dropped in ranking from a 'premium' to a "below-average" employee.[5]

The incidents at Amerco and Ditto reveal some important dynamics surrounding i-deals. Many workers seek out, though not always successfully, greater flexibility; however, more valued, high-status workers are likely to be more successful in negotiating such arrangements. At the time they are negotiated, i-deals can benefit both the worker and the firm. However, over time workers can pay a price for not conforming, particularly in firms where performance and contribution are subjectively determined. Under certain conditions, idiosyncratic arrangements form the basis for broadly available, widely shared practices, but employers and workers often are ineffective in managing and learning from the i-deals they make. Nonetheless, both Hochschild and Perlow make clear that individualized arrangements are fairly common, the products of negotiations between valued workers and their employers. Taken together, these two studies suggest a dilemma: While fast-trackers may be able to successfully negotiate i-deals to help in balancing work and family, actually executing such a deal ultimately may reduce both their perceived performance in the eyes of superiors and their actual performance ratings, resulting in diminished career opportunities down the road. This suggests that work-family balance i-deals can turn fast-trackers into slow-trackers.[6]

Wary of the career risks involved, workers often go to great lengths to avoid letting coworkers and managers know that they are juggling family demands along with work responsibilities. Scott Behson examined the informal ways in which employees address work-family conflict by making accommodations on the job.[7] Behson defined informal work accommodations to family as a "set of behaviors in which employees adjust their usual work patterns in an attempt to balance work responsibilities, without using formal work/family programs, in order to reduce the stress associated with family-to-work conflict." He notes that such tactics can modify the way in which work gets done, changing its location, sequence, or timing. Nonetheless, these informal accommodations usually maintain the same level of worker output and avoid permanently altering the structure of work. These informal accommodations are consistent with practices that working fathers are known to use, such as taking vacation days to stay home with a sick child or attending a child's school program while on a sales call so that bosses won't know they are engaging in family tasks.[8] They constitute a form of personal problem solving and role juggling—without the involvement or knowledge of the employer or its agents (e.g., managers or human resource professionals).[9]

The potential downside workers incur from altering their work roles to accommodate family demands is underscored by worker reluctance to use highly visible tactics in juggling family responsibilities while at work. In Behson's study of men and women working in a telecommunications firm, he noted that the more visible a work-family accommodation was, the less likely workers were to actually use it.[10] Thus, bringing children to work, arranging to switch duties with a coworker, and taking time off in the middle of the day to attend to family matters were lowest in frequency, while the highest-frequency accommodations were receiving family-related phone calls, working through lunch, and phoning and e-mailing family members. When used, these less visible accommodations were effective in reducing work-family conflict. Such effects were particularly pronounced for women and for those with substantial family caretaking responsibilities, regardless of gender. Workers who were highly responsible for their families' financial well-being were less likely to engage in such accommodations. Workers who reported high control over their work schedules were more likely to make work-family accommodations than those who experienced less control. Thus, it may be that workers with higher levels of autonomy are better positioned to make informal accommodations without having to negotiate an i-deal. Coworkers with less autonomy are poorly positioned to act informally to accommodate their family demands. Thus, effective use of informal tactics for juggling work and family is limited largely to those workers whose jobs make such self-initiated flexibility possible.

In theory, formal policies such as parental leave should be useful in promoting a work-family balance for workers such as those on assembly lines whose jobs otherwise offer limited flexibility. In practice, however, these policies have received mixed reactions—largely because the ways firms implement them vary widely. At the heart of employee reactions, especially judgments regarding the fairness of policies, is who the policy actually benefits. Employees who are parents or plan to have children in the future commonly view work-family policies more favorably than do employees without children.[11] In firms where workers without children can get the other supports they may need, such employees are less likely to resent accommodations made to parents. If they are to be viewed as fair, flexible arrangements need to be adaptable to the circumstances faced by the broad spectrum of a firm's workers. This principle is evident in the dilemma expressed by an executive quoted in an article on "mommy-track backlash"—"Please don't tell me that I need to have a baby to have this time off."[12]

Whether other supports accompany work-family policies also makes a big difference. When work-family policies are bundled with the training to help managers implement them, the adjustment of performance criteria to focus on contributions rather than face time, and other supportive practices, these policies create benefits while reducing the downside workers often experience from nonconformity. Such worker support packages engender greater affective commitment and intention to stay with the firm when compared to less consistently supportive arrangements.[13] Formal work-family policies are rated as more fair in settings where these policies are combined with other practices that workers experience as supportive. Especially important are managers who understand and promote policies giving workers flexibility without jeopardizing their career opportunities.[14] It's safe to conclude that the impact of work-family policies on workers, their families, and their employers cannot be understood by examining a single practice or policy in isolation. This impact needs to be examined with respect to the simultaneously occurring practices that together support or impede a policy's intended consequences.[15]

Work-family balance research has several implications for i-deals:

1. Work-family policies in themselves may invite attempts to create i-deals by signaling the legitimacy of such arrangements and the employer's willingness to entertain them.

2. Over time, an i-deal can have negative consequences for the worker who negotiates it. Adverse consequences are more likely where the arrangement is at odds with widely held work norms (e.g., negotiating shorter work days in a firm where putting in long hours is a ticket to advancement). In the case of i-deals negotiated to help juggle work and family, a worker who approaches his or her work role differently from peers, in terms of hours worked, availability to clients or colleagues, or visibility of effort, can send unintended signals regarding lack of commitment to the employer.

3. The downside of nonconforming work practices is exacerbated in work settings where performance is subjectively appraised, where performance reviews rely on judgments of worker behaviors rather than more objective criteria such as sales figures or project completion.

4. To the extent that the contributions expected from the worker with an i-deal are well specified and agreed to by the parties involved, one downside of i-deals can be reduced.

5. A supportive climate for i-deals can reduce negative consequences for workers who negotiate them. A climate that is supportive of work-family balance, and of worker flexibility in general, is likely to make it easier for workers to suggest i-deals, for managers to respond favorably to such requests, and for the potential downsides from i-deals to be managed effectively.

6. Whether coworkers view i-deals as fair depends to some extent on the opportunities those workers have to receive similar accommodations themselves. Even standardized benefits have been found to create a sense of unfairness on the part of those workers who don't need them or cannot access them.[16] Coworker sensitivities regarding inequity are likely to be even greater when accommodations arise through i-deals.

Idiosyncratic Jobs

When positions in an organization are created for and around specific individuals, these positions are referred to as "idiosyncratic jobs." Anne Miner defined idiosyncratic jobs as positions in which the job holder was employed by the organization prior to the position being created in its current form and where the job's activities match that person's perceived interests, priorities, and abilities.[17] Mark Granovetter observed that idiosyncratic jobs can also be found in more emergent, formative, or loosely structured situations, such as start-up companies, where the founders have an idea of a role they want to create but may not act upon it until they find a suitable person to fill it.[18] For our purposes, idiosyncratic jobs can be thought of as jobs formalized around their first incumbent, who remains in place regardless of whether he or she was employed by the firm prior to the job's creation.

Either the employer or the employee can initiate an idiosyncratic job. These jobs can arise all at once or unfold gradually through informal adjustments and accommodations made for a particular employee. When a current employee, as opposed to a new hire, takes on an idiosyncratic job, the process often goes something like the following: Observing that a particular administrative assistant, whom we will call Claire, has a flair for integrating computing services, her manager creates an officewide integration role with Claire as its first occupant (thus, the job change is employer-initiated). If these computer-integration activities lead to expanded use of computer systems for business functions, Claire's job may become so large that it needs to be divided into two. Claire's job becomes more specialized (through a process Miner calls "accretion")[19] if it changes to focus only on the internal systems used for accounting and human resources, while someone else is hired to handle the database management issues associated with customer transactions. If Claire subsequently seeks greater flexibility in her work in order to take care of an elderly parent, as a valued employee she may negotiate a new idiosyncratic job permitting her to work at home on a schedule of her own design (an employee-initiated i-deal). Regardless of which party initiates an idiosyncratic job, both employee and employer can contribute to the formation of its duties and responsibilities.

Research on idiosyncratic jobs is particularly informative to our discussion of i-deals because of the attention given to the organizational factors that impact the idiosyncratic job's creation, growth, and demise. Both new and growing firms are common settings for idiosyncratic jobs,[20] as are downsized firms and others undergoing major changes. Start-up firms, as well as new divisions in larger firms, are comprised of new jobs with emergent duties and responsibilities. In such settings, everyone is a newcomer and no preexisting structure constrains expectations. In her study of start-up firms, Laurie Levesque describes how Steve, a college graduate with a degree in English and little professional writing experience, became a company's first employee:

He noticed a small start-up housed in the street block where he worked and decided to drop by and check it out. The two principals were there and Steve asked them about the company. . . . By the end of the conversation, he had convinced them to . . . (hire) him to do marketing, copyediting, public relations . . . as needed. . . . Both he and they agree that if he hadn't stopped by, sold his skill set, and convinced them of the need for it, that his role would have been absent in the firm for some time.[21]

The processes by which new jobs are introduced, what they include and exclude, and how they link to others are shaped both by their occupants as well as by other people with whom they work.

Idiosyncratic jobs are easier to create in work settings characterized by ambiguous, loose, or flexible expectations, a condition Karl Weick refers to as a "weak situation."[22] Weak situations describe many work settings that are new, where the mission isn't well specified, or where some disruptive personnel movement such as a transition in management has occurred. In weak situations, individuals have flexibility to shape their own roles, molding them into activities that play to their personal strengths and preferred work styles. Not surprisingly, Steve, who joined the start-up firm that Levesque describes, liked to build Web sites and made that a major focus of his activities. In contrast to weak situations, strong situations entail a greater degree of structure and more constraints on behavior. Strong situations are typically seen in highly bureaucratic firms with stable environments and long histories. Idiosyncratic jobs are more difficult to create in such settings. Weak situations make it easier for workers to make informal accommodations without seeking formal approval because flexibility is inherent in the setting. In contrast, strong situations may necessitate formal approval of an i-deal because highly structured organizations require senior managers to sign off on idiosyncratic arrangements.

Contemporary firms contain a host of weak situations. Changes undertaken in response to competitive pressures, restructurings, and the increasing need for improvisation promote weak situations that individual workers can shape to their liking. In such circumstances, workers often are new to the firms in which they work, and their managers (if indeed they have any) may themselves be temporary, transitioning, or otherwise occupied. Whenever a boss leaves, gets reassigned, is fired, or quits, the result may be, if not a weak situation, at least a weakened one. Such conditions shape whether the accommodations workers seek must be formally applied for or can be more informally introduced.

A variety of forces affect the growth of idiosyncratic jobs—forces that operate on i-deals as well. First, many firms require a review process before job formalization or recruitment can occur, a mechanism that serves to restrain the informal practices that can otherwise enable managers or workers to take advantage of situations for the benefit of themselves and the firm. In this context, only certain managers may have the credibility or savvy to create idiosyncratic arrangements for their workers. Second, idiosyncratic jobs tend to die over time as their occupants leave or pressure for standardization asserts itself. Similarly, i-deals can also be fragile, particularly in situations where the manager with whom a worker negotiated an i-deal has left. Reorganizations, job audits, and business process reengineering efforts can induce systemwide reevaluations of jobs and employment practices, resulting in selective job retention and the rescinding of idiosyncratic arrangements. Organizational norms and values can further promote or inhibit the creation of such arrangements, depending on whether they emphasize flexibility or consistency. Thus, as research indicates that contextual factors influence the creation and demise of idiosyncratic jobs, independent of the individual worker's qualities, we see that these same forces can operate on i-deals, too.

From the perspective of i-deals, research on idiosyncratic jobs highlights the following:

1. The first occupants of newly created jobs are likely to be better positioned than are later occupants to suggest i-deals regarding job content and to initiate idiosyncratic arrangements on their own. Since the first occupant of a job typically can customize at least some of the job's duties and ways work is performed, this individual can have more opportunities to suggest and bargain for idiosyncratic terms in an employment relationship than do later job occupants.

2. Start-ups and other new organizational settings permit greater flexibility in customizing terms of employment than do established ones. I-deals that workers suggest to their employers are more likely to be accepted in start-ups and in newer settings than in more established organizations, where rules and standard procedures exist. Moreover, such flexible settings are likely to make informal accommodations easier for workers to initiate through acquiescence, without having to seek formal approval.

3. Weak situations, which are settings with few existing (or enforced) structures, are more likely to promote idiosyncratic jobs than are strong situations characterized by well-specified rules and procedures. Similarly, i-deals are likely to be less common in organizational settings with extensive, enforced rules and procedures. In more highly structured settings, informal accommodations will likely be more difficult

for workers to initiate, and workers proposing i-deals are more likely to be told no. As a consequence, it is likely that workers in strongly structured settings will propose fewer i-deals. Nonetheless, i-deals may be relied on more than informal accommodations to achieve even minor flexibility in structured settings because such settings are more likely to require approval for job changes.

4. In firms over time, pressures for standardization and consistency emerge, reducing the opportunity for i-deals. Out of concern for fairness and equity, job differences once obtained only through i-deals can become standard practices over time as they are made more broadly available to a firm's workers. Alternatively, an employer may pursue standardization and consistency by reducing or eliminating the practices that some i-deals once allowed, without extending such opportunities to other workers. Increased standardization is particularly likely where i-deals have generated coworker resentment or the firm faces particular difficulties in implementing human resource innovations. This standardization operates on i-deals in two ways. It can make certain i-deals unnecessary, offering on a broad scale arrangements to workers that once were available to only a few workers with i-deals. Or it can make i-deals more difficult to create by limiting managerial discretion and organizational flexibility.

Role Theory

Role theory recognizes the distinctive impact that workers can have on the roles they occupy. It does so through its focus on role sending (what is required of occupants), role taking (what requirements occupants accept), and role making (what requirements occupants create). Role theory is particularly pertinent to understanding the processes surrounding the creation and implementation of i-deals affecting job content (e.g., duties to be performed, performance goals). This theory also helps identify the parties an i-deal might affect.

Roles involve expectations of both the incumbent and the role's constituents regarding how the role should be accomplished.[23] Roles are forms of social demands people are pressured to fulfill. In organizations, a role's constituents—those in a position to influence the role—typically include superiors, coworkers, clients, and others with whom the worker is interdependent. Workers commonly introduce and seek changes in their roles predicated on how they anticipate its constituents to react. Some changes they attempt may be met with indifference, others with a positive reaction. Negative responses are likely to require more elaborate negotiation and problem-solving activities before being accepted.

Roles are a key part of the context in which i-deals arise.[24] Role expectations that would-be i-dealers face from colleagues, managers, and clients can constrain what can be successfully negotiated. In an established role, the web of constituent expectations is likely to be relatively stable and mutually reinforcing. Such roles constitute strong situations to which occupants are expected to conform and comply. In negotiating an i-deal that would impact how a worker performs his or her job, a worker may need to enlist the help of supportive managers or influential colleagues to gain endorsement by the role's other constituents.

Even where role expectations are strong, occupants need not conform to them completely. The newcomer encountering a preexisting set of role expectations can accept, ignore, or adapt them to fit his or her own needs. Asserting one's preference to be different, role researchers observe, can be a way to avoid being taken for granted and to express one's own distinct capabilities and individuality.[25] A recently hired technician who has successfully used a particular set of procedures before may adapt the procedures he finds in place at his new job site to better fit those with which he is familiar. Existing roles can thus adjust to accommodate the occupant. Nonetheless, as Daniel Feldman observes, new workers hired into existing roles may not be willing to suggest changes until they feel on top of their jobs. They are likely to suggest changes once they feel more confident.[26] Research on role development and how incumbents shape their own jobs suggests that certain predispositions, such as desire for self-expression or nonconformity, can motivate role change. These motives can be particularly important to the formation of i-deals, where the successful negotiation of a special arrangement can provide the worker with affirmation of personal efficacy.

Job crafting refers to ways workers alter their own roles to better align with their values, without using direct negotiation.[27] Trying to create a caring atmosphere, a custodian cleaning hospital floors may take a special interest in patients who seem despondent or unattended to. Though caregiving is not part of his formal role, the custodian who adds caregiving to his job engages in job crafting. In our framework, this activity does not constitute an i-deal if the employer and its representatives are uninvolved in this elaboration of the custodian's role. Nonetheless, job crafting highlights the opportunities workers have to adjust their work situation to their personal preferences without having to get permission to do so.

From the perspective of idiosyncratic arrangements, role theory suggests the following assertions:

1. I-deals can be part of the role-development process. As they navigate the process of taking on an existing role, new workers can influence what their role becomes. Some role changes take the form of acquiescence, as in the case of informal accommodations workers initiate by themselves. Negotiated i-deals are more likely to be sought in place of informal accommodations where workers lack the autonomy to introduce role changes on their own, or where the i-deals entail changes to which some constituents might object unless efforts are made to gain their support.
2. Negotiating with a role's constituents (such as coworkers and clients), not just with the employer, can be critical to building support for an i-deal. Managing the effect of any changes upon these constituents is an important part of effective i-deal negotiation and implementation.
3. Implementing i-deals may require workers to enlist the support of powerful others to help negotiate an i-deal's approval. Involving powerful others (e.g., senior managers or other influential organization members) is particularly critical where the requested arrangement impacts multiple parties having different interests.
4. I-deals can be motivated by the same factors that promote workers' attempts to deviate from role requirements. Deviating from an existing role can be a means of asserting one's individuality or distinct capabilities and of avoiding being taken for granted by others who have come to assume conformity to the role's demands.

Leader-Member Exchange

Managers treat individual subordinates differently depending on the quality of their relationship with each worker. Leader-member exchange (LMX) theory focuses on the relationships between managers and individual subordinates and the development of these relationships over time.[28] Its basic premise is that differences in how a manager treats individual workers are due to varying levels of trust. In effect, some workers are part of a highly trusted in-group, treated differently from the rest. This in-group is comprised of workers the manager views as competent or otherwise holds in good favor. The in-group receives better treatment than workers in the out-group. Out-group members have less influence on decision making, are less able to change their roles, receive less inside information, and generally have less attention paid to their needs. In-group members, in contrast, influence decision making, have greater latitude over their duties and responsibilities, and find their manager more responsive to their needs and interests. LMX theory addresses how new ways of organizing work can

77

emerge within a manager's span of control when a manager and his or her subordinate(s) trust each other enough to construct their roles flexibly.

LMX research largely has ignored the nature of the resources exchanged between managers and subordinates. However, LMX theory implies that more flexible job content and opportunities for growth and personal development accrue to high LMX subordinates in contrast to their low LMX counterparts. Unfortunately, to date LMX research is silent on whether the accommodations that managers make for trusted workers constitute preferential treatment or i-deals. There is also a tendency in LMX research to focus on relationships of long standing, rather than those between highly mobile workers and their managers.[29]

From the perspective of i-deals, LMX research points to the creative flexibility that becomes possible when managers and certain trusted or valued workers form stable partnerships. Indeed, having a quality relationship with one's manager or other representative of one's employer may be an important precondition for negotiating an i-deal with one's current employer.

Specifically, LMX theory and research suggest the following conclusions:

1. Idiosyncratic employment conditions are more likely to be accepted or permitted for those members of a work group who are particularly highly trusted by their manager. Note that the basis of this trust, whether it reflects worker performance or merely a special relationship with the manager, determines whether these individual arrangements constitute an i-deal or preferential treatment.
2. A manager who is reluctant to negotiate i-deals early in the relationship with a worker is more likely to respond positively to i-deals over time if he or she comes to trust the worker.

Boundaryless Careers

Boundaryless careers are extraorganizational career paths in which individual workers progressively advance themselves by working for a variety of employers. In the aftermath of downsizing, mergers, acquisitions, and widespread disruptions in employment relations, considerable attention has been given to boundaryless careers. This research focuses on highly skilled and mobile workers with skills tied more to a particular industry than to a specific firm. The experience and capabilities these workers accumulate as they move in and out of relationships with an array of employers give boundaryless career workers bargaining power in negotiating terms of employment.[30]

The power enjoyed by boundaryless career workers is sometimes equated with employability, where workers can benefit from the competencies their movement through successive firms builds.[31] From the employer's perspective, a worker's employability is enhanced when he or she makes a demonstrable value-added contribution to the firm. Such contributions can be measured in terms of project completion or a revenue gain the firm realizes from the worker's efforts. Worker contributions are exchanged for often explicit, market-based returns (e.g., profit sharing, a share of the business) and—of long-term importance to the worker—the opportunity to learn new skills that can be sold to a subsequent employer.[32]

Boundaryless career workers often perform project-focused jobs. They are exemplified by independent contractors brought together to make a television commercial, establish the physical plant of a start-up research firm, or launch a company training program. But the boundaryless career designation is often applied to regular but highly skilled employees in those firms (e.g., software, trading) that make few commitments regarding future employment. In either case, the performance of boundaryless career workers is defined in terms of results—goals met or project completion—rather than in terms of behaviors or processes. Employment may last for a specified period of time or may depend on whether the employer can use the worker's talents elsewhere once the project is complete. Employment relationships in project-focused work have two distinctive features: an emphasis on results, where individuals responsible for business results have control over how they achieve them; and renegotiability, the expectation of new or renewed contract negotiation over time. Renegotiation occurs project by project as the value of the worker to the firm shifts with the nature of the work, relationships with colleagues and customers, and opportunities that come the worker's way based on his or her skills, experience, and reputation. Assignments are negotiated in ways that enhance the worker's future employability and pay back what he or she has contributed to the firm.

Workers hoping to negotiate a subsequent assignment with the same employer do so because they want to use the assignment to develop transferable knowledge and to establish a track record of accomplishments that will signal their capabilities to future employers. Where sustained employment with the same firm cannot be counted upon, portable knowledge and skills become important resources in the employment exchange. Boundaryless career workers not only need to meet project-related goals, but must also position themselves for the next employment cycle. From a boundaryless career perspective, idiosyncrasy is negotiated into employment relations not only to reflect worker preferences but also to signal to future employers distinct—often unique—worker skills, knowledge, and experience.

The nature of a worker's future employability can itself be idiosyncratic. Workers skilled in conducting boundaryless careers are likely to have "meta-skills," which they use to learn from the experience of moving from employer to employer.[33] Such skills include the ability to learn new roles quickly and to operate effectively in the ambiguity that is common in the start of a new job. The successful worker deploys these skills to construct a personalized career in contrast to that of the stereotypic "organization man." Hall describes this concept of career as "a process which the person, not the organization, is managing. It consists of all the person's varied experiences in education, training, work in several organizations, changes in occupational fields."[34] Creativity, acceptance of uncertainty, and valuing one's uniqueness are personal orientations that boundaryless workers bring to their employment negotiation and on-the-job behavior.

Workers pursuing boundaryless careers are not expected to fit into an organizational role with a long history, let alone a future. In effect, they can be on the market at any time. Thus, the external market looms large in boundaryless career arrangements, where workers come to develop market savvy and negotiation experience by actively engaging in bargaining.

At the heart of the relationship between the boundaryless career worker and his or her employer is explicit attention to the value each adds to the other. The worker's added value lies in his or her demonstrable contributions to the firm, while the firm's added value is manifest in the learning, future financial growth, and career flexibility it provides. Indeed, the meaning of "value added" can be unique to a particular worker. A hotshot marketing manager may contribute measurably more to a high-technology firm than most other workers and receive an ownership stake, where other workers do not, as a means to both motivate and retain that manager's valued capabilities. By its very nature, effective performance of the parties in this exchange requires intermittent negotiation so that the firm's changing performance requirements are met along with the worker's emerging needs and interests.

From the perspective of i-deals, boundaryless careers research suggests the following conclusions:

1. Workers pursuing boundaryless careers are likely to have greater market knowledge, enhancing their ability to negotiate effectively with their employers. Boundaryless career workers are thus likely to be more successful than other workers in negotiating i-deals.
2. With an emphasis on personal employability, boundaryless career workers are particularly likely to seek out i-deals that provide them with future job-creating and developmental opportunities.

3. While pursuing a boundaryless career, workers tend to experience highly explicit conditions of employment. The idiosyncratic arrangements these workers seek out are more likely to be explicitly negotiated i-deals rather than accommodations arising informally.

Psychological Contracts

Psychological contracts are the individual belief systems held by workers and employers regarding their mutual obligations.[35] Every employment relationship is subjectively understood and experienced by each participant—employee, contractor, manager-employer. How each interprets his or her obligations to and agreements with others constitutes the psychological contract. Workers who form what they believe to be a mutual agreement with their employer are more likely to perform in ways they believe to be consistent with their employer's interests.[36] And where the employer is seen as fulfilling its end of the employment agreement, workers are more likely to engage in pro-employer actions, to provide quality service, and to act in ways that foster the organization's well-being. In contrast, workers who believe that their employer has failed to keep its end of the bargain can become angry and dissatisfied, reduce their contributions to the firm, and quit if they can readily do so.[37]

The *content* of the psychological contract shapes how the parties think and act in the context of their employment relationship. If the psychological contract is relational, workers tend to identify with the organization, promoting support for the organization's efforts to improve performance.[38] Relational contracts are positively related to employee perceptions that their employer supports them personally. The term "perceived organizational support" refers to the belief that one's employer is responsive to its workers' needs, a quality associated with employers of choice. Workers are more likely to believe that their employer is supportive when they have successfully negotiated i-deals with it.[39] Thus, i-deals can give rise to beliefs in a relational contract incorporating commitments regarding a worker's future involvement in the firm.

In contrast, transactional contracts, which focus on the economic exchange that employment entails, tend to be related to lower levels of worker flexibility and contribution and are less elastic in times of change.[40] These arrangements are characteristic of workers in more peripheral roles in organizations, including temporary and seasonal workers, who are likely to have relatively limited bargaining power.[41] Nonetheless, workers with bargaining power, such as valued individual contributors, can also develop transactional contracts, particularly where the focus of their negotiations is salary and benefits.

A third type of psychological contract, referred to as "balanced," is a hybrid that combines relational features of open-ended exchange along with a focus on performance-based rewards. Balanced contracts direct worker attention to continued development in response to changing performance demands; in their most comprehensive form, the worker and employer share responsibility for this ongoing development.[42] Idiosyncratic arrangements, particularly of a developmental nature, are most likely to be characteristic of workers with balanced contracts, who need a certain degree of customized development opportunities to be able to enhance their value to the current employer and to promote their future marketability elsewhere. Balanced contracts have been found to be particularly impacted by an individual worker's position in the firm's social network, being characteristic of the employment relations of those workers who are central in the informal network.[43]

Where workers in an organization, a work group, or a profession share common elements in their psychological contracts, these collective-level contracts are referred to as "normative." Normative contracts are beliefs that coworkers share regarding the terms of their exchange arrangement with their employer. These beliefs are strongly tied to the broader organizational culture, as well as to subunit-specific norms and beliefs. When a nursing home's employees feel obligated to call in and offer to work if a power failure or natural disaster hits, they share a common understanding of their performance requirements. Similarly, the staff in an office with a use-it-or-lose-it policy toward sick leave might believe that they are entitled to use all of their sick leave each year, whether they are ill or not, because they will lose it otherwise.[44] When normative contracts exist in a work group, they can influence how individual members experience their personal psychological contract. It is noteworthy, however, that psychological contract studies conducted in the United States consistently demonstrate wide intra-unit variation in how individuals interpret their employment obligations. Though agreement in the obligations associated with seniority seems to be widespread, research is needed on other forms of normative contracts.[45]

Normative contracts are important arbiters of the employee-employer relationship, because how coworkers interpret their employer's treatment of a colleague affects how they think of their own relationship with that employer. In a steel mill where a work group willingly gave more latitude to high performers who helped out their colleagues, a coworker reports:

> One guy (who was in his mid twenties but a very senior worker) had a diabetes problem. This problem enabled him to work only day shift. Other

guys were jealous (especially those with families), because the night shift was 4 p.m. to 2 a.m. In fact, some of the guys questioned whether or not his problem was a legitimate one . . . he was seen as a bit of a slacker by the other guys. . . . But, he was the type of person who played the game well. He always talked to management about the great things he did, whereas the rest of the mill would thanklessly perform, day in and day out. His personality was one where he needed recognition to perform, so he made sure people knew of his good accomplishments. He made every little thing he did sound like the greatest accomplishment the mill had ever seen. . . . So, the guys had a reason to dislike [him], and therefore questioned everything about him, including the validity of his alleged illness and doctor's orders to work only days.[46]

As demonstrated by the example above, shared norms about work roles can lead a work group to differ from its employer regarding whether a particular idiosyncratic arrangement is fair.

Despite the identification of normative contracts in certain work settings, in my own research I have found that workers in the same unit seldom have high levels of agreement regarding the terms of their individual psychological contracts. Although there may be several possible explanations for this (e.g., workers were hired at different times by different managers; individual differences lead workers to hold different beliefs), the existence of unrecognized and unmeasured idiosyncratic arrangements can be a factor in the intra-unit differences observed in psychological contracts research.[47]

Idiosyncratic arrangements are related to, yet distinct from, the *perceptions* each worker has of the employment relationship. Because each individual has a subjective experience of this relationship, reflecting his or her psychological contract,[48] two people doing ostensibly the same job can differ in their perspectives. A psychological contract refers to individual *beliefs*, while idiosyncratic arrangements refer to actual individual *treatment and resources* garnered through employment. For example, one office worker might believe she owes only an eight-hour workday, while her counterpart is willing to stay a little later if work still needs to be done. Each worker has her own distinct psychological contract. Yet this difference in individual understanding doesn't mean that an idiosyncratic deal exists *as long as their employer still treats both workers the same.* An idiosyncratic deal would arise when one worker receives employment features (or perks) that differ from those received by workers in similar roles. In our example, if the worker who occasionally stayed later came to be more trusted and relied upon by her boss, and the boss subsequently granted her greater latitude and flexibility than the other worker enjoyed on the job, an idiosyncratic deal would begin to emerge. It's the difference in actual treatment and resources accessed, not the perception of a relationship, that defines an idiosyncratic arrangement and, when individually negotiated, an i-deal.

By their nature, i-deals tend to create differences in the psychological contracts workers report. Consider how i-deals arose for two engineers:

> I received an opportunity to go to the field . . . high profile . . . includes extra allowances and travel, not available to everyone. I asked for it, and hinted that I might not stay if I didn't get it.

> I was a skilled employee, very ambitious, and sought recognition and reward for my accomplishments. Most other employees were either not as ambitious, more quiet, or not as skilled.[49]

Both engineers relate how their personal ambition and initiative prompted them to make more assertive demands of their employer than did their colleagues. Not surprisingly, such actions, over time, can lead to widely divergent psychological contracts among workers in a firm.

From the perspective of i-deals, a worker's psychological contract and its normative (collective, group-level) counterpart suggest the following conclusions:

1. Workers tend to behave in ways that are consistent with the psychological contracts they have with their employer. Idiosyncratic terms can form part of an individual's psychological contract, along with features that coworkers share. Some observed differences in on-the-job behavior among coworkers arise from idiosyncratic aspects of their psychological contracts.

2. Where employers are believed to have violated their commitments under the psychological contract, workers respond with anger, dissatisfaction, and an increased likelihood of turnover and withdrawal of effort. Once idiosyncratic terms enter into how a worker understands his or her employment relationship, failure on the part of the employer to uphold those terms risks being read by the worker as a breach of the employment agreement.

3. When a relational psychological contract exists, workers are more accepting of change and more flexible in the face of employer demands. Relational agreements often include expectations of responsiveness to individual worker needs, which can promote creation of idiosyncratic arrangements.

4. Workers with balanced psychological contracts are likely to negotiate i-deals because their contributions and value to the employer are

more demonstrable than might be the case with other workers. Moreover, such workers are likely to have a particular interest in pursuing idiosyncratic arrangements that enhance their personal development and employability.

5. It is difficult to postulate the connection between i-deals and transactional contracts. Workers with transactional contracts are likely to have relatively limited bargaining power in terms of creating idiosyncratic arrangements. However, there can be powerful independent contractors, and perhaps star employees as well, who negotiate entire employment arrangement that are both idiosyncratic and transactional.

6. Workers located in the same work unit often differ in their individual psychological contracts, leading to different interpretations of the same actions on the part of the employer. Idiosyncratic arrangements can be interpreted differently by a recipient's coworkers as a function of their own psychological contracts with the employer.

7. Where members of a work unit share a common understanding of their psychological contract, a normative contract arises that influences how coworkers interpret the employer's treatment of each of them. Social norms shape how coworkers react to idiosyncratic arrangements negotiated by their colleagues. Normative contracts can shape how coworkers view and interpret the idiosyncratic arrangements within their work group.

8. I-deals and other idiosyncratic arrangements some work group members experience can account for the lack of intragroup agreement regarding the psychological contract.

Conclusion

Workers shape their employment experience in innumerable ways, many of which are evident in organizational research on topics ostensibly unrelated to i-deals. Research on work-family balance indicates that workers do initiate accommodations with and without their employer's permission in order to manage family responsibilities while at work. This research also directs attention to the potential downsides of i-deals, ranging from coworkers resentful of these accommodations to the long-term career disadvantage that nonconformity can bring. Idiosyncratic jobs are more likely to arise in certain organizational settings than in others. In particular, newer and less formal organizations tend to promote idiosyncrasy, but the forces of standardization and consistency emerging in established firms over time can eliminate existing idiosyncratic jobs and make it difficult to create new ones. Role theory highlights the array of parties whose interests must be accounted for in understanding idiosyncratic arrangements, from individual workers themselves to their colleagues, managers, clients and customers, and the firm as a whole. How a worker negotiates with these constituents is critical to the creation, maintenance, and sustainability of i-deals. Leader-member exchange relationships are characterized by greater idiosyncrasy for high-LMX workers than their low-LMX counterparts. Individual-employer negotiation is essential to a successful boundaryless career. Its idiosyncratic arrangements can be influenced by employee contribution to the firm, market knowledge, and experience in negotiating. Psychological contracts between workers and employer can impact the way each views the negotiation of i-deals. Differences in psychological contracts among coworkers are due in part to the idiosyncratic arrangements enjoyed by some workers and not others. Psychological contracts can also shape the form i-deals take.

This review of the organizational research literature points to interesting intersections of several themes. One can only wonder what patterns might be found were these themes studied jointly. For instance, many idiosyncratic jobs are likely to arise in the context of high-quality LMX relations between a worker and his or her manager. Looking inside the black box of the exchange between workers and managers, we anticipate that some LMX relations are the basis for favoritism and preferential treatment that foster coworker resentment. In contrast, other high-LMX worker-manager partnerships, predicated on quality contributions to the firm, give rise to flexible arrangements that often take the form of legitimate i-deals. From another perspective, the nature of i-deals and the processes through which they arise are likely to differ depending on whether the idiosyncratic arrangements are undertaken for work-family balance or to fulfill a boundaryless career worker's desire for employability. Thus it is important to pay attention to the motivation behind the i-deal in understanding its negotiation and impact on the employment relationship.

There is clearly much work to be done. Nonetheless, this review demonstrates that while i-deals may have gone unrecognized in several relevant research streams, organizational research still can tell us a lot about the dynamics of i-deals.[50] Their manifest traces in organizational research provide evidence of the pervasive ways in which individual employees influence the conditions of their employment.

— 5 —

I-deal Types: Six-Plus Ways Employees Bargain

[It is] the natural tendency of the market to reward people no
more than they require.
—*Linda Babcock and Sara Laschever*[1]

I-deals take many forms. They can anticipate future contributions, pursue a payback for past efforts, or follow a threat to quit. What workers bargain for is affected by the timing of the negotiation and the circumstances that occasion it. Employees can bargain before being hired, on the job once their employer comes to depend on them, and when brandishing an outside offer. How they view their deal, whether it signals a strong relationship with their employer or an economic transaction, is a function of its timing and terms.

This chapter describes the types of i-deals employees negotiate. It begins with the actual events in the career of one highly marketable worker to illustrate the different roles i-deals can play in employment. It then maps out the domain of i-deals using a framework based on the array of circumstances in which they arise. In doing so, it offers an account of why distinctly different employment relationships can arise from i-deals. Lastly, it identifies two inherently dysfunctional forms of worker bargaining. These dysfunctional forms, status seeking and repeat bargaining, differ in fundamental ways from the functional i-deals that stand to benefit both workers and employers and which third parties may endorse.

Bargaining as a Basis for a Boundaryless Career: The Case of Steve Miller

An employee can bargain at various points in time in his or her tenure at a company; indeed, people tend to do so many times over the course of their careers. I-deals made at critical times can have powerful effects on a worker's career trajectory. Consider the critical role i-deals have played in the career of one professional, Steve Miller, who by any standard meets the definition of a boundaryless career worker.[2] Steve's boundarylessness is exemplified by the fact that his career has involved a series of employers and his marketability derives from his distinctive competencies and willingness to innovate. Steve's family values and personal goals each play an important role in his career choices. Unconstrained by traditional assumptions, Steve tends to think out of the box regarding his career pursuits. He has negotiated two major i-deals and several smaller ones during his career, with two very different employers.

1. An Ex Ante *Recruiting I-deal with Fujitsu*

Steve Miller is more formally known as Dr. Miller, with a doctorate in engineering and public policy from Carnegie Mellon University. His first professional position after graduate school was as an assistant professor in a top-20 American business school. Restless in the traditional role of a faculty member, in the late 1980s Steve decided to realize a long-standing dream. He wanted to learn firsthand the inner workings of the factory system operated by world-class Japanese manufacturers. Though he didn't know a word of Japanese, Steve had a passion for learning. He contacted several leading Japanese manufacturers and offered them this proposal: He would come to work for the firm, learn Japanese, and become deeply knowledgeable regarding the ins and outs of the firm and how it operated; in doing this, he would become a unique resource to the firm down the road. What services he might provide to the firm once this occurred were left open to negotiation later as Steve and the Japanese employer learned more about each other. Perhaps not surprisingly, his offer was repeatedly turned down.

However, one firm willing to entertain such an arrangement was Fujitsu, a manufacturer of telecommunications and office equipment. After his initial letter generated interest from senior executives, Steve exchanged a series of letters and phone calls with English-speaking Fujitsu managers. Fujitsu's chief executive indicated his willingness to have Steve join the firm. One requirement Fujitsu imposed was that the president of Steve's university be willing to agree to the arrangement. Though Steve intended to (and did) resign from the university, its president (Richard Cyert, the management scholar) wrote a letter giving his approval and support. With a clear signal that Steve had a positive, supportive relationship with his university, Fujitsu's top management entered into a unique and very open-ended relationship with him. His assignment was to work in a telecommunications manufacturing facility in Oyama, a community north of Tokyo. According to Steve,

> This was an open-ended arrangement. I would study Japanese in the morning [after taking a crash course in Japanese in the States before traveling to Japan] and then work all afternoon until late in the night on whatever projects they thought I could be useful. . . . Nothing in particular was said about the future. We left that open. Both they [Fujitsu] and I realized that once I had learned Japanese, by that time I would probably know enough about their management practices to accomplish my personal goal. Then we could see how I might become useful to them.

This unique arrangement was an experiment for both Steve Miller and Fujitsu, and one that arose without any prior relationship between the parties, a type of arrangement I refer to below as a "recruiting" i-deal. Three years later, Steve was fluent in Japanese and well versed in Fujitsu's manufacturing and management processes. At this juncture, a second i-deal was negotiated whereby Steve and Fujitsu worked to figure out how best to use his talents. This second i-deal at Fujitsu involved executives in Japan and in the United States in a negotiation process common in international transfers. As with other expatriate assignments, the human resource departments in Fujitsu's Texas plant and at Fujitsu headquarters were involved. Through their discussions, Steve and Fujitsu created a unique role, that of liaison between the Texas plant and the Japanese headquarters, a role he performed for four years. I characterize this second deal as a "performance-based" i-deal, in which Fujitsu's management recognized an opportunity to use Steve's talents, and Steve sought an arrangement to tap his special skills and bring him and his family back to the United States. After a seven-year relationship with Fujitsu, one that both parties considered to be fruitful, Steve left to join a design consulting firm on the east coast of the United States.

Steve Miller's unique initial *ex ante* i-deal with Fujitsu was sparked by his distinctive interests and nurtured by the imaginative response of Fujitsu to the unusual opportunity that employing Steve presented. In other respects, however, his i-deal is representative of many idiosyncratic arrangements in that its particular demands, opportunities, and benefits to both parties are apparent only over time. Steve's initial deal was unique both in its process (i.e., a type of hire unprecedented for Fujitsu involving sign-offs at both Fujitsu and Steve's university) and in its idiosyncratic content (i.e., support in learning Japanese and the Fujitsu manufacturing system).

His second i-deal, negotiating his transfer to the United States in a liaison role, capitalized on the time he had spent and the relationships he had built within Fujitsu. It permitted Steve to further his learning and provide a unique contribution by helping the company better manage its relationships with a key production facility. In our framework, this type of i-deal is performance-based, reflecting the potential future contributions of a highly valued current employee. The process involved in creating this second deal is less exceptional since international transfers commonly require some negotiation to create appropriate ways to use worker skills and meet employer goals.[3] However, its content was idiosyncratic in that there were few preestablished conditions for such a liaison role. Thus, Steve's two i-deals with Fujitsu differ both in their content and the process by which they were made.

2. An Ex Post *Retention Deal with IBM*

Steve Miller negotiated another distinct i-deal with a different employer a decade later. Steve, his wife, and their two children had enjoyed living in Asia and wanted to return there. After Steve had gained several years of consulting experience with the American design firm, IBM recruited him to become a consultant based in Singapore. He joined IBM with a fairly standard employment package and agreed to do sales for its Asian consulting services practice. The job entailed extensive travel and long hours. Steve, a self-confessed workaholic, built up the practice, hitting sales target after sales target. But three years after taking the job, Steve and his wife decided they wanted a more balanced family life, while still remaining in Singapore. Steve tendered his resignation to IBM and was set to take a faculty position in a Singapore university, a job that would give him more flexibility in the work he did and had fewer demands taking him away from his family.

His IBM deal arose when its management tried to keep him from quitting. Even though Steve had resigned formally, his manager at IBM asked him what it would take to get him to stay. Steve thought about his two passions: his family and learning new things. His existing IBM job's focus on sales brought with it travel and business-unit responsibilities that gave Steve little time at home and little time for creative work. Steve talked to friends within IBM, both former bosses and current colleagues, to get an idea of what he might ask for that would give him and IBM a workable arrangement. In the end, IBM agreed to a new deal that included more time off, no sales work, and the creation of a new position of chief architect that let him develop internal customer relationships to foster his design work. In my framework, this latter deal fits the category of a "retention-based" i-deal.

Implications

The i-deals Steve Miller negotiated during the course of his career exemplify some of the different circumstances under which i-deals can arise. Steve pursued the initial deal with Fujitsu in response to his goal of creating a learning experience for himself. His transfer back to the United States involved another set of negotiations in creating a new role that capitalized on the investment he and Fujitsu had made in each other. His subsequent i-deal at IBM arose under very different circumstances. After he had actually decided to quit, IBM executives worked to find a way to keep him. By asserting his preferences for more creative work and time for his family, Steve was able to negotiate another distinctive role for himself. Steve's i-deals were negotiated under the three major circumstances in which i-deals arise, at recruiting, on the job while implementing an existing personnel practice, and at termination, when the employer seeks to retain a valued worker.

The processes by which Steve Miller's i-deals were negotiated are each distinct. Initiating a special deal with a firm in Japan, without preexisting contacts there, placed the onus on Steve to find a willing employer and make his case. The whole process of his initial negotiation with Fujitsu was unique in its history, and equally so in its content. In contrast, while all i-deals involve exceptional terms, not all of them involve unusual processes. The negotiation of his transfer back to the United States involved a more established process for an international employer such as Fujitsu, though the creation of the liaison role involved unusual terms idiosyncratic to Steve and his relationship with the company. In response to IBM's efforts to retain him—an already valued employee—Steve's actions focused on making his interests known and negotiating an arrangement suitable to IBM as well as himself. Again, as in the case of his transfer back to the United States by Fujitsu, Steve's arrangement with IBM was idiosyncratic, but the process of negotiating it was not. IBM, like other knowledge-oriented firms, was accustomed to creating special arrangements when trying to retain valued employees.

An i-deal's content is in some way singular or peculiar to a particular individual and is not enjoyed by peers or coworkers. Nonetheless, the processes by which i-deals are negotiated need not be unique. Employers may have routines for creating unusual conditions of employment that may involve several executives and human resource management in the deliberations. Thus, some i-deals are negotiated through established processes. However, as in the case of Steve's efforts to get a Japanese firm to hire him in the first place, truly exceptional arrangements can necessitate exceptional processes.

Types of I-deals

Three essential features characterize the types of i-deals workers negotiate with their employers. The first is timing, the point in the employment relationship at which the i-deal is negotiated. We differentiate *ex ante* i-deals, made during recruiting, from *ex post* deals, negotiated once a relationship has formed between worker and employer. *Ex post* i-deals further differentiate into those arising when a worker quits or threatens to quit (i.e., retention-related i-deals) and those in which the worker's past performance or potential future contributions form the basis of the negotiation (i.e., performance-based i-deals).

The second feature is how the i-deal is initiated, whether the worker initiates the bargaining process (i.e., proactive) or responds opportunistically to circumstances the employer creates that make an i-deal easier to pursue (i.e., reactive).

A third feature is their content, in particular, the nature of the resources provided via the i-deal. Content is intertwined with timing since some resources such as personal support may be difficult to bargain for prior to being hired but are more readily available to a current employee.

In contrast, deals created under the same circumstances can differ in their content, as in the case in which two high performers each meet with their boss following a favorable performance review. If one employee bargains for a special bonus and the other for a challenging assignment, they may well end up drawing very different conclusions about the nature of their employment relationship, even if both get what they demanded. The first may view his attachment to the employer as largely economic while the other experiences a deeper sense of commitment. Both the circumstances in which the i-deal arises and the resources it exchanges impact the interpretations employees make regarding their employment relationship. The i-deals these features give rise to are outlined in Table 5.1.

I-deals negotiated at the time of hire (*ex ante* i-deals, cells A and B in Table 5.1) are in response to the market power and distinctive competencies of the individual worker and the prevailing industry and country norms regarding preemployment negotiation.[4] I-deals created during recruitment generally occur while employer and potential employee are negotiating the more commonly bargained-for aspects of employment, such as pay, start date, and job title. Note that not everything an individual worker bargains for is idiosyncratic. Employers often have ranges of acceptable start dates, pay, grade levels, and titles from which to create an attractive employment package for a new hire. Moreover, while workers may seek other nonstandard features of employment (e.g., special equipment, promotion opportunities), the processes whereby employers handle such requests need not be exceptional, as we saw in the case of Steve Miller's transfer and retention negotiations. Employers commonly have established routines and approval processes for handling special requests that arise during the hiring process. Managers involved in the hiring process are also likely to share information with one another regarding these negotiations. In that context, i-deals constitute part of the broader array of preemployment negotiations. In many cases, what makes the i-deal exceptional is not so much the process of its creation but its distinctive content. For example, Jim Hooley, a long-time friend and a White House staffer to President Ronald Reagan, was active in the advance planning for the former president's state funeral, begun many years before Reagan's death in 2004. When he joined a software maker in 2000, Jim negotiated a sudden-leave provision, so he could leave his job at a moment's notice when the ailing former president died, to carry out the funeral arrangements.[5] The actual provision negotiated in Jim's case was exceptional, but not necessarily the process, because firms in creative and dynamic industries, such as software, typically do considerable negotiation in recruiting.[6]

Recruiting i-deals (cell A in Table 5.1) are initiated by recruits who see themselves as having the power to propose, accept, and reject terms of employment. Consider the case of an attorney who has ailing parents who require her care and attention in another part of the country. She sought out a law firm known for its flexibility. After talking with each of the firm's partners individually, the attorney convinced them that they had much to gain from her exceptional litigation skills. The firm's partners agreed to deviate from standard practice for distributing caseloads if she were to join the firm. The attorney would be assigned cases only in her preferred location as long as her need to care for her parents continued. As in the case of this attorney, *ex ante* bargaining is endemic to highly marketable workers, particularly those in labor markets where bargaining is the norm (such as Silicon Valley during the hot job market of the 1990s). Sought-after workers are more likely to bargain—and bargain successfully. A less-established or younger litigator in the above law firm is less likely to bargain at the time of hire. If less-valued workers do attempt to bargain, they are less likely to be successful than their highly valued counterparts.

Nonetheless, *ex ante* negotiations involving unusual or burdensome ar-

Table 5.1

Types of I-deals

		Timing	
Circumstances	*Ex Ante*—Hiring	*Ex Post*—Performance	*Ex Post*—Retention/Termination
	A	C	E
	Recruiting I-deals	*Proactive I-deals*	*Threat-Based I-deals*
Worker Initiates	<u>Worker Negotiates at Hire</u>	<u>Employee Negotiates on the Job</u>	
Basis	Market power of worker	Relationship quality; employer dependence on worker	Market power of worker; employer dependence on worker
Content	Typically, employee receives economic conditions, title, job duties, hours, and location of work in exchange for accepting position and potential future contributions.	Employee receives socioemotional resources as well as economic ones in exchange for contributions past, present, and future.	Employee makes a largely economic deal, often one-sided, with no new contributions demanded by employer.
Example	An attorney with ailing parents who require her care and attention in another part of the country seeks employment at a law firm willing to be flexible in its employment arrangements. To benefit from her exceptional litigation skills, the firm's partners agree to her request to be assigned cases near her parents as long as they require her care. This agreement deviates from the firm's standard practice for distributing cases.	A young tax accountant who envisions himself a "people person" is interested in moving into the account management department of the consulting firm that employs him, to capitalize on his gregarious nature. The senior partners agree that he shows promise; although they've never done anything like this before, they agree to give him the sales training he needs to move into account management.	Marketing professor seeks outside offer from another university to use as bargaining chit. She demands substantial pay raise and reduction in teaching load as condition of declining the offer.

94

Employer Initiates	B *Opportunistic Recruiting* Employer Offers at Hire	D *Reactive I-deals* Employer Creates Circumstances	F *Retention-Based I-deals* Making It Easier for Workers to Bargain
Basis	Worker value to employer	Personnel events inviting negotiation; employer obligation to worker; employer remedy for past violations	Employer dependence on worker
Content	Employee receives higher compensation and preferred duties, hours, and location in exchange for accepting position and providing exceptional talents to employer.	Employee receives socioemotional resources, such as challenging work and developmental assignments, as well as economic resources, in exchange for contributions, frequently past ones, though deal can be future-oriented, too.	Deal parameters are broad, including socioemotional as well as economic resources; deal is often one-sided.
Example	Star professor recruited by another university refuses to consider job offer unless faculty appointments are also extended to his wife as well as her former husband, with whom she shares joint custody of their children.	An international banker is reluctant to take an overseas assignment for fear that it will interfere with her musical training. Because the company needs her talents elsewhere, they agree to pay the special packing and shipping for her custom-made grand piano (at a cost several times what it normally requires to move an expatriate's household effects).	Manager of nonprofit resigns in order to spend more time at home with young child and work on his MBA. Employer counters and offers the individual more flexible hours and support for MBA if he stays on part-time.

rangements for the employer require greater care and effort on the part of the recruit to create a process culminating in employer acceptance. As in the case of the attorney who negotiated an unusual arrangement, *ex ante* i-dealers might need to develop a special rapport or knowledge regarding the employer and its interests in order to achieve their desires. Thus, a new marketing director who wishes to commute each week from Toronto to the company headquarters in North Carolina or a graphic designer who demands special equipment for a home office would each be aided in their pursuit of an i-deal by building a relationship with their potential employers (e.g., through a series of meetings) to complement their strong job qualifications. Though valued skills or distinctive contributions are necessary conditions for an i-deal, those workers better at negotiation or relationship building, or both, may be more effective at creating i-deals than their equally qualified but less interpersonally savvy counterparts. Note, however, that relationships aren't enough to create an i-deal; an individual must have valued competencies to create an arrangement intended to benefit the employer as well as him- or herself. Relationships are not required to negotiate an i-deal successfully, however, as was seen in the case of Steve Miller's first, recruiting i-deal with Fujitsu. When he first contacted Fujitsu, Steve knew no one there and couldn't even speak Japanese. The driving force behind i-deals is the distinctive value the worker offers the employer.

Opportunistic recruiting (cell B in Table 5.1) occurs when the employer proposes the i-deal. In our example, a star faculty member, whom we'll call Cameron Dale, was recruited by a top business school, which upon learning of his complex family situation, extended an unusual offer. Cameron's wife, a fellow business school professor, shared joint custody of her children with her former husband, who also happened to teach at the same business school. The recruiting university offered to hire all three of them. This i-deal is unusual because it involved hiring a third person to resolve a dual career problem. The sought-after recruits clearly had a say in the terms and conditions of such an arrangement, since the very fact that the employer initiated the arrangement suggests the high regard in which the potential hires were held. In this case, the professors bargained for attractive economic payouts from the recruiting university, including high salaries, benefits, reduced teaching loads, and generous research support. Such opportunistic recruiting is often exceptional in both process and content. When market conditions are extremely competitive, this mode of recruitment epitomizes creative ways of hiring talented workers.

The content of *ex ante* i-deals tends to focus on basic conditions of employment that are of concrete and universal concern, such as pay, benefits, duties, hours, and location. While *ex ante* arrangements may be exceptionally generous, their terms are often limited to monetizable features of employment. Few recruits are in a position to bargain for more personal resources such as support or socioemotional concern. Also, negotiating for more particularistic or socioeconomic resources such as developmental assignments or special support requires some degree of inside knowledge and affinity between the parties. Insofar as insider status is a necessary condition for obtaining socioemotional resources, i-deals made during recruiting are unlikely to include them. In consequence, the resources bargained for *ex ante* tend to be monetary or tangible and reflect information worker and employer possess about the worker's market value. Not surprisingly, workers who successfully negotiate i-deals tend to view their terms as part of their larger compensation package, incorporating conditions that normally affect pay such as work hours and duties. *Ex ante* i-dealers commonly attribute their i-deal to their own market value rather than something special about their relationship to their employer. As such, it is not surprising that research suggests that *ex ante* i-deals are not viewed as a strong signal regarding the quality of the employment relationship per se.[7] The meaning workers attach to *ex post* i-deals is another story.

Ex post i-deals arise once a worker has been hired. We distinguish two different facets in their timing. Performance-based i-deals are negotiated by current employees when contributions they have made to the firm or their potential future contributions form the basis of their efforts to gain employer support for idiosyncratic arrangements. Retention/termination-based i-deals are negotiated with the prospect that the worker might quit unless an agreement is reached.

Proactive i-deals (cell C in Table 5.1) are performance-based negotiations initiated by workers. They arise when the worker believes he or she is sufficiently valuable to the employer to negotiate successfully. Managers who respond positively to such *ex post* requests often have developed a high-quality relationship of trust and mutual reliance with the subordinate, making it easier to entertain a special accommodation.[8] In such supportive circumstances, individuals can actively seek out ways to meet personal needs that their employer's standard practices don't fulfill. In the example in Table 5.1, a young tax accountant fancied himself a people person rather than a number cruncher. Despite his successes in this field, he asked his manager whether he could switch to account management. His own boss was reluctant to grant this unusual request, but when the matter was brought before the firm's senior partners, they saw it as an opportunity to develop the tax accountant and preempt the potential future loss of this promising young employee, and they agreed to give the accountant sales training and mentoring in preparation for the move.

It can be easier to negotiate an i-deal after the worker has established a relationship with the employer than it is at the time of hire. Workers unable to negotiate during recruiting may try again once they are on the job. While she was being recruited for a teaching position at a Singaporean junior college, Soon Lee tried to get the college to hire her part-time so that she could study for an advanced degree. Soon admits, "I am not typical for a Singaporean. I don't want to just accept where they put me." At that time, the employer refused her request, saying it was not consistent with company policy. After two years on the job, however, the teacher made the same request of her immediate boss, who granted it. In the case of Soon Lee, timing impacted her employer's responsiveness to her efforts to obtain a special arrangement.

When an employee is proactive in creating an i-deal, the resources involved run the gamut from economic to socioemotional, from work-family flexibility to expanded job duties geared toward strengthening promotion chances or salary growth potential.[9] The bargaining process commonly is bilateral, with worker and employer each negotiating what they will receive. As such, proactive i-deals can reinforce a high performer, promote beliefs in the supportiveness of the employer, create new roles, fill gaps the employer didn't realize it had, and provide resources that have particular meaning to individual workers. It can strengthen and reinforce relational terms of the psychological contract, particularly when the resources exchanged are of a socioemotional or developmental nature.[10]

Reactive performance-based i-deals (cell D in Table 5.1) arise when workers respond to circumstances the employer has created that make it seem likely that a proposed i-deal will get a favorable response. Three circumstances that lead workers to believe employers may respond particularly favorably to an i-deal include:

1. personnel-related events in which the employer is posed to take action (e.g., promotion or transfer);
2. worker contributions that place the employer under obligation to reciprocate (e.g., upon completion of a special project);
3. remedies for past employer violation of promises or commitments (e.g., when a promised promotion didn't materialize).

Personnel-related events in which the employer is seeking a willing worker to fulfill an important assignment or take a difficult-to-fill position are prime circumstances for i-dealing. Such events permit employees to link their requests to circumstances that make it clearly in the employer's interest to agree. Job postings or new project start-ups can make it easier

Table 5.2

I-deals in Personnel Decisions and Events

Event	Example
Recruiting	Unique role for applicant with distinctive talents Applicant for senior managerial position who commutes from home in another state
Performance review	Special assignment or project to motivate and challenge worker High ratings used to lever request for preferred hours or duties
Compensation	Special bonus negotiated for early project completion Equity share for valued marketing manager in start-up firm
Training	Employee who seeks education in special competencies (e.g., technical, managerial)
Promotion	Make acceptance contingent on special preferences (e.g., different hours, change of location, choice of projects)
Retirement	Phase-in process for valued worker who begins reducing workload and hours Special consultant role created to keep retiree with valuable skills and knowledge available to employer

for employees to argue that their request for an i-deal benefits the employer, too. By tying an i-deal to circumstances that make employers more willing to accommodate special requests, employees can construct more personally rewarding work arrangements with less risk of rejection. Such personnel events include performance reviews in which workers have received high ratings; job openings that the worker uses to negotiate development, support, or preferred working conditions; and other circumstances in which the employer is motivated to gain the worker's cooperation (Table 5.2).

Michaela Bell took advantage of one such personnel event, the posting of a vacancy in a managerial job, to propose an arrangement she had wanted for some time. A thirty-five-year-old manager, she had worked for her employer for a dozen years before asking for an i-deal. Originally, she had been hired to work full-time in a program development job. After taking on several difficult assignments that established her value to the organization, Michaela decided to make a shift. She sought to become the only manager (out of ten) who worked half-time. Going part-time had been on her mind for a while. When the management position opened up, Michaela saw an opportunity to pursue the change with her employer.

To make this transition, Michaela approached her immediate boss when the managerial position opened up in an area in which she had client experience. She expressed her interest in that position and began a negotiation that focused on her preferred work schedule and the variety of tasks she

99

would be able to accomplish in that time frame. Her choice of workdays (Tuesday, Wednesday, and Thursday) and hours (9 a.m. to 4 p.m.) was predicated on her family's activities and her desire to volunteer in her children's after-school programs. This shift also required her to negotiate boundaries, that is, which tasks she would be responsible for and those she wanted off her plate. At about the same time that Michaela got the go-ahead to become a part-time manager, a coworker with a more limited track record sought a similar deal but was unable to win approval from the company's management. In Michaela's case, her employer filled an important position and kept a valued professional happy and motivated. Michaela's situation demonstrates how workers often wait for an opportunity to suggest an i-deal when the circumstances give them leverage, making it the right time to ask. As a result, her employer gained an effective manager with ample knowledge of the organization to launch several new programs while maintaining satisfaction among existing clients. Michaela was able to enjoy a higher level of family and community involvement than would have been possible had she continued to work full-time.

Reactive i-deals also arise after workers have made special contributions at the behest of their employer, thereby positioning themselves to ask for something special in return. A case in point is the young faculty member who asked for a semester off and increased research funding after teaching two courses outside her area when an older instructor fell ill. Because she had stepped up to help the school at a critical time, her department head was pleased to agree to an i-deal for a hardworking junior person. Insofar as rewarding high performers is a common practice, it might seem odd to link this practice to i-deals. Nonetheless, such a reward is an i-deal if the worker influences the form it takes, thereby introducing idiosyncrasy into his or her employment relationship. Indeed, i-deals are ways workers can adapt established practices, such as recognizing and rewarding high performers, to better suit their needs. In a similar way, personnel actions such as performance reviews and promotion discussions can invite workers to bargain for special arrangements by making their past contributions or future potential salient to the employer.

Circumstances under which workers have gone the extra mile, completed a difficult assignment, made sacrifices, or otherwise performed exceptionally can obligate the employer to respond with special recognition. Workers can use their employer's obligation to reciprocate their contributions and thereby create unusual arrangements that would be difficult to gain acceptance for otherwise. In some cases, the employer might have actually promised a reward in advance, while leaving the details open-ended. The chief information officer at an express mail company challenged the leaders of various systems development projects to streamline the company's information systems, allowing local people to operate them without elaborate centralized supports. He promised, "Work yourself out of a job—and there will be a place for you." Richard Neuhaus, a manager of information technology special services, took on the CIO's challenge. In less than a year, he had the new system he was in charge of up and running smoothly. When he talked with the CIO about what he could do next, the CIO responded, "What do you want?" Richard negotiated a two-year leave to complete his doctorate, with the opportunity to rejoin the company in a new role. Two years later, Richard Neuhaus, PhD, returned as director of systems development. I-deals made in circumstances such as these represent a form of reciprocity, where it is understood that the worker is entitled to a payback.

Reactive i-deals also can be used as a remedy for treatment that may have been unfair, as when workers believe their efforts have gone unappreciated or the employer has broken a promise. In a study of psychological contract violation, individual workers responded differently when they believed their employer had broken a promise, whether for a promotion, more challenging assignments, a raise, or another attractive reward.[11] Some complained to their immediate boss or senior manager, while others simply quit their jobs without complaining first. Those workers who complained typically had relational psychological contracts involving mutual loyalty and support. In contrast, those who quit without complaining had more economically focused transactional contracts. Workers with relational contracts were generally more upset when their employer failed to keep its commitments than were their counterparts with transactional contracts. Nonetheless, workers with relational contracts were committed to remaining with their employer *if* the violation could be remedied. For example, when he was recruited, one study participant had been promised a promotion if he performed successfully in his first year on the job. After receiving a stellar performance rating, Gary Masson, a thirty-year-old MBA in a small consulting firm, was upset when his boss told him there were no promotions available; because of the now sluggish economy there were cutbacks instead. Gary complained to a senior partner. He was offered a slight pay raise, but on pressing the partner regarding the importance of career opportunity, he was able to negotiate a set of more visible accounts and a promotion within six months. Gary stayed with the firm, was promoted, and believes he made his point: "I wanted recognition of my value to the firm and that I deserved the promotion." Workers who are loyal often prefer to voice their discontent through informal channels, asking their supervisor and others to help work out problems and resolve situations they see as unfair.[12] Such circumstances can lead workers to seek i-deals in compensation for previous inequitable treatment.

For many people, i-deals are easier to request and obtain after they have worked at a company for a while than before joining the company. Although workers can proactively pursue i-deals in circumstances of their own making, as in the case of Soon Lee, others, like Michaela Bell, prefer to wait until opportunity makes an i-deal easier to suggest. Some workers—many women and minorities in particular—are reluctant to ask, assuming that what their employer offers to them is fixed and not subject to negotiation. Other workers, including those who are experienced negotiators, are more proactive in raising issues with a current or would-be employer. Less-skilled negotiators are more likely to avoid proactive negotiations, electing to negotiate only when a situation appears to require it or the likelihood of success is particularly high (e.g., when the integrative potential of a negotiation is obvious).[13] Being able and willing to ask for what one wants can spell the difference between a work experience that complements an individual's needs and values and one plagued by frustration and silent suffering. As the quote at the outset of this chapter indicates, negotiating may be essential to getting a person's needs met. Not doing so may be taken as a signal that what a person has is sufficient.

Workers seldom make requests unless they believe it is appropriate to do so. Such is the case when proactive workers drive the process of creating i-deals, as Soon Lee did.[14] Other workers are more reactive, capitalizing on opportunities that special circumstances create for requesting an i-deal (e.g., when an employee is asked to accept a transfer or new assignment). It is easier for employees to speak up when they recognize an opportunity to get something they want while also benefiting their employer. In contrast, those workers with a special need but no obvious way to make a case may not raise the issue until that need becomes especially salient (their child-care arrangements have collapsed or an evening class's group project is approaching its deadline). The important point is that not every worker feels that it is okay to ask.

Successful performance-based negotiations arise once an employee has built a relationship and performance record with an employer. These types of negotiations have more powerful implications for how workers construe the relationship with their employer than do *ex ante* negotiations. Performance-based *ex post* i-deals occur in the context of ongoing give-and-take in the employment relationship. Unlike i-deals negotiated while the worker is on the job market, the external labor market is often not salient in performance-based *ex post* arrangements. What matters more is the track record the worker has created as well as evidence regarding his or her potential future contributions. An employer who grants an i-deal in recognition of past contributions sends a signal of reciprocity and appreciation, while granting an i-deal based on future potential can signal a commitment to the worker's career development and personal growth. In effect, asking for what one wants can have different meanings in the middle of a relationship than at the beginning of one.

Ex post negotiation for idiosyncratic arrangements appears to be more common than *ex ante* bargaining in employment.[15] The greater frequency of i-deals made for current employees can be attributed to several factors. First, introducing an unusual or nonconforming practice may be easier later in a relationship. Employers who might be reluctant to accommodate special requests from workers they are unfamiliar with or who have little leverage at the time of hire (i.e., the young, inexperienced, and uncredentialed) can over time come to depend on these individuals and take steps to accommodate them when the need arises. Second, only highly marketable workers are likely to successfully bargain during recruiting. Their less-marketable counterparts, if they bargain at all, tend to do so on the job, after their employers have come to depend on them. Even a reluctant i-dealer can attempt to negotiate if an employer takes steps that make it easier to do so. Third, because the employer has less information about the worker during recruiting than after, workers are concerned with what signals particular requests might send regarding the kind of worker they are likely to be. A worker seeking to make a good impression might be willing to demand promotion opportunities during recruitment to convey his or her ambitions but not to ask for an extra week's vacation. Since employers might construe the latter request as an indication that the worker lacks commitment, such requests are likely to be made once the worker has a track record with the employer, increasing the likelihood that the request will not be misconstrued. Fourth, evidence suggests that those who bargain for i-deals during recruitment continue to do so later, on the job.[16] By negotiating *ex ante,* the firm is hiring workers predisposed to negotiate later, too. Lastly, there are numerous opportunities in the course of their employment relationship for workers to successfully negotiate i-deals. Workers after all are usually hired by the same employer only once. Taking all these tendencies together, it is not surprising that more i-deals are negotiated *ex post* than *ex ante,* and the majority of these appear to be performance-based.

Performance-based i-deals arise under the broadest array of conditions and involve a greater mix of resources than do other forms of i-deals. The circumstances and resources involved affect the meanings workers attribute to i-deals. In contrast to *ex ante* i-deals, arrangements negotiated once a worker is on the job are more likely to be taken as an indicator of the quality of the employment relationship. While market factors dominate worker attributions regarding their employer's motives in granting them a special deal during recruiting, these external factors are less salient in performance-based i-deals.[17] Workers tend to attribute their success in negotiating a performance-based i-deal more to the quality of their relationship with the employer.

Performance-based i-deals are an important component of a firm's human resource practices. They provide employers with the opportunity to target particularly valued rewards to high performers. When these i-deals give employees socioemotional resources such as special concern and personal development, workers tend to see their employer as supportive.[18] I-deals that remedy injustice can serve to restore trust in the employment relationship, particularly in cases where workers believe that the employer has honored the spirit (if not the letter) of the employment agreement.[19] Through the capabilities employers develop in making performance-based ideals, these arrangements have the potential to create positive externalities by enhancing the employer's capacity to motivate its workforce.

I-deals also arise when workers quit or threaten to quit. *Threat-based i-deals* (cell E in Table 5.1) arise when a worker threatens to quit unless his or her demands for a raise, promotion, or other changes in employment conditions are met. Workers who leverage outside offers or other evidence of their mobility (e.g., calls from headhunters, outside requests for their resume) commonly bargain over the economic conditions of employment. The marketing professor who went on the job market to get outside offers she could take to her dean leveraged the evidence of her marketability to demand a substantial raise. Such bargains are often one-sided, unilateral deals in which the worker gains valued employment terms without being required to provide anything new in return. (However, if the professor negotiated to be groomed for a leadership position, the i-deal could involve investment on both her part and the employer's.) Threat-based i-deals have a downside for the employer, who risks rewarding bargaining behavior while creating inequity among coworkers who make comparable contributions. A worker who leverages an outside offer to get an i-deal is likely to view the employer's response as consistent with a transactional approach to employment, where the i-deal augments his or her compensation package but not necessarily the worker's attachment to the firm. In consequence, though the worker may remain with the company, the employment relationship is not necessarily strengthened by a threat-based accommodation. There are also risks for the employee, who may learn that he or she is less valuable than anticipated. Moreover, if once successful in leveraging an outside offer, the employee who continues to use this tactic to bargain repeatedly can create a pattern that coworkers both resent and mimic, creating negative externalities for both third parties and the employer. Below we address the implications that threat-based i-deals have for repeat bargaining.

Retention-based i-deals (cell F in Table 5.1), in contrast, are initiated by the employer in an effort to retain an employee who has quit or plans to quit. They are distinct from threat-based i-deals in that the employee is not deliberately leveraging his or her mobility to bargain for a better deal. Indeed, in many cases the employee might not believe such a deal would even be forthcoming. A case in point is the scientist with an outside offer he believed his employer would never match. He tried to quit only to be talked out of it by company representatives who were more than willing to give him what he wanted.

When an employer reacts to an employee's attempt to quit by proposing an i-deal, that employer is often highly motivated to retain a valued worker and willing to offer a broad array of conditions. Evan Davis, a manager in a nonprofit organization, had asked for a reduced workweek to have more time with his young daughter and to complete the MBA he had begun at night. The chief executive refused, telling him she gave reduced workweeks only to people approaching retirement. A month later, Evan decided to quit so he could finish his MBA faster while still having more time with his family. The day before his farewell party, the chief executive offered to let him work thirty hours a week. He refused. She then offered to pick up the tab for his night-school tuition and let him rebalance the projects he was juggling to make it all more manageable in a thirty-hour week. Evan finally agreed to stay. In this case, a retention-based i-deal followed the employee's failure to negotiate a performance-based i-deal.

Retention/termination-based i-deals can reveal a disconnect between what workers value from their employer and the existing reward system. If workers need to go outside the firm to be paid a market-based wage, the existing compensation system may not be competitive or equitable. Unless there are offsetting conditions (e.g., location, flexibility) that make the current employer particularly attractive, workers will use their valued capabilities to improve their employment conditions. Firms that rely on outside offers as a basis for determining wages punish workers who are loyal, less mobile, or both, while creating internal inequities that are difficult to legitimate among workers making comparable contributions. As such, the occurrence of retention/termination-based i-deals, especially if widespread, is an indication of inadequacy in the firm's compensation scheme and related management practices.

Implications

The information workers and employers have about each other differs across the circumstances and timing of i-deals. Employers rely on market-based information to deal with individuals at the time of hire, including the abilities and demands of other applicants, difficulties faced in recruiting suitable workers, and special opportunities provided by workers with rare talents. More detailed and person-specific information is available in dealing with current employees. Workers, too, have access to richer, more detailed information about employers after they have been hired, making it easier then to request idiosyncratic arrangements that require organization-specific knowledge (e.g., opportunities for particular developmental assignments). Differences in the information that is available to both parties before recruitment and after hiring are compounded by differences in the motives for granting i-deals. Although i-deals at hire are likely to be made only for potential employees with special competencies, employers may be willing to make subsequent i-deals with many other workers as well once they grow to value and trust them. It is important to recognize that for current high performers, a broader array of resources—from economic to socioemotional—are likely to be allocated via i-deals than is the case in i-deals created during the hiring process. The broader mix of resources available through i-deals made with current employees affords them greater opportunity for meeting their diverse personal needs. Retention-based i-deals are problematic: They often indicate that the firm's existing reward system is inadequate, and their continued use can heighten the sense of inequity among the firm's workers.

Dysfunctional I-dealing: Bargaining for Status and Repeatedly Bargaining

To this point, we have addressed workers' bargaining in pursuit of tangible ways to meet their special, personal needs while making valued contributions to their employer. However, i-deals have their own dark side when they are used to meet individual needs that themselves are dysfunctional. In particular, i-deals can be counterproductive when their purpose is to foster a worker's competitive position relative to his or her coworkers. Typically, these are one-sided exchanges wherein the worker demands more money or other rewards than coworkers receive, without a substantive difference in his or her contribution or a promise of greater future contributions. Note that these dysfunctional arrangements can occur in any of the six types of i-deals this chapter describes.

Individuals may seek i-deals out of hypersensitivity to status differences or a need for reassurance that others esteem and respect them.[20] I-deals sought for status are typically one-sided: the worker makes demands without offering to do anything more in return. These deals are the result of a worker wanting more, where "more" is defined as obtaining resources in

106

excess of what his or her peers receive. One such example is a professional baseball player with a multimillion-dollar contract who seeks perks for his family and friends as further indication of his success and renown. I-deals that individual workers seek to feel special are particularly precarious, as they are based on an individual's predisposition to be set above his or her peers. As psychologist Robyn Dawes puts it, the pursuit of status is a "hedonic treadmill," where each successful boost in status becomes a new zero point, a status quo that the individual soon takes for granted. Having adapted to each new status level, the individual seeks even more in pursuit of that special position over others that is never fully realized.[21]

Some workers are chronically sensitive to status issues, repeatedly seeking out equalizing treatment anytime they learn of benefits a coworker accrues.[22] A case in point is the professor who learns that a colleague has been given a reduced teaching load and storms into the department chair's office to demand the same deal. When i-deals are sought for status reasons, as in the case of this equity-sensitive professor, workers are unlikely to frame the deal in terms of its benefit to the employer, believing they are entitled to special treatment with no sacrifice on their part. As such, i-deals based on status seeking are often difficult to justify, particularly to the would-be i-dealer's coworkers. As the department chair later commented, the sensitive professor had only half the story: His colleague had accepted a cut in pay in exchange for the reduced workload.

Secret tests are an informal, circumspect way of monitoring when individuals believe they cannot obtain the information they need by asking directly.[23] A person who feels insecure about a relationship with another can indirectly seek information about the health of the relationship by creating secret tests to evaluate its status. In a dating relationship, a secret test might entail the thought "I'll know he loves me if he takes me to the movies on Friday and to my favorite restaurant." Of course, this is supposed to occur without the partner ever being told what he needs to do to pass the test! The chances of a partner or spouse actually passing this test are pretty low, making it likely that the person constructing the secret test is going to be disappointed. We see similar behavior in the workplace. In one company, coveted parking spaces were offered as rewards for group accomplishment. Group members sometimes put off deciding among themselves how to share the spaces, hoping instead that their boss would offer a space as a perk to some of them.[24] To workers seeking affirmation of whom their boss values most, seeing who gets the parking spaces constitutes a secret test.

Workers sometimes float the possibility of an i-deal by their managers as a secret test, when what they really seek is assurance of their standing in the eyes of their manager and in the larger firm. Secret testers can propose i-deals to test the waters and to gauge the quality of their relationship with their employer, their status, and their potential bargaining power. In an employment relationship, a worker might formulate a secret test such as "I will know my boss appreciates my contributions if he praises *me* when I praise the efforts of my coworkers." As in the dating relationship test discussed above, because the manager had no idea he or she was being tested, the worker is likely to be disappointed when the boss says nothing in support of her contributions. Seeking i-deals as assurance of one's special status is risky for both worker and employer, not least because this motive is difficult to satisfy and thus often leads to repeat bargaining.

Repeat bargaining is another dysfunctional aspect of i-deals. So far, our discussion of i-deals has focused on discrete arrangements made on single occasions. However, the meaning of i-deals potentially can change with successive bargains made over time. Although initial i-deals are likely to be offered and interpreted as special, subsequent i-deals can come to mean something different. Diminishing marginal returns can result for both worker and employer when repeat bargaining occurs, as each subsequent deal is less special. Moreover, workers who repeatedly propose i-deals risk damaging their personal reputations and being seen as players motivated primarily by the thrill of gaming the system.[25] Employers also may be unwilling to make repeated i-deals that provide ever-increasing levels of a particular resource, usually pay or status, to the same employee, because they risk being manipulated, being seen as practicing favoritism, acting capriciously, or irritating other employees. This sensitivity suggests a trend toward limited, selective use of i-deals. However, while some workers would be reluctant to bargain repeatedly out of loyalty or fear of reputation loss, others are willing to play the field by threatening to quit if their demands aren't met. In such cases, firms not only risk being held hostage to the instrumental behavior of a few workers but also risk eroding the loyalty of coworkers who do not play this game. Managers themselves can institutionalize such status-seeking behavior by demanding market-based information as a criterion for granting an i-deal to a current employee. A case in point is the business school dean who would not raise the salary of faculty members *unless* they came to his office with an outside offer in hand.

There is a big difference between repeat bargaining and intermittent renegotiations over time. Throughout the course of a worker's tenure with an employer, there are numerous occasions when negotiation may be needed. These intermittent renegotiations of the employment relationship can be legitimate and beneficial, allowing the deal to be periodically updated. Over the course of several years with the same employer, an individual worker might seek special development opportunities at some point and flexible hours at another as part of the normal demands of work and home life over time. Such negotiation constitutes intermittent bargaining because it entails a mix of resources appropriate to different points in a work career—not the escalation of demands for the same resources (e.g., pay) that comprises repeat bargaining. Intermittent bargaining can be beneficial when it reflects reciprocity, meeting the needs of both the firm and the worker, enhancing their mutual contributions and each other's well-being.

Conclusions

I-deals make it possible for workers to meet needs that their employer's standard practices do not fulfill. They also enable employers to adapt their existing human resource practices to changing employee needs by broadening the mix of recruiting tactics, performance incentives, and developmental opportunities they offer workers. I-deals provide employees with valued personal choice and flexibility while permitting employers to attract, motivate, develop, and retain valued workers. The timing of an i-deal and the content exchanged impact whether workers attribute their success in bargaining to their market value or to the generosity and supportiveness of their employer. While *ex ante* requests are likely to be attributed to the worker's standing in the labor market, *ex post* i-deals, especially performance-based ones, signal the quality of the firm as a supportive employer as well as the value both parties place on the employment relationship.

The typology of i-deals calls attention to the many ways in which i-deals enable an employer's human resource practices. Recruiting i-deals enable employers to respond to dynamic labor markets by permitting employers to offer novel arrangements. Such arrangements help employers attract talented workers from backgrounds that differ from those the firm's human resource practices usually target. Performance-based i-deals enable employers to customize rewards to meet the distinctive needs of individual high performers. These i-deals can also make it possible for a firm's existing human resource practices, such as performance reviews and promotion processes, to accommodate emerging employee demands without having to be formally altered. Retention-based i-deals permit employers to take action to retain workers they would otherwise lose and to identify ways to update their current human resource practices to be more competitive.

There is also a negative aspect to how individual workers approach i-deals. I-deals can be created to reassure status-hungry individuals, creating a short-term fix for what is likely to be a more chronic personnel problem. Repeated bargaining by the same worker over time can erode the quality of the employment relationship and drive a wedge between the repeat bargainer and his or her peers. Repeat bargaining can, in effect, be a reward for disloyalty, for example, when workers repeatedly look for outside job offers to use as a bargaining chip, and can also be viewed as a symptom of inadequacies in the firm's system for allocating rewards. In contrast, intermittent bargaining over the course of an employment relationship can create a sense of healthy flexibility. The effectiveness of an i-deal is gauged by its capacity to meet the needs of employee and employer both when it is negotiated and over time.

— 6 —

How Employees
Negotiate I-Deals

He that cannot ask cannot live.
—*Thomas Draxe*[1]

Employees speak with many voices in negotiating i-deals. They can assertively demand, calmly inquire, or subtly hint. Before, during, and after negotiating i-deals, workers can try to foster employer acceptance and coworker support. How workers pursue i-deals can have profound effects on their relationship with an employer, whether it is strengthened or compromised, expanded or diminished. I-deals can help employers attract, retain, motivate, and develop valued workers. Yet they also can be costly when they result in work arrangements that put the worker at odds with standard criteria for gauging performance—or create envy in coworkers. Subject to the forces operating in conventional firms that promote standardization and suppress deviance, i-deals can be difficult to sustain over time. As such, i-deals can entail an ongoing process of adjustment and renegotiation, feedback and redesign, challenging the ingenuity and goodwill of workers and employers.

This chapter describes the processes workers use to initiate, create, and maintain i-deals over time. It examines the three phases of i-deal formation: prework, negotiation, and managing the aftermath. How these phases are executed impacts both employer acceptance and coworker endorsement of an i-deal.

The Processes Workers Use to Create I-deals

The processes involved in creating i-deals have three phases, first identified by Vivien Clark (Figure 6.1).[2]

1. *Prework* refers to those activities that lay the groundwork for successful i-deal negotiation, including information gathering and relationship building. Gathering information about the employer and its practices and those of other firms can help the worker formulate the specific arrangements he or she seeks (e.g., uncovering precedents to create legitimacy for an i-deal). It can enhance the effectiveness with which workers articulate their requests, explain why the deal is in their employer's interest, and address how potential obstacles can be overcome. Relationship building affects the level of directness workers use in formulating their requests and can increase the likelihood of acceptance by the employer and those affected by an i-deal (e.g., by helping out one's peers or manager to show good faith and commitment to the organization).

2. *I-deal creation* refers to the communications (e.g., requests, demands, negotiation tactics) exchanged between worker and employer (and relevant others) to obtain approval for an i-deal. These communications include the request tactics, negotiation strategies, and creative problem solving used to reach agreement and set expectations regarding employer and employee obligations in the i-deal.

3. *Managing the aftermath* refers to how workers and their managers act toward coworkers, superiors, customers, and other constituencies to maintain idiosyncratic arrangements once they have been established. Activities in this phase are intended to reduce negative externalities and promote positive ones. They can serve to sustain the i-deal over time or end it in the face of change (e.g., new management, escalating performance demands, changing personal circumstances). Activities designed to sustain an i-deal include evaluation and feedback, renegotiation, and redesign of the i-deal's terms.

The processes whereby an i-deal arises can involve these phases to varying degrees, with their greatest likelihood of elaboration in the performance-based i-deals employees initiate.[3] Employee-initiated performance-based i-deals are made with less emphasis on external market and more on internal factors than are recruiting and retention i-deals. The former typically necessitate more preparation in building a case, identifying options, and promoting managers', coworkers', and customers' acceptance. Our focus in this chapter is on the negotiation process employees use to create the

Figure 6.1 **Phases of I-deal Negotiation**

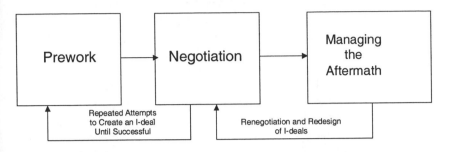

most complicated and carefully planned of all idiosyncratic arrangements, employee-initiated performance-based i-deals.

Prework: Preparing to Request an I-deal

Prework improves a worker's chances of successfully negotiating an i-deal. The i-deal's feasibility, the conditions under which others might lend their support, and the prospects for backlash or political complications often become known only once the worker has gathered information to help in formulating the request for an i-deal.[4] To avoid the risks that come with asking directly, such as rejection or embarrassment, initial groundwork can be used to feel out and indirectly assess an i-deal's viability. When information gathering is combined with relationship building, prework can help employees build a case for an i-deal while promoting it to those whose support it requires. In negotiation terms, prework leads employees to adjust their aspiration levels and improve their best alternative to a negotiated agreement (BATNA).[5] It also makes it possible to turn a negotiation into a problem-solving process.[6]

Identifying What Is Negotiable

Prework can directly impact worker beliefs regarding what is negotiable. For example, an accounts manager considered asking his boss for time off to attend executive education sessions. In gathering background information about opportunities the employer had provided other workers, he learned that one person in another department had gotten the firm to pick up 100 percent of the tab for the education that led to his professional certification. Armed with this knowledge, the worker went to his manager and requested time off and full tuition reimbursement for executive education, which he argued would improve his ability to serve the firm's clients. Indeed, such prework can reveal that one's request is not particularly unusual, or even idiosyncratic, if there is local precedent for it.[7] When precedent exists, prework can focus on developing alternatives to strengthen the worker's bargaining position. It can also focus on the employer's perspective (i.e., getting inside the employer's head) to understand how to effectively reach agreement.[8]

Insights into the negotiability of one's employment conditions are useful to every potential i-dealer. Personal networks can provide important information regarding what others have negotiated in the past.[9] This information is especially valuable for women, who often believe they have to sacrifice professional goals to achieve personal ones. Prework can help employees realize that they don't need to sacrifice as much as they might think in pursuit of an i-deal.[10]

Personal initiative differentiates many of those who request i-deals from those who don't—and one major difference may be in the use of prework.[11] Workers displaying strong personal initiative actively search for ways to achieve their goals, alert to early signals of obstacles that must be overcome. Initiators tend to believe it is up to them to find work arrangements that meet their needs.[12] They display this belief in the efforts they undertake to gather information and build relationships in preparation for creating an i-deal.

Looking Outside the Organization: Market Research and Benchmarking

Fact-finding regarding alternative employment options can form the basis for negotiating i-deals. Many workers monitor the job market regularly, looking for better alternatives. Workers in many countries read help-wanted ads daily to find out what other companies are offering.[13] Approximately 16 percent of the U.S. workforce has signed up on Monster.com, where the search for job information peaks on Monday between noon and 4 p.m.[14] Insofar as younger people and those with fewer local ties or geographic constraints are likely to find mobility more attractive than colleagues who are rooted in the community, they are more likely to seek out and use market information to lay the groundwork for an i-deal. Less-mobile workers are unlikely to pay attention to or seek out market information.

External searches are not used just for job-hopping. They also make it easier to negotiate with a current employer by providing external benchmarks. A private banker working in a small Swiss firm conducted a Web search of various executive education programs. His search revealed that several private banking firms were sending their staff to international programs tailored to bankers. The banker downloaded one school's brochure and put it on his boss's desk. Though initially taken aback because the firm had sent no one to formal training, the manager ultimately agreed that if its competitors were training their staff, it was reasonable to honor the banker's request. As in this case, external information can provide a benchmark for workers to use to influence their employers' beliefs regarding appropriate employment conditions, motivating a positive response to a request for an i-deal.

Identifying Where Innovation Is Possible Inside the Firm

Gathering information inside the firm also lays the groundwork for requesting an i-deal. Indeed, internal information gathering can be eye-opening. Recall Vicky King, the manager described in chapter 4, who coined the phrase "coral reefs" to identify the i-deals she uncovered after she learned how to spot the array of special deals that other valued workers in her company had negotiated (including sabbaticals to do underwater photography).[15] Prework can lead workers who start off with one view of their organizational reality to change that view as they encounter exceptions to the rules. An even more powerful psychological change occurs when the worker realizes that there are in fact multiple realities (i.e., from the vantage points of workers in different positions, departments, etc.); through this realization, the worker learns just how varied and multifaceted are the employer's arrangements with its workforce.[16] Such psychological changes are an example of what Argyris and Schoen call "double-loop learning," in which individuals come to question and test their assumptions regarding employment, a learning process that I as a researcher and employee have come to personally appreciate.[17]

Employment conditions that once appeared to be fixed and immutable can turn out to be variable and negotiable when subjected to careful scrutiny. Information searches tend to focus on patterns and established practices. However, it can be even more helpful if the would-be i-dealer highlights exceptions and new opportunities. As Margaret Wheatley argues, to create effective responses to a world that is constantly surprising us, we need to embrace the living properties of information:

> We haven't been interested in newness. We've taken disturbances and fluctuations and averaged them together. . . . We live in a society that believes it can define *normal* and then judge everything against this fictitious standard. We struggle to smooth out the differences, conform to standards, measure up. Yet in life, newness can only show up as difference. If we aren't looking for differences, we can't see that anything has changed; consequently, we aren't able to respond.[18]

I-dealers and their managers can scout out ways to learn and innovate, looking for ways to redesign the employer's structures and practices. Following a series of downsizings at a U.S. Air Force base, civilian employees and managers who survived the layoffs sought ways to get necessary tasks done while also restoring unit morale. Knowing that their workload was now greater than ever, and with few promotion or development opportunities in sight, layoff survivors at the base reexamined each unit's set of accountabilities and deliverables. They had started to question their old assumptions about critical tasks when a senior manager responsible for filing a monthly report with the Washington, D.C., headquarters failed to do so one month—and no one at headquarters noticed or asked about it. The manager never filed that report again; he and his fellow managers began scrutinizing their other tasks to determine which were really critical to their mission. Building and strengthening interunit relations across the base, they found ways to reprioritize or share existing work. While achieving each unit's newly rearticulated mission, this informal process led to individual workers negotiating assignments and duties to make them more personally interesting. This negotiation was predicated on the employer's need to retain survivors and sustain their motivation despite trying circumstances.

Gathering information prior to negotiating an i-deal can reveal the "white space," that is, the opportunities for flexibility that exist in the organization.[19] This flexibility can arise in several different forms, from readily acceptable arrangements in innovative settings—the highest form of flexibility—to workarounds in cases where flexibility is highly constrained (as described in chapter 2). A would-be i-dealer in a highly bureaucratic organization might look for a precedent in work groups or areas whose practices differ—knowing that precedent often trumps otherwise inflexible rules and procedures in justifying decisions. Workers looking for i-deal opportunities may check out those places where the organization already does things differently. (Animal lovers take note: In my university, the Robotics Institute keeps a pet cat, but the business school does not, though my colleague down the hall brings his dog to work everyday. If ever I decide to try to bring my favorite pet to school, I know at least two places I might look to make my case.) Identifying innovation islands can be as easy as reading the organization's newsletter or talking with colleagues in other parts of the firm.

Another method of finding flexibility involves identifying gaps in existing duties, tasks, and organizational activities, and using that knowledge to create a new role whose focus hasn't previously existed in the firm. Such arrangements may involve solving a problem the employer doesn't know it has. As his idiosyncratic arrangement with Fujitsu evolved, Steve Miller and his senior managers identified—and filled—a gap in the interface between the Japanese firm and its American subsidiaries, as described in chapter 5. I-deals based on gap filling deploy worker talents in novel ways, helping the employer become more adaptive.

Workers seeking flexibility may also use their existing zone of acceptance to find ways of reinterpreting their current role. As described in chapter 2, when a behavior or employment arrangement falls within the zone of acceptance, neither the worker nor the employer will raise an objection if one acceptable behavior is substituted for another.[20] The prework conducted to identify this zone involves talking with one's role constituents (including internal as well as external customers) to create alternative ways of accomplishing the same tasks and goals. It may involve getting a clear sense of which role responsibilities certain constituents believe to be critical and feeling out each constituent's willingness to go along with the changes sought by the would-be i-dealer. A certain degree of testing the waters helps workers identify what constitutes acceptable behavior in creating i-deals. These explorations can lead the worker to initiate the change on his or her own, as in the case of a worker who realizes that his manager has flexible hours and decides to emulate the boss's schedule. A worker who fears to assume that the behavior is acceptable without checking first can do some fact-finding to see where the zone of acceptance lies, thus becoming better able to formulate a request so as to appear more normal. This can be accomplished via direct inquiry as well as indirectly through observation. Workers who note that a boss works variable hours can see a higher-up's departure from the standard as precedent for their own flexibility.

Not every employee has the resources to do prework effectively. Prework often involves tapping one's organizational network. Though this can be a useful way to begin preparing to negotiate an i-deal, it may not be adequate when a worker's network is limited or biased. Women, for instance, need to be especially careful to gather information broadly in preparation for i-deals, since they often hold gender-segregated jobs, which can provide a limited perspective on what types of i-deals are possible.[21] The same can be true for minorities with limited organizational networks or others without ties to people in powerful positions.[22] Not surprisingly, workers are more likely to directly obtain information about a possible i-deal from friends, colleagues, or managers with whom they have a relationship. This is true of expatriates who compare notes on each other's compensation packages when working abroad as well as among workers who joined a firm at the same time.[23] Workers are particularly likely to pay attention to the flexibilities their coworkers enjoy, especially those whom they view as equal in stature, as in the case of workers with similar duties or titles, and those who act as their substitutes by attending meetings for them, covering the same clients, and the like.[24] Employers for their part are known to take steps to reduce awareness of i-deals by creating social or physical distance among workers.[25] For this reason, workers pursuing i-deals may need to build new relationships to access otherwise unavailable information. Prework can help people access information not readily available through their existing social contacts.[26]

Social distance between information seeker and source (e.g., a fellow employee with an i-deal) leads to reliance on indirect information gathering, a process referred to as "monitoring," in which people observe others to obtain information they are unable to inquire about directly.[27] This process entails close scrutiny of how others behave. Monitoring is not something everyone does all the time. Rather, people pay particular attention to others when they have few other sources of information and are vigilant about their own standing. Disgruntled workers who think their employer plays favorites may pay close attention to how coworkers are treated. A worker interested in being promoted might carefully observe a potential rival's job performance and be sensitive to any positive attention, perks, and support that rival receives. Personality also plays a role in monitoring, where equity-sensitive individuals can be chronically vigilant about their standing relative to others.[28] Finally, organizational practices can exacerbate monitoring. In a firm characterized by rampant secrecy regarding personnel decisions such as pay and promotions, monitoring is more likely than in organizations with more transparent processes.

Because it is less accurate than direct inquiry, monitoring poses a potential problem where i-deals are concerned: the actual terms of another's i-deal may not be readily discernible. Nonetheless, monitoring is likely to be used when the target is a senior manager or a worker with whom one has an adversarial relationship, or when no relationship exists at all.

Building Relationships

Relationship building, particularly with the key constituents of one's role or job, can generate political support for an i-deal.[29] Constituents can include clients, coworkers, immediate managers, and others with whom one is interdependent. Communicating with one's constituents in laying the groundwork for an i-deal can help identify ways to head off adverse reactions. Prework focused on relationship building can promote understanding of why an i-deal would be legitimate and how to make it more broadly beneficial. This effort can help to remove obstacles, offset negative reactions, and establish what the employer and others want in return.

As an example, a private banker seeking to enroll in an advanced-degree program that would take him out of the country for several weeks at a time raised the issue first with his clients. Once he had responded to their concerns regarding his continued accessibility to them, he was able to assure his boss that he had an appropriate plan for remaining available when clients needed him.

Relationship building also can be used to solicit support for an i-deal. A worker might use an informal network to identify allies, such as a sympathetic manager or powerful people in the firm, who are likely to support the i-deal. In her study of part-time professionals, Clark describes how workers used their social network to determine whether a manager was "good" or "bad" when it came to approving part-time work arrangements.[30] This network was particularly important because the human resource departments in the firms studied often were unable or unwilling to identify others with the particular type of arrangements workers were seeking, be it working part-time, job sharing, or some other accommodation.[31]

Sam, an accountant in Clark's study, took pains to build support prior to approaching his manager:

> I went to quite a bit of effort to discuss my idea with quite a few people. And so it was pretty well known throughout our team and the organization that I was interested in this idea before I actually asked about it. . . . So politically I think that I had set it up so that it would have been impossible to say no.[32]

One challenge to successful i-deals is anticipating how coworkers will react. Workers often recognize that failure to involve coworkers in the process of creating an i-deal can make it difficult to make an i-deal work. Clark describes Barbara's concern when coworkers were not involved in her move to a part-time position:

> I'm just starting in a new team, and the one thing I had to do, and still haven't actually done it well . . . [is] to sit down as a group and really make sure that everyone shares, you know, that they're holding hands on this . . . that they support you being part-time, that it is not just an entitlement.[33]

Failure to effectively involve coworkers in the prework phase is illustrated in a counterexample that occurred at the Lakeside Leadership Institute, a management training facility. Two days after she was hired, Naomi Patterson asked the institute's executive director whether she could work from 7 a.m. to 3 p.m. rather than the usual 8 a.m. to 5 p.m. The executive director told her it was fine with him, but she would have to work it out with her coworkers herself. The following Monday, Naomi quit after two of her new coworkers told her that if she didn't work until 5 p.m. she'd just as well not work there at all. In effect, the executive director put Naomi in the position of having to negotiate an i-deal with coworkers who scarcely knew her. The circumstances made it impossible for Naomi to build a relationship with her coworkers, let alone to negotiate with them.

Implications

Prework can change how workers understand the opportunities for i-deals in the firm that employs them. In fact, prework can affect what workers are willing to bargain for, depending on how the obtained information expands or deflates their aspirations in the negotiation. Employees who follow up prework with attempts to negotiate an i-deal are likely to have higher aspirations regarding what to ask for and greater success in their negotiation compared with those who do little or no prework.[34] When workers know what flexibilities others in the firm enjoy, they are more likely to believe that the negotiation pie is larger and that they have greater leverage than workers who have not laid the groundwork for negotiation. On the other hand, prework can nip an unworkable i-deal in the bud if it leads to the realization that a sought-after arrangement is untenable to coworkers or customers. Prework also can identify which critical constituents need to be brought on board if the i-deal is to be sold successfully to one's employer. By learning customer and coworker concerns, i-dealers can make sure these concerns are addressed in the negotiation and can look for creative solutions to resolve them.

I-dealers can cycle through prework and negotiation several times, since initial attempts to negotiate an i-deal can fail (see Figure 6.1). Though many would-be i-dealers begin prework only after an initial request is denied, others continue to gather information during the actual negotiations.[35] Throughout the negotiation process and its aftermath, successful i-dealers are likely to update their understandings regarding the possibilities for and consequences of i-deals for themselves, their employer, and coworkers.

Creating an I-deal via Request and Negotiation

The word "request" comes from the Latin for "require" and "quest" (in effect, a search for what is needed), referring to the act of asking that something be given.[36] Of course, asking for an accommodation may be difficult; special requests are exceptions that can create difficulties for the employer who grants them because of the costs of fulfilling them (e.g., special effort, norm violation, coworker resentment). The worker who requests an i-deal often recognizes both the social costs associated with asking and the organizational and personal constraints surrounding the request itself. For these reasons, our understanding of how workers negotiate i-deals is informed by two areas of research: request making and negotiation.

Request Making: The Role of Politeness

How the request for an i-deal is tendered influences how people react to it. Making a request in a manner that is likely to engender cooperation and reduce the employer's social costs of granting the i-deal calls attention to the rules of politeness. Politeness is a way of maintaining social harmony, motivating others to cooperate, and avoiding conflict.[37] Asking politely increases the odds that the target of the request (e.g., manager, coworker, or human resource representative) will cooperate in granting a personal accommodation. To illustrate various levels of politeness, Table 6.1 shows some different ways a worker might request getting out of doing direct sales, a type of work he dislikes. Note that as the worker is increasingly polite, his request for an i-deal becomes more indirect and therefore less likely to be as clearly understood. The trade-off is that polite requests may be more acceptable to the person being asked, assuming he or she interprets them correctly.

Politeness has been conceptualized as "face protecting," in which communication is designed to protect the self-esteem and social standing of both speaker and target. Politeness theory differentiates between two different forms of face, positive and negative, which represent an individual's twin motives of fostering relationships and preserving independence.[38] *Positive face* is the desire to be approved of by others. *Negative face* is the desire to be unimpeded in one's actions. Power and social distance shape the levels of politeness people use in request making, with greater politeness displayed in situations where the two parties have different degrees of power and are separated by greater social distance.[39]

People tend to be more polite with their superiors or others with whom they lack a close personal relationship. When the manager is a personal friend and not an individual with significantly higher status, the i-deal can be requested in a much more direct and informal way.[40] Less-polite strategies also tend to be used when the target of the request is a peer or a subordinate. The greater the target's power, the greater the social distance, and the greater the level of imposition posed by the request, the more polite the requester will be. For those workers who formulate their requests more politely, one potential downside is that very polite requests obfuscate the requesters' motivation and the intensity of their desire. This obfuscation can cause the target to misconstrue the importance of the

Table 6.1

Politeness Strategies

1	2	3	4	5 Most Polite
Bald and on the record	**Negative politeness**	**Positive politeness**	**Off the record**	**No communication**
Stating the request baldly with no politeness to couch it ("I don't want to do selling any more. I just want to fill orders.")	Displaying politeness by indicating solidarity with the target while asserting one's preferences ("I know you don't like to sell either. I'd rather just focus on customer service and order fulfillment instead.")	Displaying politeness by respecting the target's freedom of action, using restraint, and being formal and self-effacing ("I'm sorry to do this to you, but I am really not a salesperson. I am a lot better at detail work than I am with people. What would you suggest I do?")	Indirectly requesting via hinting, subtlety, or understatement ("Perhaps it would be better if I did something else.")	The most polite of all, not saying anything.

122

request. In general, workers with more power are likely to incur fewer social costs from asking and are more likely to be direct (i.e., less polite).

Politeness works in two ways, protecting both the person asking and the person being asked from uncomfortable confrontations that would make it difficult for them to continue their relationship. People are polite not only because it is normative to be so, but also because it can be strategic. By protecting the target of the request (e.g., the manager) from embarrassment or overt threats to his or her authority, politeness helps the requester achieve his or her goals. Sometimes this means using modesty and self-effacement (positive face), with the goal of making oneself acceptable to a superior. At other times, it means using joking rudeness and acting like one of the boys or girls (negative face).

Image is a concern for would-be i-dealers, especially because their requests might be confused with an attempt to get preferential treatment or to break a rule. Initiating a request by saying "I don't want to put you [my boss] in an awkward position" couches the request in a way that reduces the threat to each party's face or image. "If there is an opening in Customer Service, would you be willing to consider me for it?" puts the target in the driver's seat, with wide flexibility to say "No," "Maybe," "Under certain conditions," "If I can," or "Yes." Contrast this request with the demand "The next time there is an opening in Customer Service, I want it." In terms of the target's response, the reverse can also be true. A very polite response can be used to mask the manager's true intent: "You are a very valuable member of this department, and we appreciate all that you do. We'll see what we can do." It is important to note that management's failure to fulfill requests that workers believe have been agreed to is a significant source of psychological contract violation.[41]

Context affects the use of politeness strategies. In innovative settings where flexibility is encouraged, workers may tend to be more direct in requesting an i-deal. Employment arrangements are more elastic in innovative settings. The strategies workers use to create such arrangements are thus likely to be more regularized and routine, requiring less attention to politeness or concern over image than in circumstances where i-deals are more unusual. In contrast, politeness rituals are more likely to be followed in bureaucratic settings because flexibility is unusual and requesting an i-deal an exception to the norm.

Achieving Agreement Through Negotiation and Problem Solving

Recall that in the context of i-deals, negotiation has two meanings: accomplishing an intended result through mutual agreement and overcoming some obstacle through dexterity and skill. Both meanings are pertinent to understanding whether workers are able to successfully negotiate i-deals when a lot depends not only on the extent to which interests overlap between the worker and the employer but also on the worker's ability to negotiate and problem solve effectively.

Negotiation processes. Successful negotiations build trust, share information, and creatively package issues to reflect the interests of each party.[42] To the extent that workers ask diagnostic questions to identify the interests of their employer and the manager with whom they are negotiating, they are more likely to successfully identify a bargaining zone in which they can create a mutually beneficial agreement. This approach reflects a high level of concern for both the worker's own interests as well as those of the employer, often achieved by adopting a cooperative orientation and focusing on the long-term relationship. One risk of this approach is that the worker's own interests may not be effectively communicated. Polite expressions of concern for the other party can be ineffective unless the worker also clearly expresses the actual terms and conditions he or she seeks. Because both parties negotiating a performance based i-deal usually expect to interact in the future, they tend to downplay hard tactics and instead work to achieve a suitable solution while maintaining their relationship.[43] If the parties can creatively package the issues that concern them, they can expand the bargaining zone and may approach the negotiation with an emphasis more on problem solving than on bargaining.[44]

Single-issue negotiations are often thought of as distributive (i.e., as a fixed pie, where what one gains the other loses). Multiple-issue negotiations have greater potential for integration because they increase the pie, allowing worker and employer to trade things they value less for other things they value more. Moreover, adding new issues as the parties come to better understand relevant concerns, and fractionating existing issues into separate elements, can lead to creative solutions.[45] Judy Levine sought a leave to work on a favorite candidate's election campaign. Her employer was concerned about the leave's timing and impact on the workload of others. It was an important part of the negotiation that concerns were raised over the precedent being set. Judy agreed to delay her leave's start date to relieve some of the burden on her coworkers. Recognizing her employer's concern regarding the precedent the i-deal might set, she also agreed to use the time to carefully formulate a process of managing her client and coworker relations so that others might emulate it in requesting a similar arrangement. By taking on this additional role, she helped her employer create a routine to better manage the impact of leaves on coworkers. As in Judy's case, negotiations can turn into problem-solving exercises with several issues on the table, some of which are distributive (e.g., the start date and extent of burden on coworkers) and others integrative (e.g., how the issue of precedent might be handled). The result can be mutual accommodation and creative packaging to achieve an agreement that meets the needs of all parties.

Alternatives. As in the case of effective negotiations generally, workers can more successfully negotiate an i-deal when they have a well-defined BATNA.[46] For example, after deciding to spend more time at home with children, a worker might begin to identify various alternatives to continuing to work full-time: taking a part-time position in another firm or living off savings or support from a working spouse. By generating alternatives in case the i-deal is not accepted, it can be easier for the worker to convey his or her demands in a clear and compelling way. Workers who have already made a decision to seek the particular employment arrangement they need, as in the case of Steve Miller's *ex post* i-deal with IBM (described in chapter 5), are in a better position to negotiate with employers than those who raise the possibility more tentatively. If the BATNA is poor, the individual is not in a particularly good position to bargain.

Workers who know they have alternatives are in a better position to assert their interests, particularly when their employers' alternatives are less attractive than their own.[47] To maintain a good relationship and willingness to be flexible, workers may communicate their options in ways that avoid the appearance of threat. Maire Kiernan, a benefits consultant, made the decision to follow her fiancé and move from London to Spain by the end of the year. She believed that she would be able to freelance from Spain because many companies needed benefits consulting as a result of the newly created European Union. Maire informed the company she worked for that she was thinking of moving (though she'd actually already made the decision to do so) but would make sure that all her projects were complete before she left. As new projects came up, she reminded her employer that she might be leaving so a decision needed to be made regarding whether she should accept any new projects. When the company pressed her to do so, Maire indicated she was willing to do the additional work *if* she could do it from Spain. Wanting to keep this valued employee, her employer agreed.

In seeking an i-deal, workers can gain an advantage from making a strong first offer. Clark's research found that successful i-dealers often tended to be tough early on, requesting the part-time arrangement they preferred even when they doubted their employer's willingness to agree to it. By being tougher early, these workers set the tone for the subsequent negotiations.[48] It is easier for workers to make a high first offer when they have done the prework needed to identify what options they and their employer really have. I-dealers in Clark's research made concessions later, if warranted, on issues that were peripheral to their interests. Thus, some part-timers agreed to come into the office at the end of the month on their scheduled days off when there were deadlines, or let their colleagues call them at home when problems warranted it.[49] Another good strategy is engaging the employer in brainstorming to determine how to solve the problems involved in fulfilling both the worker's and the employer's needs (e.g., "I need X. How can we accomplish this?").[50]

Exchanging information during the negotiation increases the odds of success, particularly if this information is used to identify possible options around which an agreement can be reached.[51] It helps when workers convey their own interests, particularly if their employers are likely to be unfamiliar with their concerns. For example, an employee who sought a more challenging assignment made it clear that his goal was not to gain status or be reassigned to another manager. It also helps to get information from the employer. Asking "What problems does this create for you?" can make it easier to reach agreement if the answer is used to remove obstacles or expand the issues under consideration. Successful i-deal negotiators commonly take steps to ensure that conversations with the employer and its agents are collaborative rather than adversarial. These negotiations lead to solutions, often by the parties together identifying options that neither thought of independently.

A negotiation evolves differently depending on whether it is proactive (e.g., selling the employer on granting flexibility in response to a worker's special need) or reactive (e.g., using the offer of a promotion as a basis to negotiate further training). When an obligation has been acknowledged—in reactive performance-based i-deals—workers are likely to be very explicit in their requests and often directly demand an idiosyncratic arrangement. ("I'd like to take Thursday off" is easy to say directly if the requester has put in three ten-hour days in the past week.) There is less need for face saving in such situations, making it easier to tender a direct request. Similarly, when request legitimacy is high, the need for positive face support is less essential. The operations manager in a software firm saw accommodation as a way of life in her company:

> As things grow, opportunities or needs for different sets of skills . . . a role that nobody has had before [arises], and you say, "Well that is something I'd like to do, that I can do. Can I move into it?[52]

Generally, the more attractive the alternatives they have, the more likely workers are to be direct, to the point of making a take-it-or-leave-it offer.

As an example of the tough negotiating stances Clark describes in her study of part-time professionals, Mark wanted to work part-time to continue his MBA while having more time at home with his young son. Framing what Clark refers to as a "dramatic request," Mark presented the company with a take-it-or-leave-it proposal after offering a detailed, personal account of why he needed to work part-time.

> "I've come to terms with what my values are. . . . I believe in parents partici- pating more in the rearing of their children, so that's important to me. I be- lieve in continuing education, and I think now is the opportune time for me to do that. I started with that and then said what I'm offering to OilCo, the non- negotiable thing, is two days a week . . . to continue as a technical consultant for 16 hours. But if you think that's an awkward arrangement or whatever, that's fine too. And I'll move on." And it was accepted right away without any real debate. . . . But general agreement that, you know, that my manager, project manager understood why I was approaching it and there was nothing OilCo could say that would change my mind because it wasn't monetary and it wasn't job-content related. It was outside of what OilCo could influence.[53]

By making it clear that he was willing to walk away if OilCo did not ap- prove his request, Mark had the power to negotiate successfully.

Threats. Threats are more likely to be employed when the i-deal sought is economic or monetary in nature and would be largely ineffective in the pursuit of socioemotional resources (e.g., mentoring or personal support). Threats are implied when workers attempt to leverage outside offers to get a raise. Their use is more likely where there is little or no personal relation- ship between workers and their managers, or where each is from a different cultural or social background (e.g., majority- versus minority-group mem- bers). In particular, there tends to be mistrust when members of different social groups negotiate (in contrast to negotiations involving members of the same group), leading to greater use of threats relative to promises.[54] However, a threat sometimes can be framed as a positive (e.g., "Can you do X so I can stay?").

Because threats focus on economic employment conditions and tend to arise in situations of weak or limited relations between the parties, they characterize transactional employment relations to a greater de- gree than relational ones. Where employment is relational, workers are less likely to use threats to bargain with employers. Nonetheless, there is one circumstance in which threats and other hard tactics have been used in relationship-oriented employment. When workers demand remediation after the employer has violated a commitment made to them, direct demands accompanied by threats are not surprising. Indeed, the use of threats accompanied by anger and other emotions associated with betrayal can demonstrate that the worker truly believes that a violation has taken place.[55]

Negotiating i-deals through third parties. Using a third party to negotiate an i-deal lets the worker keep his or her distance from the bargaining process, which can be especially useful for novice or reluctant negotiators. Third parties can include one's manager, coworkers, and even a personal agent. By one account, more than 5 percent of workers who earn more than seventy-five thousand dollars (U.S.) a year have agents negotiate their employment contract.[56] A worker who proposes an i-deal risks losing face if the request is declined. If workers are otherwise reluctant to assert their own interests, the thought of asking for accommodations can cause them distress. Moreover, some individuals are simply not good negotiators. These factors often make it attractive to negotiate an i-deal through a third party. Idiosyncratic arrangements involving third parties arise in hiring highly paid workers ("stars") whose particular demands might require a good deal of effort and investment on the part of the employer.

Agents in sports and publishing fill this third-party negotiator role, but increasingly we see specialists who represent all manner of professionals who contract independently. These individuals, often professional agents or lawyers, bargain on behalf of their clients, as in the case of special deals granted to star employees and CEOs. Other workers may elect to go through friends, an intermediate manager, a mentor, or a trusted human resource representative. Experts recommend the use of third parties in cases where workers are worried about damaging a relationship by asking for too much. Some people do a better job asking on behalf of others than for themselves. Moreover, since both men and women concede less when their negotiating partner is a woman, women seeking an i-deal may benefit from use of a third party.[57]

Third parties can make requests differently, being less burdened by issues of face and politeness or worries about the relationship's future. A classic tale of third-party bargaining is found in Wilkie Collins's Victorian novel *Woman in White.* The sinister Sir Percival sends his solicitor, Mr. Merriman, to negotiate a marriage settlement with wealthy (and, of course, orphaned) Laura Fairlie. Mr. Merriman demands for his client the entire estate of his fiancée, should she die before him. In response to pleas that he withdraw this audacious request, the solicitor says:

> I am not a hard man. . . . But if Sir Percival will blindly leave all his interests in my sole care, what course can I possibly take except the course of asserting them? My hands are bound . . . my hands are bound.[58]

Any reader of Victorian novels will surely anticipate that things don't go well for Laura Fairlie in her marriage settlement. The point is that third parties can ask for things without taking the same social risks as workers bargaining on their own behalf.

Managing Expectations

Successful negotiations involve effectively managing expectations. The management of expectations often entails continued interactions between the parties after an i-deal has been generally approved. The purpose of these interactions is to explicate an i-deal's terms and conditions in line with the old English proverb "Make every bargain clear and plain, that none may afterward complain." Because i-deals are nonconforming, it helps to create some structures that make the i-deal more workable over time. Special efforts to manage expectations can take the form of preparing a formal proposal, writing a job description, or implementing a trial period. Taking these steps at the time the i-deal is created can help to reinforce its terms. Before an i-deal is agreed to, conversations with manager, coworkers, and clients can contribute to the formation of shared expectations. Nonetheless, writing out the i-deal's terms after they have been approved evokes a familiar ritual—contract making.[59] When agreed-upon terms are explicitly specified up front, it is more likely that the parties to the i-deal will hold similar beliefs about what each owes the other. These terms typically include the worker's availability to the organization (e.g., time and location), milestones to be accomplished, and supports the employer will provide. In the case of Michaela Bell, the first part-time manager in her firm, whose case was described in chapter 5, "There was no job description when the job was offered to me. My boss thought it was unnecessary, but I insisted one be written. I have been careful to avoid assuming duties not central to the job." Writing a memorandum of agreement not only clarifies expectations but also can help legitimate the i-deal to new parties in the event that the original manager who approved the arrangement leaves.

To avoid one common risk of i-deals, workers might need to anticipate expectations associated with future personnel decisions affecting them. Because i-deals are nonconforming practices, they can create inconsistencies in contributions and job-related behaviors. These inconsistencies make it difficult to rely on established personnel systems in managing workers with i-deals, particularly if the i-deal involves reduced time or limited contact between the i-dealer and the boss. Nonconformity complicates personnel decisions (e.g., performance evaluation, promotion, development opportunities) because comparisons between workers can be difficult to make using the same criteria. I-deals that reduce employee hours or permit them to work at home can send inadvertent, negative signals regarding that individual's commitment or career aspirations. Workers with reduced hours can find themselves rated lower than peers who work standard hours, even if their prorated performance is comparable or higher. Workers doing their jobs at a distance may provide less visible evidence of their career commitment and thus become more likely to be passed over when training or promotion opportunities arise. If such future personnel decisions are discussed during the i-deal's negotiation, some of these problems may be alleviated.

Implications

Proposing an i-deal and deciding its fate can be done in a single conversation. Alternatively, an initial request may represent only the first of several rounds in a more involved negotiation. More complex negotiations are undertaken when the i-deal is particularly exceptional or burdensome. Employees proposing i-deals are more likely to be direct when they believe themselves to be in a powerful position and when they believe the employer owes them a positive response to their request. Effective negotiations often include special efforts to create shared expectations on the part of the parties involved. In doing so, they set the stage for more effective management of the negotiation's aftermath.

Managing the Aftermath

The process surrounding an i-deal doesn't end with its creation. The next challenge is to sustain the i-deal and make it work effectively over time. Because of their exceptional nature, i-deals are subject to organizational pressures for consistency. I-deals are more likely to be sustained if they are viewed as legitimate to begin with, that is, consistent with shared values and beliefs among organization members. Such might readily be the case in a workplace known for its innovation and employment flexibility. In other circumstances, where flexibility is less acceptable on its face, i-deals are more likely to be viewed as legitimate *if* they are consistent with organizational culture based beliefs, such as supporting employees with special needs or enhancing customer service. In all cases, the reasons motivating the i-deal need to be conveyed clearly to coworkers and other third parties. Nonetheless, even in such favorable environments, workers can be find it difficult to sustain their i-deals over time.

Workers with i-deals often must manage the aftermath to keep the arrangement from eroding (e.g., protecting its boundaries) and to manage their relations with coworkers (e.g., promoting beliefs in the i-deal's fairness). In the words of a worker who transitioned from full-time to part-time, "Some people perceive that I am less than a full-class citizen . . .

that I'm cheating the system. I always feel so vulnerable since I've gone part-time, not wanting to make myself too visible, not wanting to make waves."[60] Because they are exceptional, i-deals will be successful from the perspective of both worker and employer when efforts are made to reinforce appropriate expectations and to put in place processes that sustain them over time.

Involving coworkers and customers when appropriate in the i-deal's ongoing redesign constitutes a key part of a sustainable i-deal. I have noted that some i-deals backfire, as in the case of workers who take family leave or temporarily shift to part-time only to suffer career-wise. Workers can be labeled as different and can be passed over for development and social activities. Even when an i-deal is not particularly burdensome to them, coworkers can resent its lack of precedent. The nonstandard contributions an i-dealer makes (e.g., in assignments, client service, etc.) can become less valued over time, threatening the i-dealer's continued employment. The reasons for the i-deal may be forgotten as the original manager and coworkers leave. Therefore, it is in the interest of workers to attend to problems arising in the aftermath of their i-deal's creation.

Protecting Boundaries

When one's role has been changed via an i-deal, the job's new boundaries need to be managed. For example, a professor with a dual appointment in different departments still may be exposed to single-appointment expectations. Making the actual demands of the *role* proportionate to the nature of the appointment can require an ongoing effort on the part of the i-dealer. The worker may schedule regular hours in both work settings, use technology to stay in touch, and seek to adapt office meetings to conform to a dual-appointment schedule.[61]

An employee with an i-deal may manage its boundaries with the assistance of others. Part-time manager Michaela Bell sat down with her assistant and worked out what issues required her to be available and what the assistant could handle alone. Of course, boundary management takes time and has its own limitations, as in a case where Michaela's manager assumed (incorrectly) that she would be unwilling to travel to a conference and therefore asked someone else to go in her place. In general, periodic discussions with managers and coworkers may be important for i-dealers in maintaining boundaries consistent with the spirit of the i-deal, while benefiting both themselves and their employer. Boundary management serves to sustain and reinforce the i-deal's actual terms and conditions.

Managing the Rap

Any deviation from standard practice invites unwanted attention and unpleasant conversation about the i-dealer's motives, contributions, and personal relationships. Managing how clients and colleagues interpret one's i-deal is important to sustaining cooperation, trust, and subjective beliefs regarding the i-dealer's performance.[62] To reduce coworker resentment, a worker who negotiates reduced hours may frame the i-deal as an economic sacrifice. Other workers may say they are "away from the office" rather than "on their day off" when they cannot be in for a meeting. In contrast to boundary management, managing the rap influences third-party perceptions but not the actual terms of the i-deal.

Perceptions can become reality, however. For example, many organizations minimize the contributions of a part-timer. Part-time professionals are sometimes denied the opportunity to participate in bonus programs and get the short end of the stick when office space is allocated, being seen as outsiders rather than full-fledged work-group members. In time the worker's standing in the organization can be diminished. To avoid these adverse perceptions, i-dealers can go to great lengths to manage how others view them. As Michaela Bell says, "I don't publicize that I am not here certain days. I don't say, 'I am part-time.' Instead, 'I am out of the office.' Don't want [clients] to think there aren't resources for their program."

Workers manage office chatter regarding their i-deals by actively maintaining their social network and relationships with colleagues. They may deliberately use lunchtime and coffee breaks as a time for relationship building. Don Blake, a professor who negotiated a joint appointment in two departments, acted as a liaison between them. He worked to build ties with colleagues in both departments, even though it involved double the meetings, traveling back and forth between two buildings, and constant shifting between two dissimilar sets of cultural norms. He made sure that each week he spent time in each building and socialized with colleagues in both departments.

Promoting Fairness: Managing the Impact of an I-deal on One's Coworkers

A serious issue in creating i-deals is their impact on coworkers. From the above discussion it should be apparent that i-deals can be a burden to coworkers, requiring them to make extra efforts to coordinate with the i-dealer, whose schedule, tasks, or priorities—or a combination thereof—often differ from their own. A worker who is more discriminating about the meetings she attends or delegates tasks and responsibilities to others in order to protect her i-deal's boundaries can justifiably be resented by those who pick up the slack. An i-dealer with a dual appointment who expects co-workers to keep him in the loop adds to their burden. For good reason, many managers are reluctant to grant an i-deal unless a worker agrees to manage its impact on coworkers. The more interdependent a worker is with his or her coworkers, the more important it is that those coworkers be involved in the process of creating the i-deal in the first place, a topic to which we turn our attention in chapter 7.

Renegotiation with Successive Managers

Idiosyncratic employment arrangements are vulnerable to changes in management. A worker's relationship with his or her employer depends to a great extent on the particular boss, supervisor, or manager for whom he or she works (in some cases, there may be several of them at the same time). In previous research investigating how employers had violated their psychological contracts with workers, workers in the study offered three words to summarize the most common explanation for these violations: "My boss left."[63] When a manager departs, the new person who fills that role is likely to be unaware of all the efforts and contributions the previous manager's subordinates made on the firm's behalf—and any special arrangements the former manager might have made with them. Indeed, new managers often are uninterested in the agreements their predecessors made. In a telling example, Lisa Horwich negotiated a four-month maternity leave. But a week after she gave birth, she couldn't get anyone to acknowledge the agreement, since her boss had been laid off. No one had kept track of employee leaves of absence, and Lisa wound up quitting her job.[64]

All of this indicates that idiosyncratic arrangements may need to be renewed or renegotiated as administrations and managers change. Along these lines, in the 1990s several of the top fifty women in the United Kingdom's civil service negotiated with their boss, a cabinet minister, for Fridays off. Each time the administration changed, the women approached the new minister to ask for the same deal. Though they were repeatedly successful in bargaining for Fridays off, each new minister they negotiated with told them not to tell anyone else about the deal. Consequently, every time the cabinet minister changed, the women had to renegotiate the arrangement.[65] Maintaining an i-deal across a succession of managers takes work, and there is a risk that subsequent managers may not be receptive.

Finally, i-deals aren't always meant to last. Some i-deals are intended to be temporary, as in the case of a worker granted reduced hours until his daughter began first grade. Other i-deals are open-ended, as in an i-deal for a more challenging assignment, but even these arrangements can come to an end. An i-deal's functionality for the worker or the employer can change over time. A part-timer might decide to go full-time, the employer may no longer need the particular capability the i-dealer brings, or the clients an i-dealer served may have left the firm. Thus, there is an advantage to periodically revisiting an i-deal, its terms, and the conditions that gave rise to it. Over time, it may make sense to redesign or end the deal.

Redesign

The need for flexibility is ongoing, particularly in the dynamic settings in which i-deals commonly arise. Their exceptional nature means that i-deals can have unanticipated consequences for the worker, employer, and others. As in any innovation, from new information technology to a novel way of organizing, there is no reason to assume that the i-deal at its outset is perfectly designed with all necessary features in place and its contingencies and bugs worked out. A worker who originally bargained to work at home Monday and Friday may learn that important meetings seem always to be scheduled on Friday, and accordingly need to readjust to a Monday/Thursday schedule at home. Coworkers may find themselves unduly burdened by the i-deal, or certain of its features, necessitating a closer look at how the i-deal is set up. Redesign is a problem-solving process. It identifies ways to make the i-deal more effective once worker, employer, and other constituents have experience with it. Incorporating a redesign process into the initial i-deal recognizes the likelihood that making it work well will require refining and adapting it over time.[66] If the i-deal creates disruptions that cannot be remedied, it ultimately may need to be discontinued.

Implications

After i-deals are agreed to, negative consequences can accrue to i-dealers who deviate from workplace norms. As a result, i-dealers need to make ongoing efforts to protect and manage their arrangements. Creating and maintaining shared expectations with managers, coworkers, and other constituents can mean working to preserve the deal's boundaries and reinforce its terms. Since i-deals are by nature exceptional, what people anticipate the deal to involve and what actually turns out to be the case can be quite different. Updating and redesigning i-deals is important to their sustainability. Further, how others think about and describe an i-deal also can affect its long-term viability. Workers with i-deals need to pay attention to how they represent themselves and their i-deals to others. Whether they seek to publicize the deal's specialness or downplay it depends on the nature of the deal and the factors shaping its acceptability to others. Maintaining an i-deal over time can be difficult, particularly when a worker's manager changes. Since circumstances do change, it is reasonable to revisit and if necessary redesign i-deals periodically.

Negotiation Phases Depend on the Type of I-deal

The attention workers give to the three phases of i-deal negotiation depends on the kind of i-deal involved. As described in chapter 5, workers can bargain for i-deals at the time they are hired, once on the job, and when they consider quitting or have an outside offer. They do so in ways that vary in their directness and the degree of effort extended to formulate a request.

Employees who proactively seek performance-based i-deals to redesign their current employment arrangement tend to formulate their requests with care.[67] They tend to engage in more elaborate prework, gathering information on opportunities for employment-related innovation in the firm, and they also attend more to managing their i-deal's aftermath, particularly its impact on coworkers and other important constituents on whom their performance depends. While proactive i-dealers might work more systematically through the negotiation process, more reactive i-dealers are less likely to engage in prework, relying instead on the opportunity their employer affords them to suggest an i-deal. Workers seeking i-deals more reactively are likely to put less effort into formulating their requests.

Market issues dominate in i-deals made during recruiting, where prework is typically limited to gathering labor-market information. Since coworkers are more accepting of the role that market factors play in new-hire compensation than in that of current employees, there may be fewer issues to manage in the aftermath of a recruiting i-deal than in the case of a pay raise given to retain a current worker.

When retention issues are the catalyst for i-deal creation, prework may be undertaken by the proactive worker, who seeks outside offers, but not by the reactive one, whose efforts to quit are stalled by employer attempts at retention. In retention-related i-deals, less attention may be given to coworker-related issues, which can create resentment and a sense of injustice in the i-deal's aftermath.

Conclusion

The three phases of the negotiation process, prework, negotiation, and its aftermath, call attention to how workers can create exceptional employment arrangements even when they lack the authority to introduce them on their own. The special effort an employee makes to manage this process can result from failure of initial efforts to bargain, causing the would-be i-dealer to change strategies to negotiate more effectively. I-deals require skills on the part of individual employees to negotiate them in the first place and challenge the capabilities of both worker and employer to sustain them over time in ways that are a net benefit for both. The process of managing the aftermath of an i-deal provides opportunities to redesign and refine it. Concerns that coworkers are likely to have also motivate i-dealers and their employer to attend to the aftermath. Implementing the three phases of the negotiation process well requires savvy and ongoing learning. Employees and their managers need to be both quick learners and good problem solvers to realize the benefits i-deals offer.

— 7 —

Coworkers: The I-deal's Most Interested Third Parties

> The liberty of the individual must be thus far limited; he must
> not make himself a nuisance to other people.
> —*John Stuart Mill*[1]

Justice in the employment relationship is seldom a matter between a worker and the employer alone. Coworkers are the third side in the triangle of workplace justice.[2] I-deals can disturb the relationships coworkers have with their employer and the peers who negotiated the deals. Negative coworker reactions are widely anticipated when i-deals are requested, making them inherently difficult to negotiate. If an i-deal is agreed to, apprehension regarding coworker reactions colors the way it is implemented. Anticipated and actual coworker reactions are at the root of the complexity and challenge of negotiating i-deals.

The traditional organizational response to coworker concerns is to hide i-deals and swear i-dealers to secrecy, promoting a sense of favoritism and duplicity in the eyes of coworkers. Alternatively, concern over coworker reactions can prompt employers to avoid i-deals altogether, limiting the organization's flexibility and ability to innovate. The traditional under-the-table approach and its i-deal-avoiding alternative have one feature in common: both make it difficult to learn how to implement i-deals in a manner benefiting worker and employer while being fair to coworkers. This chapter explores i-deals from the vantage point of coworkers, who often are an i-deal's most interested third party.

I-deals challenge traditional notions of effectiveness in negotiations. In a world of free agency, whatever a worker can negotiate from an employer is viewed from a win–win perspective: employers and sought-after workers are expected to bargain with their own interests in mind, period. When workers are employees whose performance depends on the efforts and good-will of coworkers, however, it is not that simple. Employers can typically ill afford to satisfy the demands of one worker at the expense of many others. Failure to manage the impact of an i-deal on coworkers can cancel out its benefits to employer and worker. It is for this reason that all employment contracts aren't idiosyncratic. The presence of peers on whom workers depend in order to perform and the cooperation productivity requires necessitate selective use of i-deals. Nonetheless, i-deals are an essential ingredient on the menu employers use to compensate, reward, and support their employees. To create i-deals that balance the interests of the employment relationship's three parties, we must shift the focus from win–win to win–win–win or at least win–win–no loss.

This chapter's central argument is that coworkers need not necessarily judge i-deals to be unfair. I-deals can be a winning proposition for coworkers in certain circumstances. In others, they can be cost-neutral, or "no loss." Coworkers tend to react favorably to certain i-deals and unfavorably to others. The outrage resulting from an i-deal that paid thousands of dollars to move an expatriated Swiss banker's grand piano vividly contrasts with the ringing endorsement coworkers gave to their company's arrangements to support an office manager undergoing chemotherapy. Nonetheless, in other cases the same deal can generate different reactions from individual coworkers. Coworkers are not monolithic—they are individuals with their own vantage points and experiences. Colleagues can diverge widely in their acceptance of a fellow worker's i-deal for a challenging assignment, reduced workload, or shift in schedule. Moreover, their reactions can change over time as coworkers experience the day-to-day impact of the i-deal in their work lives. This chapter provides a framework that explains why individual coworkers react as they do. It specifies conditions under which coworkers win, lose, or draw in the making and implementation of i-deals.

Organizing Framework

Understanding coworker reactions requires us to attend to factors shaping the information and perspectives coworkers have regarding i-deals. Despite the incomplete information they often have, coworkers commonly do observe and form judgments about i-deals. Maria Baumeister, a Swiss banker,

Figure 7.1 **Factors Shaping Coworker Reactions to I-deals**

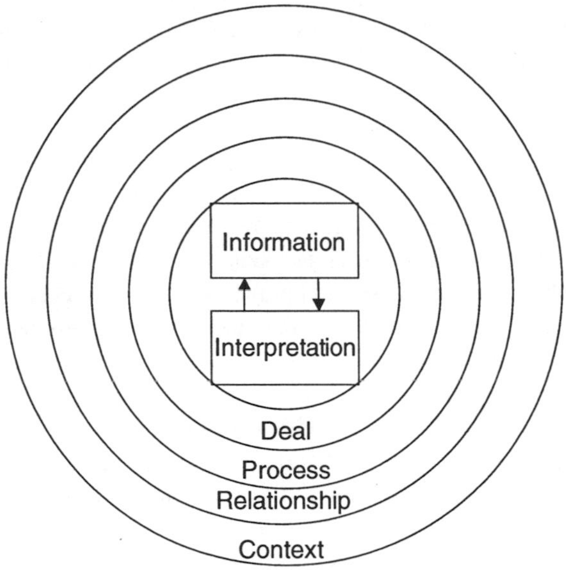

refused to accept an overseas assignment until the bank paid to ship her German-made grand piano. News of her i-deal was spread via email to her expatriated colleagues, who were livid at the several-thousand-dollar tab the bank had agreed to pick up. Maria's bargain was resented by fellow expats, who viewed the bank as less than generous with them. Several contacted the bank's human resource department to demand a cash payment equal to the piano's shipping costs. (Interestingly, only the bank's expatriates seemed to care about this deal. Maria's colleagues who remained in Switzerland were largely unmoved by news of her i-deal.)

The judgments coworkers make ultimately affect whether they accept the i-deal and, consequently, how they relate to both their i-dealing colleague and their employer. Coworker information and interpretations regarding i-deals are shaped by four factors (Figure 7.1):

1. the *organizational context*, including the nature of the work the i-dealer performs as well as its symbolic and physical structure; the work setting's collective climate, characterized by shared beliefs regarding the employer's trustworthiness and fairness; and social norms associated with the use of i-deals
2. a *coworker's relationships* with the i-dealer and the employer

3. the *processes* used to negotiate the i-deal and influence the judgments made regarding it
4. the *nature of the deal* itself, including the type of i-deal (*ex ante* or *ex post*) and the basis on which it is made (e.g., need, retention)

Organizational Context of I-deals

The organizational context's key role in influencing coworker reactions is through its impact on the comparisons coworkers make between themselves and the i-dealer. Comparison is more likely when the i-dealer's role, status, or personal characteristics make that person relevant to the coworker's own employment relationship. Bertrand Russell expressed this tendency well: "Beggars don't envy millionaires; they envy other beggars who earn more than they do."

When comparisons across individual employees are difficult or irrelevant, i-deals are unlikely to generate adverse coworker reactions. Differences in time, territory, and technology were once hailed as the bases for boundaries between work groups (e.g., a factory's day and swing shifts, the north and south branches of a business, or an organization's sales, manufacturing, and graphic design departments), creating distinct identities, information flows, and social processes. Despite the greater interdependence of contemporary work (where virtual teams bridge the boundaries of time, space, and organization), the remaining boundaries—task and social—often reduce the information available about i-deals, thereby limiting social comparison. Colleagues are less likely to concern themselves with an i-deal negotiated by someone in another department, unless they work with that person.

In contrast, interdependence promotes comparison, since interaction is often necessary when workers need to cooperate. Interdependence is tied to beliefs that the setting's distribution rules should be the same for all—a view that makes any differences more salient.[3] Where parties formally compete with one another (e.g., sales personnel competing for bonuses, junior lawyers trying to make partner), the likelihood of monitoring and social comparison increases.[4] On the other hand, highly differentiated work with dissimilar hours, tasks, and accountabilities downplays comparison.

People make comparisons when they have access to information about where they stand relative to others. Insofar as social boundaries limit information flow, they reduce the likelihood of comparison. Placing people in separate positions within an organization downplays their differences in pay, benefits, career options, or perks. For instance, two engineers whose jobs differ in their titles, duties, and required credentials are less likely to compare themselves to each other in evaluating the fairness of their employer's treatment than they are to rely on comparisons with other engineers in their same position doing the same work. This is one basis of dual hierarchies for engineers and other professionals, who can advance up either a technical or managerial career ladder.[5]

Coworker responses to i-deals may be neutral (if the result to them is no-loss) or more favorable (if the result to them is a win) in workplaces where a lot of differentiation already exists. In a study of part-time professionals, Corwin and colleagues found more favorable coworker reactions in highly flexible work settings where workers faced little pressure to conform. Workplaces that emphasize results (e.g., publications, sales) rather than behavior (e.g., attendance), such as research labs or sales units, can make flexibility easier by virtue of their tolerance for nonconformity. Tolerant settings where status differences are downplayed make it easier for coworkers to accept peers whose employment arrangements differ from their own.[6]

The nature of work impacts comparisons fellow workers make. It is easier for employers to treat two contractors differently than to treat two employees differently. The inherent individualism associated with project-based contracting downplays comparisons between contractors, who often share few personal or professional ties. While coworkers in similar positions are more likely to compare themselves to one another, contractors have little basis for doing so because what each does is different and their interactions tend to be limited. This may be why many firms discourage or ban contractors from socializing with regular employees.[7] The constraints employers face when they treat two employees differently are noticeably absent among independent contractors.

In settings that invite comparison, both employer and would-be i-dealer are expected to take greater care in negotiating an i-deal and in managing its aftermath. Employers can create symbolic boundaries to reduce comparisons across workers. The creation of a new position tailored to an i-dealer's skills and interests (e.g., "special consultant") can place the i-dealer in such a different role that he or she effectively has no peers to which he or she might be compared. One basis of the idiosyncratic jobs described in chapter 4 is exactly this: a symbolic boundary to legitimate differential treatment. These arrangements can be used to take advantage of a worker's special capabilities, providing challenging assignments to high performers.

Faced with the challenge of especially demanding high contributors, employers may augment symbolic boundaries with social distance, placing difficult high contributors outside the normal range of interaction with other employees who do similar work. For example, a star scientist who is interpersonally difficult may be assigned a unique role (a symbolic boundary) and report to a different manager (social distance) from other scientists. The scientist may be unable or unwilling to effectively manage his relations with peers in order to justify to them the special recognition and accommodations he is accorded. In such a case, giving him a different title and assigning him to another manager, which removes him from a situation in which he has any direct peers and eliminates his day-to-day contact with similarly employed coworkers, thereby reduces comparisons. Symbolic strategies and social distance are important tactics to reduce comparison when a highly valued i-dealer is unable or unwilling to effectively manage his or her relations with peers.

Another important feature of the organizational context is the collective beliefs work-group members hold regarding the employer's fairness and trustworthiness. Settings in which members believe who you know is the basis for favorable treatment make it difficult to legitimate special treatment even for a person others view as a high contributor. Collective perceptions of injustice are a counterindicator for i-deals if the employer seeks to stave off adverse coworker reactions. When employers are viewed as untrustworthy or biased in the way they allocate rewards, i-deals are likely to be a growth medium for perceived injustice. Coworker cooperation can be critical to an i-deal's success, as when colleagues must pick up the slack or adjust their work habits to accommodate the i-dealer. Adverse reactions can include coworkers withholding their help or support. In this way, a negative collective climate can cancel out an i-deal's expected benefits.

Collective beliefs regarding the use of i-deals exist in many work settings. The dean with 150 faculty and 147 different i-deals created a setting where employee bargaining was a way of life. This practice tends to reduce overall trust between workers and employer. In a let's-make-a-deal work setting, finding out that a coworker has struck a new deal tends to prompt a gold-rush effect, as others try to capitalize on their coworker's deal in making their own special bargain. By contrast, where i-deals are used more judiciously, coworker reactions are more likely to vary depending on other conditions surrounding a particular i-deal, as described below.

Coworker Relationships with the Employer and the I-dealer

In the triangle of relationships in which i-deals are embedded, coworkers' reactions are shaped by their relationships with the employer and the worker who has an i-deal (Figure 7.2).

Figure 7.2 **Triangle of Exchange in I-deals**

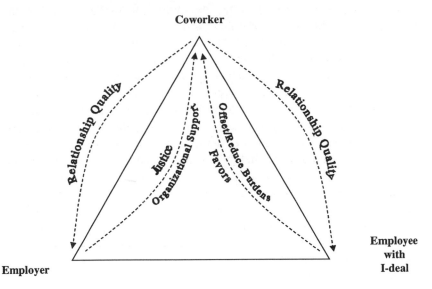

Relationship with the Employer

Coworkers with a high-quality relationship with their employer are likely to be more accepting, other things being equal, in response to news of another's i-deal. Key features shaping the quality of this relationship include justice, that is, whether coworkers believe the employer treats them fairly; the psychological contract between the coworker and the employer; and the resultant support the coworker experiences from the organization.

A coworker who feels well treated is less likely to question the fairness of another's i-deal. In contrast, coworkers who do not feel they are rewarded adequately, provided resources in an unbiased manner, or otherwise treated with respect tend to greet an i-deal with suspicion.[8] Such sensitivity is evident when coworkers monitor the behavior of their managers and peers because of a history of inequity or perceived injustice.[9] Monitoring occurs in situations where personnel practices have created mistrust and a prevailing sense of inequity. Problematic practices can include past i-deals that were poorly implemented. Thus, a department whose former manager made dozens of i-deals over the years with its employees while disregarding coworker resentment is a difficult setting for a new manager to formulate i-deals that are viewed as fair, at least until new patterns of fair treatment and trustworthiness are established.

The employment relationship affects how coworkers interpret another's i-deal. In particular, coworkers can ascribe different meanings to an i-deal depending on the nature of their own psychological contracts with the employer, and whether these have been fulfilled. For example, a coworker with a relational contract who exchanges socioemotional support with the employer is likely to be tolerant of i-deals for a peer, since relational agreements embody a commitment to be responsive to member needs.[10] Expectations of reciprocity played out over time, coupled with responsiveness to one another's needs, characterize well-functioning relational contracts. Coworkers are more likely to accept i-deals when their own relational contracts are coupled with a history of fair treatment. In part because relational contracts are based on the belief that the relationship will continue into the future, they lead to fairness being parsed over a longer time frame. It then becomes easier for workers to accept treatment that favors a colleague because comparable treatment may be theirs down the road or might have been theirs in the past.[11] In contrast, since relational agreements tend to downplay overtly self-serving behavior in the interest of the overall relationship, repeated bargaining on the part of a colleague can be especially distressing to coworkers with relational contracts.

When intermittent negotiation is the norm, as in the case of balanced contracts, coworkers may view an i-deal as part and parcel of a responsive employer's repertoire for managing its workers. This would be the case especially when a deal involves developmental opportunities or other factors shaping employability. Balanced contracts combine relational features of mutual concern with responsiveness to changing demands. They can result in a different mix of resources among coworkers since individual bargaining is more common in balanced contracts.[12] Coworkers with balanced contracts are likely to be even less upset by the individual bargaining than those with relational contracts, since they tend to view it as the norm. Moreover, they can accept differences in employment arrangements among their peers, as long as the resources are basically comparable (e.g., challenging assignments for one person and support for formal education of another). Note that in the case of both relational and balanced contracts, if the employer is seen as having fulfilled its commitments, coworkers can be expected to adopt a more positive perspective on the employer's actions generally. As a result, to these coworkers, a peer's i-deal is likely to be more acceptable than to other coworkers with unmet relational or balanced psychological contracts.

The dynamics of transactional psychological contracts are another matter. These focus primarily on economic factors such as pay for performance and market value and give rise to weaker worker attachment to the employer. Workers with largely transactional arrangements tend to get little unless they bargain for it. Though bargaining may be the norm in transactional arrangements, especially on the part of workers whose capabilities give them leverage, an i-deal granted to one can create a gold-rush effect on the part of peers who seek to match a colleague's i-deal.[13] The escalating compensation packages of sports stars are a classic example.

Coworkers tend to view another's i-deal through the lens of their existing beliefs regarding their own employment relationships. While an i-deal may signal a supportive organization to a colleague with a relational contract, it can be interpreted as a competitive allocation by another worker with a transactional contract and might be seen as everyday self-management by one with a balanced contract.

Organizational support is an important element of a positive relationship between worker and employer and tends to characterize relational and balanced contracts. When workers believe their organization provides them with support in meeting their personal needs, they feel more obliged to promote their employer's interests. This support reduces the employee's monitoring of employer decisions and promotes greater trust and acceptance of organizational actions and changes.[14] Coworkers who experience their organization as supportive are more likely to greet another worker's i-deal with acceptance than are their counterparts who perceive the organization as less supportive. Under conditions of high organizational support, coworkers generally spend less time and effort evaluating a peer's i-deal and worry less about the employer's motives in granting it.[15] In effect, they are inclined to trust that the employer's decision to grant an i-deal is basically fair.

A supportive employment relationship affects coworkers' reactions to i-deals in another way, via the time frame used to evaluate the employer's actions. Coworkers in highly supportive employment relationships are inclined to take the longer view, evaluating their situation less in terms of where the exchange stands in the present, and more in terms of its likely standing over the foreseeable future. Coworkers who conceptualize their employment as a relational exchange over time may view short-term disparities in treatment as less meaningful than workers who make a mental accounting each day. Note that this is particularly true when coworkers do not have pressing concerns that the employer has otherwise failed to meet. Insofar as the coworker continues to view the employer as supportive, day-to-day disparities in treatment can be downplayed or ignored.

Employers viewed as supportive by coworkers also tend to engage in practices that reduce coworker sensitivity to i-deals. As I describe in more detail in chapter 8, a supportive employer tends to offer a broad array of standardized benefits (e.g., health-care coverage and tuition reimbursement) and position-based resources (e.g., promotion opportunities) to workers, providing these valued resources automatically, without negotiation. Supportive employers also tend to have well-developed human resource practices and credible performance appraisal processes that promote a sense of justice and fair treatment among organization members.[16] When employers are perceived to be supportive, coworkers are predisposed to give the employer the benefit of the doubt and view it as just, absent evidence to the contrary.

Relationship with the Worker Who Has an I-deal

Coworker reactions are also shaped by the personal relationship they have with the i-deal recipient. People who enjoy a close, caring personal relationship with an i-deal recipient are less likely to resent their peer's good fortune than are those who lack such a relationship.[17] The special treatment a close personal friend receives via an i-deal is likely to be more acceptable than that received by a less intimate coworker or distant other, ceteris parebus.[18] Indeed, an i-deal can be gratifying to a coworker who cares a good deal about the recipient, for example, a close friend, a mentor who has shown his or her coworkers the organizational ropes, or simply a kind and generous person whom others like and respect.[19] In contrast, an i-deal negotiated by an employee a coworker absolutely cannot stand can be particularly grating. The important point is that the recipient of an i-deal can have several coworkers, and their individual reactions are in part predicated on the particular relationship existing with each.

Coworkers are more likely to accept i-deals for fellow workers whom they hold in high esteem, regardless of whether they are close friends, if accomplishments, integrity, and other laudable attributes are seen as entitling that person to special treatment.[20] Such was the case for Vandana Shah, a human resource manager who enjoyed the respect of peers even after she bargained for a special promotion: "They were well aware of it [the i-deal] and they would also take advice from me. . . . After my resignation, one has been promoted." Vandana had tried to be supportive of peers prior to her promotion, and afterward she became a mentor to them, allowing them to benefit from the experience she gained in her new position.

Close relationship and respect are often intertwined in accommodating a colleague. An American law firm's office manager, Sally Perry, was diagnosed with cancer. She asked her boss for time off during her chemotherapy treatments and a reduced workweek over a period of eight months. While Sally's boss granted this formal request, her staff stepped up on their own to perform some of her duties to lighten her remaining workload. "It's nice to know they'd [management] do this for a staff member because you know how crazy this place can be," one of the staff said in describing their reaction to the i-deal. As another said, "We need to help each other and Sally has been there for me." In contrast, an employee in a health-maintenance organization, Rita Olin, had asked for a change in responsibilities and a more flexible schedule because migraine headaches made it difficult for her to cope with irate patients. Her fellow workers were annoyed by Rita's repeated absenteeism and resented what they saw as her effort to take advantage of their supportive boss's goodwill. Some doubted that the migraines were real. In this case, absence of both close relationships and trust led colleagues to react negatively to Rita's request for accommodation.

Some workers may be better positioned than others to engender good relations with coworkers and acceptance of an i-deal. Workers who do on-the-job favors for their colleagues are generally held in higher esteem than their less-generous peers. Those who do favors for coworkers also tend to be more productive.[21] Productive people may be better positioned both to grant favors (such as the high-performing worker who talks to a manager on a coworker's behalf) and to ask for them (including requesting that colleagues support their i-deal). Indeed, regular and frequent exchange partners may be allowed to request even bigger favors from one another over time. By relying on norms of reciprocity to create future opportunities for favor exchange, workers can build supportive relationships with their colleagues.[22] Acceptance of a colleague's i-deal can be a form of granting a favor, a way of reciprocating support that a productive colleague has provided.

When an i-dealer has standing in the eyes of his or her coworkers based on past contributions, dues paying, or prior willingness to help and support peers, coworkers are more likely to accept an i-deal in the classic manner afforded by Hollander's idiosyncrasy credits.[23] A case in point is coworkers' acceptance of special arrangements for veteran employees or those who have made extensive contributions or sacrifices on the organization's behalf. After the Vietnam War, many American ex–prisoners of war (POWs) who had been held for years in the Hanoi Hilton prison camp were given the option of staying in the military, even when their skills were out-of-date or no longer in high demand, such as flying aircraft that had been discontinued. Typically, they found their way into military staff or teaching posts. When I taught at the Naval Postgraduate School, I recall asking a military colleague what sort of job an ex-POW on our faculty had; he replied, "Whatever he wants it to be. Those guys [ex-POWs] can write their own ticket." Workers who are seen as having paid their dues tend to be held in high regard by their colleagues, creating greater willingness to accommodate them.

Processes in Creating and Implementing I-deals: The Coworker's Vantage Point

Unless they are directly involved, coworkers tend to have incomplete knowledge regarding the i-deals their peers negotiate. As opposed to the principals who negotiated the deal and thus possess firsthand knowledge, individual coworkers can hold differing perspectives from one another because they are not always privy to the same information.[24] If only the employer and employee who negotiated the deal know its exact terms, others will learn about them incompletely and inaccurately, often through rumor and innuendo. Coworkers are likely to fill in the blanks in their understanding of another's i-deal using the cues they derive from the way the i-deal was created.[25] Though each may have his or her own perspective, coworkers generally are biased against perceiving these deals as fair if they are made behind closed doors, because this secretive process raises suspicions that there is something to hide. In contrast, an i-deal negotiated with actual coworker involvement sends quite a different message about its potential fairness.

I-deals signal their fairness in the way they are created, in secret or publicly, and with or without coworker involvement. Processes that take coworkers' interests into account when formulating the i-deal promote coworker acceptance. As such, how individual coworkers react depends on whether they perceive an i-deal's creation and its aftermath as appropriately reflecting their interests. Matters of justice are important insofar as repeated complaints about the unfairness of i-deals ultimately may lead to their prohibition, thereby denying an employer and its employees a key benefit and source of flexibility. In judging the fairness of i-deals, coworkers consider how those arrangements were made—the issue to which we now direct our attention. I-deals can be considered fair by coworkers when any of a number of features are present (Table 7.1).

Consultation: Do Coworkers Have Input?

First and foremost, whether coworkers are consulted prior to the creation of an i-deal is critical to creating i-deals that serve the interests of their three parties. Consulting with coworkers entails seeking out information regarding their perspectives on a potential i-deal; doing so can reinforce and strengthen the relationship coworkers have with both the employer and the colleague seeking an i-deal. It may be valuable even if the i-deal has little direct effect on coworkers to reduce differences in information coworkers possess regarding the i-deal. Seeking coworkers out is also a sign of respect

Table 7.1

Coworker Acceptance of I-deals

Low Acceptance	High Acceptance
Organizational Context	
Interdependent work	Independent work
High interaction	Low interaction
Same positions	Differentiated positions
Relationships	
Low trust in employer	High trust in employer
Low psychological contract fulfillment	High psychological contract fulfillment
Low organizational support	High organizational support
No or poor personal relationship with i-dealer	Good personal relationship with i-dealer
No respect for i-dealer	Respect for i-dealer
Process	
No input or consultation	Consultation on i-deal
No comparable choice available	Comparable choice available
Coworker endures loss	Coworker enjoys benefit
Deal	
Tangible resources	Intangible resources
Competitive resources	Noncompetitive resources
Coworker values same features	Coworker doesn't value same features
Illegitimate allocation rules	Legitimate allocation rule

with regard to their feelings and concerns. It is a critical first step in creating a transparent process for vetting and designing i-deals. Having input into decisions relevant to one's interest is a central feature of procedural justice.[26] Though input does not necessarily imply veto power, it does mean that interested parties can express their concerns. Additionally, because input cannot occur without advance notice that an i-deal is being considered, it meliorates the secrecy commonly associated with i-deals.

One important concern in the employer-coworker relationship is whether coworkers have the same view of the i-dealer that their employer has. Robert Kelley, author of *How to Be a Star at Work,* says that some would-be stars are really prima donnas, that is to say, stars only in their own minds.[27] These individuals tend to actively promote their own interests, working hard to create a good impression with their boss. Prima donnas seek ever-greater status in the organization and thus may bargain repeatedly, as described in chapter 5. Insofar as prima donnas skew the allocation of rewards in ways that create losses for coworkers, whatever benefits they bring to the organization do not offset losses coworkers incur. A real star is more likely to be widely seen as adding value to his or her work group and organization. In that case, stars encounter greater coworker acceptance in response

149

to a request for an i-deal than do prima donnas. By consulting with coworkers, the employer can quickly learn whether there is a common perception regarding whether the individual deserves an i-deal. Consultation with a would-be i-dealer's colleagues prior to granting an i-deal can influence their belief that the basis on which the i-deal is granted is legitimate and fair. (Note that perception is not reality and there are reasons why coworkers might be envious even of a star employee, an issue we discuss below.)

Employers who seek information from coworkers before granting an i-deal can promote fairness while improving the quality of the decisions they make. Consider the case of an investment banker from Taiwan who had worked for an American company for about eighteen months. An above-average but not star performer, Ted Huang was somewhat older than his peers. He had been brought in to sell financial instruments to an expanding market of overseas Chinese investors.

Ted asked the managing partner to assign him a private office when one became available because it would allow him to meet with his Chinese clients in a setting more suitable than the cubicles he and his coworkers occupied. Before making a decision, the managing partner asked the other bankers how they felt about this proposed arrangement. She learned that the banker's peers had very different views regarding both him and his request for a private office. Some viewed the banker as status-seeking and stuffy, while others saw him as a traditional older Chinese businessman and were uncertain how to read his behavior. While most thought of a private office as a badge of success, some were indifferent to office-space arrangements as long as they themselves made money. One noted, "If the office makes money, we come out ahead, so will giving this guy an office be a net benefit or not?" Others raised concern about whether the company was really committed to expanding its business overseas. In the end, the manager informed Ted that he could not have the private office at that time. Instead, she told Ted that his work was central to the office's international initiative and that his request made her realize that there was an opportunity to create a space that would impress clients and convey the firm's global interests by displaying Chinese and other international artifacts there. The manager initiated a redesign of the existing conference room (expanding it to include space from an office next door) to make it more attractive and comfortable for staff and visitors. Though Ted still would have preferred his own office, he nonetheless appreciated recognition of his work's importance.[28]

By giving Ted's colleagues a chance to express their views, the manager learned that giving him a private office would be a sensitive issue to some, and that the value Ted brought to the firm was not universally perceived. She realized that this was partially her responsibility and that she needed to do more to develop the office's international capability while signaling its strategic importance to her staff. In this case, a problem was addressed without resorting to an i-deal.

Consulting with coworkers can also improve an i-deal's effectiveness and implementation. Pierre Leclerc, a computer game developer, wanted to spend part of the year in the south of France remodeling an old farmhouse. He proposed a telecommuting arrangement with the office manager whereby he would spend six months a year in France and the remainder of the time in the firm's Montreal office. Since work in the office was organized around client teams, the office manager worried that letting Pierre telecommute might disrupt the teamwork that made the office run smoothly. The manager first polled other team members individually to get their reactions. Though reactions were mixed, enough support was evident for this respected designer that the manager decided to have Pierre work with his team members to create a plan that would permit him to telecommute without disrupting the group. Over a two-week period in which several one-on-one conversations and an all-hands meeting occurred, a plan emerged. Along with arrangements for assigning and coordinating work, one recommendation was the purchase of collaborative work software to assist team members with communication, file updating, and information tracking. Adoption of this plan led to improved coordination of work within the team. Over time its approach for coordinating distributed work, including a now-customized version of the collaborative software, was adopted by several office teams.

By giving the team an opportunity to express its views, the manager made the whole office aware of the i-deal under discussion. Turning it into a problem-solving process put the designer in a position to better appreciate the implications his i-deal had for peers and to gain their assistance and support in making it work. In the course of this process, the designer was able to convey his willingness to be flexible on some aspects of the plan, such as return trips to Canada when the team considered it important. The office manager signaled a variety of important values to his staff, including flexibility, transparency, and shared responsibility for the group's work arrangements.

I-dealers stand to benefit from consulting with coworkers, and many do it as a matter of course. Such was the case for a financial adviser who wanted to get an advanced degree. He sought to manage his relations with an array of third parties, including coworkers: "I got their approval (spouse, colleagues, partners) . . . by telling them that I would not apply if they objected. . . . I asked my largest clients if this would trouble them . . . they were very supportive." Consultation, as argued in chapter 6, is an important feature of the prework that successful i-dealers undertake. Consulting with coworkers provides information about their concerns regarding the i-deal. Such concerns can include whether coworkers think a deal is fair to them individually and as a group, and whether the time is right for such a request to go forward. They can also apprise the would-be i-dealer regarding situational factors that might affect the i-deal's appropriateness and ease of implementation. For instance, coworkers who might find an i-deal unacceptable for a rookie could advise that person to wait a few months to prove his or her worth, and only then go forward with a request that would have their support.

Consultation is particularly important when an i-deal would burden coworkers. A fund manager who wants a leave to attend executive training but agrees to delay that leave until after a new hire is brought on board can help both his coworkers and his employer manage the consequences of the i-deal. Effective i-deal negotiations are often part bargaining process and part problem solving, working out in advance ways to carry out an i-deal without creating undue problems for others. Consultation is easiest when coworkers perceive the employer to be supportive and when they have good relations with the peer who seeks an i-deal.

Consultation can have a direct effect on fairness perceptions by publicizing the i-deal under consideration and providing coworkers with an opportunity for input, two features that promote a sense of procedural justice.[29] Moreover, when coworkers have advance input, the potential costs to them can be reduced by up-front problem solving, which in turn promotes more effective implementation. Realistically, consultation may be difficult to implement in certain circumstances. In a large work unit, individual consultation with each coworker may be impossible. Moreover, the nature of the request (e.g., a leave for medical reasons) may preclude a public discussion. Employers and i-dealers must consider whether consultation involves a few well-regarded coworkers or the whole department. Regardless of how it is conducted, the process of consultation affects whether an i-deal is seen as a stealthy backroom deal or an appropriate and aboveboard personnel action.

Can Coworkers Make a Similar Choice?

Making the negotiation of an i-deal a public process can, in turn, foster the belief that coworkers, too, might create their own i-deals. Coworkers are likely to perceive i-deals as fair to the extent that they believe they have the opportunity to make similar arrangements for themselves.[30] In effect, a coworker's belief in the fairness of another's i-deal is positively related to the degree to which he or she believes it is possible to receive equally desirable outcomes.

Having comparable ability to negotiate puts the onus on the coworker to choose whether or not to seek an i-deal. One downside of situations in which employers provide little unless workers ask and everything must be bargained for is that workers can resent being forced to bargain. After successfully getting her manager to comply with her request for a new computer, an employee encouraged her colleague to do so, too. Her colleague responded, "If I have to ask, I don't want it." Rather than being forced to bargain, her colleague preferred to do without. However, some resources are rare, special, or not valued by all (e.g., special assignments, unusual responsibilities) and thus are better allocated individually. In these cases, coworkers' understanding of their chances of obtaining the same accommodation is critical to their sense of fairness.

To make use of comparable opportunities for themselves, coworkers need to understand the conditions that motivate an employer to agree to an i-deal in the first place. Such conditions, as described in chapter 5, occur at various points in the employment relationship. It is not uncommon for workers who successfully complete a difficult or challenging assignment to have the opportunity to discuss their next project with their boss. These conversations can provide an opportunity to negotiate a new career challenge or a shifting of gears to let workers pursue their work and private lives more in tune with their personal preferences.[31] Coworkers can more readily recognize their own opportunities for creating idiosyncratic arrangements, if they are so inclined, when they understand that such negotiations are available to them, too, upon project completion. Similarly, communicating that i-deals arise under conditions ranging from project completion to highly favorable performance reviews provides important signals regarding coworkers' opportunities for choice. Note that the intermittent negotiation opportunities discussed here are distinct from coworker attempts to match another's i-deal. Subsequent arrangements may not be considered idiosyncratic, since matching arrangements are motivated by factors (e.g., equality) other than those motivating the initial i-deal (e.g., personal need, skill development, value to the firm).

Employers can capitalize on the incentive value of flexibility by publicizing the performance criteria that must be met in order to negotiate it. For example, a firm may offer i-deals for workers who make an exceptional contribution, as in the case of the express mail firm's executive who offered a continuing spot in the company for any managers who "worked themselves out of a job" by helping their departments become more autonomous. Alternatively, a firm may seek to create internal entrepreneurs by publicizing the possibility of special arrangements for workers who identify an opportunity for new business growth. Whether i-deals are offered in exchange for past contributions or are based on future potential, coworkers are more likely to believe that they have the opportunity to exercise choice if the criteria for granting i-deals are communicated up front.

As a counterexample, consider work settings in which i-deals are granted only when a worker presents an outside job offer or threatens to resign. Coworkers are less likely to believe they have comparable opportunities in such cases because it requires visible competition with peers and confrontation with their employer to demonstrate their worth. Even coworkers who are otherwise highly mobile can resent having to go through the trouble of getting an outside offer to obtain treatment comparable to that of an equally performing peer, particularly since self-serving biases make it likely that most workers will view themselves to perform as well as the i-dealer. Obtaining an i-deal in this manner is more of a "forced" choice for coworkers who seek to be treated in a way they view as fair.

Do Coworkers Gain or Lose?

Externalities are costs and benefits from a decision that are borne by individuals and groups other than those making that decision. I-deals can be negative, neutral, or positive in the externalities they generate.

One person's i-deal can create costs for others, particularly when the parties are interdependent. These costs can be difficult to offset, creating negative reactions from coworkers. In fixed-pie situations, where resources are constrained, coworkers are more likely to experience a loss whenever a peer's i-deal takes up some of those resources. Time off for one person, for example, may result in more work for others. A worker who gets a raise because he or she received an outside job offer can reduce the pool of money available for raises to others. Negative consequences from i-deals in resource-constrained situations are amplified by the tendency for human beings to be more sensitive to losses than to gains.[32] Costs that coworkers incur when a colleague receives special treatment can generate considerable acrimony, and such costs can be hard to downplay.

In addition to tangible costs such as more work or lower raises, i-deals create symbolic losses to the extent that they impugn the worth or value of others. Hospital administrator Marc Torino had extra nurses scheduled to attend his ailing mother upon her admission to the hospital. This staffing change generated outrage among the hospital's nurses, who were insulted by the implication that their usual standard of care was not adequate.

Symbolic losses are particularly likely in the absence of any expressed justification for differential treatment. In the cases of both Michaela Bell and Vicky King, each had a female coworker, one a junior person and another at a lower rank in the firm, who had sought flexibility similar to that which Michaela and Vicky received. Their requests were denied, without any explanation of why flexibility was given to other workers but not to them. Absence of explanation is a breach of interactive justice.[33] It conveys disrespect for the nonrecipient and raises concern regarding the (unknown) basis on which the employer grants flexibility and entertains requests.

An i-deal that benefits coworkers and minimizes the burden on them is more likely to result when the employer and would be i-dealer recognize at the outset of negotiations the impact an i-deal can have on coworkers.[34] If these principals to the deal have information regarding its benefits and burdens, they are more likely to be able to take the coworkers' perspective. Perspective taking is the capacity to put oneself in the place of others and empathize with their experiences. It is a cognitively complex process that requires active efforts to understand another's perspective and to integrate it into one's own thinking and decision making.[35] Evidence suggests that when their own interests are affected, decision makers are more attentive to the perspective of the other party in the case of burdens than in the case of benefits. Thus, an i-dealer is likely to be more sensitive to the longer hours a coworker puts in to permit the i-dealer to enjoy a shorter workweek but less sensitive to the fact that a raise he or she negotiated might make colleagues feel inequitably paid. I-dealers can be expected to more willingly share burdens with their coworkers (e.g., come into the office on scheduled days off when work is particularly hectic) than benefits (e.g., give back or decline part of a raise).

This sensitivity to burdens is evident in the way i-dealers and their employer often manage their relations with coworkers. The i-dealer and his or her employer can engender a more positive response when each takes steps to minimize their deal's adverse impact on coworkers. Insofar as coworkers perceive i-deals to be less fair when they result in costs to themselves than when they are cost-neutral, both i-dealer and employer can work to offset these costs, thereby promoting distributive justice. Both the i-dealer and the employer can manage relations with coworkers in a way that enhances their perceptions of fairness, by maintaining a friendly, supportive relationship with them, doing favors, or providing additional help when needed.

I-dealers can be thought of as incurring obligations toward their coworkers so as to avoid unduly burdening them, particularly in the case of *ex post* i-deals in which the worker already has a relationship with his or her peers. At the very least, enlightened self-interest applies in cases where i-dealers may need to manage their relationships with others to promote the cooperation and trust that are critical to getting work done. Managing peer-to-peer relationships is easier if the parties were in good standing with each other before the i-deal was negotiated. Obtaining support from colleagues is difficult if there is no relationship and more difficult still in situations where the parties are adversarial or hostile to one another. Actions employers and i-dealers take during the prework, negotiation, and aftermath phases can reinforce or undermine the quality of their relationship with coworkers.

Out of social obligation or enlightened self-interest, i-deal recipients have a role to play in reducing the deal's negative consequences to coworkers. Humility and modesty don't hurt, consistent with norms of politeness.[36] Recipients of i-deals can also add new or unknown information that might not be available to coworkers about their deservingness (e.g., conveying the contributions, sacrifices, or broken promises of the past that motivated their special treatment).[37] They can also act to reduce the burden their i-deal imposes on others. Vivien Clark's part-time professionals, while careful to manage the boundaries between their work and nonwork lives, often took pains to make themselves available to their coworkers if needed. Some would come into work on their scheduled days off during crunch times or for particularly important meetings. Most encouraged colleagues to call them at home if questions arose that only they could answer.[38]

As mentioned earlier, there is evidence that employers and i-dealers develop an etiquette or code of conduct for managing relations with coworkers when idiosyncratic arrangements exist.[39] An employer might provide an educational leave for a valued worker but require the i-dealer to e-mail a summary each month of what he or she has learned that might help the company, a common practice among my MBA students from Japan. Before taking that leave, the worker also might be required to document his or her work in order to ease the leave's effects on coworkers. Such actions are particularly critical in instances where i-deals increase the workload or coordination costs incurred by coworkers. Similarly, a prescribed code of conduct for managing coworker relations is evident in one manager's decision not to give a worker time off to attend a son's baseball game:

> Mr. Quesnel couldn't say yes without hampering the work of six other employees and risking disrupting production. . . . The man had violated the plant's informal "no surprise" policy, asking workers to inform managers of time off needs as far in advance as possible. "He didn't give us enough time to react," Mr. Quesnel says.[40]

The costs arising from i-deals are not necessarily fixed but depend on whether efforts are made to manage or offset them.

At times, coworkers actually can benefit when a peer receives an i-deal. Consider the case of the star faculty member being wooed away by a more prestigious university. Here is one university administrator's account of the role coworkers played in creating an i-deal for that star:

> His colleagues came and demanded that we take action . . . whatever it takes to keep him, no teaching, twice the money . . . space, whatever. It's the bragging rights they're after, to be able to say that they work with [that individual].

By storming the provost's office, the coworkers of this faculty star promoted an i-deal for their high-performing colleague. The costs of this deal to coworkers, less laboratory space to go around and higher teaching loads, was in their view offset by the cachet of having the star professor remain in their department. The star's special treatment was justified by his coworkers' shared belief in his value to the organization. In such cases, coworkers benefit from an i-deal because the status of their group is enhanced by retaining a valued member. In local hierarchies, status may be a thing of considerable value, as in the case of the proverbial "big fish in a small pond."[41] Moreover, while being at the bottom of a hierarchy has negative consequences, lower-status members of a prestigious social unit can benefit from its standing and whatever other benefits come with it (e.g., munificent resources). When members realize gains simply from being in a high-status group ("bragging rights"), being at the bottom may be less of an issue.

I-deals that create benefits for coworkers are more likely to be accepted as fair than those that have no positive implications for other workers. As the saying goes, "No man is happy but by comparison."[42] Because i-deals can have comparison effects, implementing them fairly means attending to the needs coworkers have for social standing and esteem, because even workers without high status expect to be treated with respect. Protecting the value of the organization with which they identify may itself be a benefit from an i-deal if it attracts or retains a worker who adds to the organization's reputation and value.

Respectful treatment also is conveyed when the employer and i-deal recipient offer an acceptable explanation to coworkers as to why the arrangement was merited.[43] Such explanations convey that coworkers are individuals worthy of consideration in the employer's decisions. Explanations are offered in recognition that coworkers might be concerned about their own standing in the eyes of the employer and perhaps in the eyes of their i-dealing colleague, too. An explanation of personal need or merit reduces coworkers' need to guess, monitor, or otherwise fill in the blanks that the i-deal might otherwise appear to have.

Although i-deals can have neutral or positive effects on coworkers' social standing, coworkers often view another's i-deal as a threat. Some threats are not easily offset. Mouly and Sankaran describe the case of the "tall poppy," a professor in New Zealand whose status, visible accomplishments, and esteem within the university were envied by colleagues. Her jealous peers complained that the scholar was successful because she was selfish in pursuing her own research and failed to mentor them:[44]

> Tara is so good, she makes us feel inadequate. . . . She selfishly publishes to advance her own career. . . . Tara does not mentor us enough for us to come up to par with her. . . . She is not a "team player."

Mouly and Sankaran use this case to exemplify the confusion of egalitarianism with mediocrity, where lower-contributing coworkers receive less recognition and fewer rewards, generating envy destructive of not only their own well-being but also that of the high achiever. In the above case of Tara, her research prowess earned her recognition and special support from the university. Nonetheless, she was ultimately denied a promotion due to the negative impression of her contributions generated by repeated peer complaints.

Note that this case of the tall poppy—one who stands out above others and thus is cut down—serves as the antithesis of the acknowledged star professor whose peers rushed into the provost's office to demand a special deal that resulted in his retention. These contrasting situations illustrate the different ways in which high contributors can impact the interests of their coworkers. In the case of the star faculty member whose coworkers wanted to retain him to protect their bragging rights, the employer and coworkers shared the same values, desiring to retain a high contributor. In the case of the tall poppy, the interests of the university employer and coworkers were at odds. While the university sought to improve its research productivity, its non-research-oriented faculty wanted to protect their positions by fighting off a shift in the university's focus from teaching to research. A core issue in i-deals awarded to high contributors is whether coworkers buy into the form that those contributions have taken. Where there is disagreement regarding the work group's or organization's goals, that lack of consensus can play out in coworker reactions to rewards given high performers.

The kind of i-deal that is negotiated (i.e., recruiting, performance-based, or retention-related) can have different effects of perceived gains and losses. In the recruitment of a new hire, the pressure to respond to market demand can result in a downplaying of coworker concerns. Nonetheless, coworkers are often willing to accept an i-deal used to recruit a valuable worker. Differences in treatment based on market factors can be more legitimate in *ex ante* i-deals than they might be once that worker is on the job. In *ex post* i-deals, coworker perceptions of gain and loss are more complicated.

The attention given to coworker concerns varies with the circumstances surrounding *ex post* i-deals. When pressure is strong on either the employer or the employee to create an i-deal, the i-deal's impact on coworkers tends to receive short shrift. For example, an employer who experiences considerable obligation to be responsive to a high contributor's request may overlook or downplay the i-deal's impact on coworkers. Pressure to reciprocate can be especially great when the person seeking an i-deal has made considerable sacrifice and contribution on behalf of the firm. Along these same lines, a worker who believes that compensation has been promised or is deserved because of a past violation may view an i-deal as something he or she has earned and pay less attention to its impact on coworkers. In these cases, both employer and worker may fail to factor coworker concerns into their deliberations.

More systematic attention to coworker concerns is likely when an i-deal is sought in a proactive way by a worker trying to meet a current need or pursue a future opportunity. The worker seeking an i-deal under these circumstances is more likely to actively gather information from coworkers to build his or her case. Concomitantly, the employer is more likely to question whether an i-deal is warranted when no organizationally pressing circumstances exist. In these cases, the employer is more likely to deliberate carefully before responding to such a request, allowing more coworker feedback and greater consideration of a deal's likely impact on others. The proactive worker is also more likely to seek out, consult, and otherwise involve coworkers in the process of negotiating the i-deal. Thus, the process associated with the formulation of i-deals contributes in many ways to the reactions coworkers have to them.

The Deal Itself

The particular nature of the i-deal, the resources it involves, the basis on which it is granted, including the reasons employers offer, and how these are communicated all impact how coworkers react to news of an i-deal.

The resources involved in an i-deal impact coworker reactions through their visibility and the extent to which they affect coworker interests. It is easier to obtain information about visible resources, such as flexible hours or special training, than about less visible ones, such as access to information or emotional support. However, visibility is not just a factor because of the information it conveys. Coworkers tend to more generally value visible resources, such as goods and services, or pay and training opportunities. Less-visible resources, such as information and emotional support, tend to be particularistic, valued by some but not all, and under certain conditions and not others. As such, coworkers are likely to judge distributive fairness to be lower when i-deals involve visible, tangible resources as opposed to more invisible, intangible ones.

Uriel Foa and Edna Foa developed a model of resource exchange based on degrees of similarity and appropriateness for exchanges between two parties (e.g., money can change hands for services or goods but not for love).[45] Status-based exchanges may be more likely to be associated with love, services, and information (as opposed to money and goods, two more tangible and readily monitored resources). Resources that are more abstract, less tangible, or less visible are more difficult to monitor and evaluate. In contrast, tangible resources tend to more often be a fixed pie, creating a sense of competition in which allocating certain resources means that less is available for others. Tangible, fixed-pie resources include overt differences in status (e.g., titles), material goods (e.g., equipment), and forms of support that are readily noticeable (e.g., different work hours). In contrast, relatively intangible accommodations, such as providing some workers greater access to information than others, might go unnoticed. If these differences are blatant and the content of the information is something coworkers care about, their reaction will be more negative.

As a general rule we expect coworkers to be accepting of i-deals involving resources that they personally don't care about. An accommodation is more likely to be viewed as acceptable when it involves resources others don't value. For example, workers with a low need for growth may not care that a particular colleague seeks out and gets more responsibility, as long as other conditions about which they do care remain the same.[46] In effect, i-deals are more acceptable when they create accommodations other workers don't want anyway and leave an i-dealer no better off than his or her coworkers with respect to those resources coworkers value. Although people are likely to feel bad when they are less well provided for than their peers, the meaning of "less well" is subjective. An i-deal's fairness is likely to be affected by how much coworkers themselves value its specific features and whether they, too, are in a position to access them.[47]

Legitimacy of Distribution Rules

Reward distributions are viewed as political by those workers for whom they create a disadvantage, especially if the ways in which rewards are allocated are at odds with the distribution rules workers believe are legitimate.[48] Insofar as the i-deal's appropriateness depends on the facts of the situation, one relevant fact is the basis on which the i-deal is made and its consistency with the allocation rules accepted by members of the setting.

The idiosyncratic treatment one person receives may be acceptable when coworkers view their employment to be a relationship of sharing and community among themselves, their employer, and their coworkers. When workers are strongly identified with the organization, how well individuals are treated, especially those with particular personal needs, reflects on the "special" relationship all members have with the firm. This is the case in those firms labeled "employers of choice" for the quality treatment they offer their workers. For example, Fel-Pro, a manufacturer of gaskets in Skokie, Illinois, for many years had a munificent employee benefit program that was a source of pride even to workers who did not partake of its provisions.[49] Such settings tend to be characterized by allocations based on equality for most rewards and need under special circumstances.

In contrast, in settings where a market focus predominates, personnel decisions often revolve around external benchmarks. Thus, workers in a firm with a long history of raising salaries for employees with outside offers can share normative beliefs about the appropriateness of negotiating idiosyncratic terms based on one's market value.

Ultimately, reward systems succeed only when the parties involved believe that the rewards are appropriate.[50] I-deals as a particular form of reward allocation can be evaluated by coworkers according to their shared beliefs regarding reward appropriateness. In particular, a work group's view of whether a peer deserves an i-deal is often predicated not only on present performance but on other preconditions, such as time in the group, previous efforts made on behalf of the group or organization, and quality of the relationship the i-dealer maintains with his or her peers. Ford and Newstrom refer to these socially shared beliefs regarding deservingness as "dues paying," which they define as the process of meeting the collective expectations of relevant organizational observers as to what a particular person must do (or should already have done) to deserve an award, promotional job assignment, formal or informal status, interpersonal cooperation, social deference from others, reward, or other recognition.[51] They offer the following case:

> Mary Beth was on the top of the world. Her second promotion in less than year was being announced by her boss at the weekly departmental meeting, and she was thrilled. However, as she glanced around at the faces of her coworkers listening to the announcement, she spotted a number of thinly veiled scowls. After the meeting broke up she received a few polite remarks of "Congratulations," but noted an absence of enthusiasm. Later that day, as she was entering the cafeteria, she thought she heard one colleague whisper to another, "Mary Beth didn't deserve the first promotion, much less this one." The other responded, "You're absolutely right, she hasn't paid her dues yet."[52]

Dues paying typically includes one or more of the following: possessing some minimum qualifications, performing a series of tasks at a better than satisfactory level, spending an appropriate amount of time in the firm or in one's current position, doing the grunt work expected of others, showing respect for one's coworkers (especially senior ones), and not acting superior. Managers are not always in the best position to determine whether dues have been paid, especially when multiple definitions of dues exist. Ford and Newstrom recommend what they term an "integrity-based" approach to incorporating dues paying into decisions regarding special treatment. To be integrity-based, firms should take care to frame the i-deal in terms of whether it is in response to past contribution or in anticipation of future ability to provide an important service, to clarify the criteria used in deciding to grant the deal, and to open the judgment process to neutral observers.[53] The perspectives of several respected organization members can provide an indicator of the an i-deal's potential acceptability by coworkers generally. While dues paying is socially complex and context-specific, paying attention to it can be important to maintaining the goodwill, trust, and cooperation of coworkers.

The legitimate conditions for granting *ex ante* and *ex post* i-deals can differ. Market factors tend to be legitimate considerations in *ex ante* negotiations, and coworkers may accept differences in employment conditions generated by labor market factors at the time a higher-paid colleague is hired (as in the case of salary compression).[54] However, other things being equal, reliance on market factors to negotiate an *ex post* i-deal is more likely to generate adverse reactions on the part of coworkers who see themselves as making comparable contributions to the firm. Employers, however, are inclined to treat mobile workers more generously than their equally competent but nonmobile peers[55]—a practice that can generate outrage among peers, inspire them to pursue their own outside offers, and create resentment on the part of those whose life situations make them nonmobile. We expect that coworkers will react more positively to the assertion that market factors motivated an i-deal their employer grants to a new hire, than if the same justification is offered for granting special accommodations to a current employee.

The resources involved also shape the distribution rules third parties believe are appropriate. Some benefits are best enjoyed collectively, and equal distribution is preferred as in the case of security-related resources such as health insurance and pensions.[56] These resources tend to be allocated to workers as a group because of shared need and the elaborate infrastructure required to administer them. On the other hand, offering pensions only to high performers violates worker normative beliefs regarding fair allocation.[57] Other benefits are inherently competitive, as in the case of rank or status (e.g., highly differentiated titles and job grades). Competitive resources tend to require legitimate criteria, such as performance or seniority, to be allocated in ways employees view as fair. I-deals involving competitive resources are more likely to generate negative coworker reactions unless appropriately justified, because their allocation to one person limits their availability to others. Lastly, some benefits are meaningful only to particular workers (e.g., work suiting a unique skill set) and are more likely to be allocated on an individual basis. I-deals are likely to have their most legitimate application in this case.

Implications for Relative Standing

Whether coworkers accept or reject an i-deal depends in part on what it signifies regarding their own standing as work-group and organization members. When a star employee negotiates an i-deal, his or her coworkers may accept that their status is lower than the i-dealer's, being more junior, less skilled, or otherwise not comparable in skills or contributions. The key feature is that the star employee's status exists prior to the negotiation of the i-deal. On the other hand, when a competent but not necessarily stellar fellow worker negotiates an i-deal that gives him or her special opportunities others don't receive, the i-deal itself raises that person's standing relative to coworkers. If the latter i-deal allocates unearned competitive resources, it creates losses for coworkers with respect to their own competitive position, which in turn generates perceptions of unfairness. Even when a fellow worker has a disability or some other compelling personal need, coworkers can resent accommodations that bestow unearned competitive resources such as promotions on those individuals.[58]

Conclusion

Anticipated negative coworker reactions are the reason i-deals are difficult to negotiate and are so often kept secret. Nonetheless, coworkers who learn of an i-deal do not always react negatively. Coworkers are likely to react positively to i-deals that bring benefits to a colleague they respect or care about. Similarly, they are inclined to accept i-deals made by an employer to which they are personally committed and with which they enjoy a positive relationship. In such circumstances, coworkers may be inclined to view an i-deal as a win for themselves as well as for a colleague and the employer.

On the other hand, even an i-deal that is not exactly a win from the coworkers' perspective can be acceptable if it can be implemented in ways that do not disadvantage them. I-deals can create losses for coworkers by the burdens they place on them (e.g., doing extra work to make up for a colleague's reduced hours) and by loss of status and relative standing in relation to the i-dealer (e.g., reducing the coworker's odds of being promoted). Potential coworker losses can turn into a draw or "no-lose" situation if coworkers are consulted in an i-deal's design and implementation.

Coworkers accept accommodations for peers they judge to have paid their dues, have high seniority, or otherwise have earned special treatment. They resent special accommodations involving scarce, desirable resources. Those accommodations that generate particular resentment are those that put i-dealers in a better position to obtain future raises, promotions, and other rewards that are in limited supply. In effect, coworker reactions reflect in part whether they judge the i-deal to impact their standing relative to peers. These judgments are not a strict calculus of wins and losses but reflect in part the synthesis of cues and sentiments regarding coworker relations to the employer and i-dealer.

— 8 —

Organizational Perspectives on I-deals as a Human Resource Practice

> The market is very creative in providing individualized
> rewards. Companies should be equally creative.
> —*Peter Cappelli*[1]

> A reputation for following through on implicit contracts
> is...a valuable asset.
> —*J.A. Ritter and Lowell J. Taylor*[2]

> Tell me why it's legitimate.
> —*Manager to would-be i-dealer*

I-deals are more effectively used as a personnel management tactic by some employers than others. They help employers meet their human resource (HR) needs particularly well when they complement the firm's other human resource practices and when they are aligned with its business strategy and supported by its culture and managerial actions. All employers at times must decide whether to make exceptional arrangements for a prospective or current employee. How often employers face this decision largely results from the extent they compete for qualified employees and the diversity among those highly sought-after workers. This chapter addresses the factors that shape whether it is in the employer's interest to make i-deals as opposed to relying on more standard arrangements. Three internal organizational factors affect the ease with which i-deals are implemented and whether it is in the employer's interest to make them:

1. *HR practices* provide the menu from which to choose ways of recruiting, motivating, and retaining workers, and shape whether i-deals are substitutes or supplements to more standardized arrangements. How effectively the firm's HR practices, including its use of i-deals, support its business strategy, shapes the functionality of i-deals for the employer.
2. *Individual managers* are typically the key decision makers in enacting these solutions—and play the central role in deciding whether to grant an i-deal. The coherence and consistency of managerial actions are critical to the functionality of i-deals.
3. *The organization's culture* provides a basis for legitimating i-deals by providing a lens through which managers and workers interpret the firm's use of idiosyncratic arrangements. These interpretations affect the ease with which i-deals are used and their impact on cooperation within the firm and the quality of the employment relationship.

This chapter begins with two cases illustrating how organizational factors impact i-deals' effective use. It then examines how human resource practices, individual managers, and organizational culture influence whether granting i-deals is in the employer's interest.

Two Cases: Organizations Implementing I-deals

To illustrate how human resource practices and strategy, managerial action, and organizational culture impact the use and sustainability of i-deals, the following cases provide a study in contrasts because features of each setting lead i-deals to function very differently.

The Lakeside Leadership Institute: Barriers to Effective I-deals

At the Lakeside Leadership Institute (LLI), a for-profit managerial training facility in the midwestern United States, program manager (PM) Ellen MacFarlane approached the director and threatened to quit unless she was given a raise. Her pay was comparable to that received by the other dozen or so program managers: a monthly base salary and a bonus based on the number of program days she coordinated over the annual minimum of sixty-five days. The institute tended to give few raises, despite the fact that staff workload had been steadily increasing over a period of years. Ellen was more mobile than her fellow program managers because she had no family locally. Her threat to quit was credible. Swearing Ellen to secrecy, the director raised both her salary and her bonus rate.

Background

Compared with wages in the larger metropolitan area in which the LLI was located, the wages LLI PMs were paid fell below the median. LLI offered the PMs relatively limited benefits—except for something they particularly prized, challenging professional work without having to commute into the city. The institute employed more than a dozen program managers, all women, typically with children still at home. Most PMs previously held administrative or managerial positions in firms located in a large city nearby but chose to work at LLI because of its convenient suburban location. The PMs were responsible for organizing leadership training programs providing customized development for major national and global firms. These staff members provided a high degree of program support and attention to detail that was widely remarked on by program participants.

In the twenty-five years since its creation, the highly successful institute had grown at an accelerating rate. Nonetheless, its management structure was minimal—the chief executive officer, who founded the institute, controlled all major decisions. Jay Edwards, the facility director who supervised the PMs, was broadly seen as a figurehead. In this awkward role, Jay sought to avoid interpersonal confrontations. He frequently told the PMs that they were on a pedestal in comparison to other institute staff, such as kitchen help and cleaners, many of whom were immigrants with little education. When the PMs complained about their growing workload, however, both he and the CEO told them that they were replaceable, with the CEO saying, "You are not on a pedestal to me." The PMs often spoke bitterly about the lack of respect they received from the CEO, despite what they saw as their crucial role in the institute's growth and success.

In the institute's early years, the PMs were a small collegial group. Their original director, Marie Dupont, created a supportive environment, where pay and perks were comparable for all PMs. "Marie had her favorites but it didn't manifest in pay and benefits," said one program manager. After Marie died, the PMs still conducted themselves very informally despite an increase of more than 50 percent in their workload.

Although their fixed pay was low, the PMs received bonuses for any work beyond the sixty-five program days they were obligated to complete each year. This overtime bonus system motivated the PMs to do more work without requiring the institute to hire additional staff. One consequence of the bonus structure was to make it difficult for PMs to move to another part of the institute, as even a promotion to a higher grade would result in a pay decrease.

The Aftermath

The director gave Ellen a raise in her base pay and her bonus rate. This deal was kept secret until another PM noticed the disparity in LLI's accounting statements. When her fellow PMs confronted Ellen about the difference, both she and they became upset. Ellen told them about the pay raise and bonus differential she had negotiated. The other PMs went to the director, telling him that morale was breaking down and that people resented the lowering of their pay and status relative to that granted to Ellen. The PMs had expressed their discontent with the freezing of their pay to the director and the CEO many times before. This time, the revelation regarding Ellen's raise became a catalyst for confronting the matter with greater resolve.

Implications

The Lakeside Leadership Institute based its human resource strategy on lowballing the PMs, providing few rewards except for their salary and bonus, and taking advantage of the premium these women placed on having challenging jobs located near their suburban homes. If he had acted consistently with that strategy, Jay would have let Ellen quit rather than make an i-deal to retain her. I-deals out of sync with a firm's human resource strategy are difficult to justify. At LLI the PMs' egalitarian norms might have made them even more unacceptable. The original director, Marie Dupont, was careful never to compensate her individual staff members differently, knowing the CEO would not let her raise everyone's pay. The culture Marie developed was one of teamwork sustained by equal treatment. In contrast, Jay sought to placate Ellen by offering her a secret pay raise, disregarding its implications for her work group. He didn't attempt to provide an alternative arrangement that her colleagues might have found more acceptable.

The i-deal Ellen negotiated reflected her mobility as a single woman, rather than any unusual contribution to the institute. The director granted her i-deal despite his awareness that the PMs all felt inequitably paid given their ever-expanding workloads and the institute's continued revenue growth, to which they contributed. The director did not react to Ellen's renegotiation of her compensation by recognizing that others doing similar work were now considerably underpaid. Paying people for mobility rather than their market value or contribution reflects opportunistic behavior on the part of an employer who takes advantage of those workers for whom quitting is particularly costly. Because there was no difference between the other PMs' work product and Ellen's, there was insufficient justification for granting a pay raise to her alone. Ellen probably would have been much better off working elsewhere, since LLI's location was of no special benefit to her.

Fulfilling a request only for a worker who threatens to quit and not for other equal contributors violates basic principles of equity. It often is pointed out that markets tend to pay no more than what workers demand; however, such a criterion applied to *internal* personnel decisions is more difficult to justify and erodes trust and internal equity. By raising the pay for someone who threatened to quit, the institute's management ignored the implications of its actions for other, less-mobile PMs. There is little that Ellen could have done in this case to offset negative reactions by her peers, but her employer could have done a lot. By swearing Ellen to secrecy, the director effectively acknowledged that he knew her coworkers would react negatively, but he accepted no responsibility for factoring their concerns into his decision.

Feather River Science Systems: Facilitating a Shift in Business Strategy via I-deals

At Feather River Science Systems (FRSS), a software development firm specializing in packaged statistical programs used in social science and biomedical research, senior scientist Dr. Nikil Reddy approached the company's chief executive with a set of concerns. FRSS executives had seen a growth opportunity through product diversification, accomplished by developing data-mining software for use in marketing research. FRSS's strong reputation for quality in scientific and industrial research gave it distribution opportunities competitors lacked. The data-mining job market was hot, with corporations, universities, and information-technology consulting firms competing for newly minted computer science graduates. Nikil, the leader of FRSS's data-mining initiative, was struggling to ramp it up since only a few current employees had the required technical capabilities.

Nikil wondered whether FRSS could successfully staff this initiative. Its long-standing human resource practices suited its current labor force and not the hot market he sought to recruit from now. Complicating matters, FRSS's recruiting efforts had made its interest in data mining known. Nikil had been approached by several firms trying to woo him away. Though he and his wife, a software designer, had been critical members of FRSS for the past eight years, he had started thinking about his own future given his alternatives and the challenges FRSS faced. Was FRSS ready to do what the diversification required?

Background

A privately held business located in the rust-belt section of the United States, FRSS was comprised of an array of workers—designers who developed and maintained the programs, marketing and customer support staff, and administrative personnel. FRSS was known in the industry as a place that attracted highly educated people with a strong analytic bent, techies who liked to think of themselves as on the leading edge of applications development. In its twenty-plus-year history, FRSS had translated breakthroughs in statistics and information technology into successful tools at the high end of capability end users sought. Designers were widely understood to be FRSS's critical employees. They worked together on an array of projects in a setting known for its camaraderie and low turnover.

FRSS offered good benefits, profit sharing, and pay that was above-average for the region, though not for the industry. It had a high retention rate among its design staff, attributed to its supportive, collaborative culture and emphasis on staying at the leading edge of new technology and applications. FRSS designers worried less than others in the industry that too long a stay with the company might make them less marketable. The FRSS environment was known as "the campus," where seminars and project-meetings involved lively and cutting-edge exchanges of knowledge. Every noon hour, designers gathered in the lunchroom for a well-attended free-form discussion, a reason many gave for why they preferred to work in the office rather than at home. Designers continually honed their skills and visibility in the industry through conference presentations and publications, in many of which they participated collectively. The array of applications FRSS designers had created allowed flexibility in the projects they worked on. The advantages designers enjoyed by virtue of their critical positions at FRSS contrasted with the lower pay and benefits provided to nontechnical personnel. While turnover was greater in these positions, FRSS was a sought-after employer because of its overall positive work environment and reputation for producing high-quality products.

The expansion into data-mining software challenged FRSS's historical recruiting strategy. Recent computer science graduates with training in this area differed in many ways from the traditional FRSS designer workforce. These graduates tended to be foreign-born and not necessarily motivated to spend a career in the community where FRSS was located. In contrast to the typical FRSS designer, they often were in dual-career situations. Finding a suitable professional job for a spouse was a challenge given FRSS's rust-belt location. Recruits into the data-mining initiative came with demands that differed from those of FRSS's traditional job candidates.

Typical of FRSS employees, the CEO, Carole Duchesne, had been with the firm since the start of her career. Working her way from design to marketing to CEO, Carole was committed to continuing FRSS's collaborative culture while undertaking new ventures that took advantage of its reputation and distribution capabilities. When Nikil met with Carole, he asked whether FRSS could meet the salary, career opportunity, and other perks new recruits demanded. He felt that it was impossible to anticipate what it was going to take to attract data-mining experts and that it was likely that there would need to be case-by-case arrangements. Several potential candidates he had spoken with indicated that they couldn't consider the position unless their spouse was able to find work. Some had immigration and visa issues, while others worried that without a track record in data mining or marketing software, FRSS might not provide them the kind of career opportunities they were looking for. When Carole asked him about possible solutions to the career issue, Nikil raised his own recent experience of being approached by several prospective employers. Despite strong ties to FRSS, Nikil expressed his sense of being at a crossroads where decisions needed to be made about the goals both FRSS and he had for the future. Wanting to go forward with the data-mining initiative and to retain Nikil as its vital leader, Carole committed to implementing solutions that worked for the initiative, Nikil, and FRSS's critical employees, the designers.

The Aftermath

Carole spoke with FRSS's designers, dropping by their offices individually or buttonholing them in the hallways. In talking to the most senior designers and several rising stars who were opinion leaders, Carole raised the dilemma she faced in considering substantially greater salaries for new recruits than many current designers enjoyed. Consensus had existed in the decision to launch the new initiative; the question now was how the changes in the company's practices mandated by this shift would be viewed.

Most designers Carole spoke with understood the market issues behind the salary differences. They discussed the future of FRSS if it didn't innovate. There was general agreement that growth was critical to FRSS's future. Though FRSS was not a high payer, other features FRSS offered had built a stable collegial design team. After getting a sense that these influential designers were on board, Carole decided to offer Nikil the opportunity to manage his own business unit with a substantial raise. Together she and

Nikil mapped out the structure of a separate data-mining subunit, where new recruits and current designers who shifted over would be part of a distinct project group. Separating data mining from statistics would allow Nikil to focus on building the initiative in a greenfield environment. The recruiting process went forward, targeting the median market salary level to be competitive but not to exacerbate equity concerns among the statistics group. Leveraging the generous standard benefits and campuslike learning environment, FRSS was successful in recruiting several recent graduates. Individual arrangements were made for recruits seeking green cards and employment for spouses. Several new hires came with special project interests for which FRSS provided support on condition that they educate the broader FRSS community to contribute to its ongoing professional development efforts. Three years after the initiative began, FRSS was one of the top three businesses in this niche.

At FRSS, i-deals were clearly tied to a business need and the possible benefits that successfully implementing the new initiative would bring to the entire firm. Separating data mining from statistics reduced day-to-day comparison and legitimated the differences in pay between the two groups of designers.

Organizational Context Makes the Difference

The functionality of FRSS's i-deals from the firm's perspective and the lack of it at LLI resulted from differences in the way the two firms stacked up on key organizational features (Table 8.1). First, the shift in the relevant labor pool FRSS tapped to implement its new business strategy legitimated human resource practices that departed from its conventions.[3] At LLI the relevant labor pool remained suburban women with professional skills whose mobility was limited by a lifestyle choice. The market factors that increased bargaining in the case of young computer science grads at FRSS reduced it for LLI program managers, whose competitive position was weak.

FRSS had a more elaborate HR system than LLI, offering a broad spectrum of standard benefits and a campuslike environment employees enjoyed. Designers who did not participate in the i-deals that were granted to their data-mining counterparts were more sanguine given their overall satisfaction with the resource package FRSS provided them and their understanding of why a pay difference existed. In contrast, PMs at LLI were dissatisfied with their salary and bonus package to start with, and received few other benefits from their employer aside from its convenient location. Raising the pay of a worker who threatened to quit made the other PMs even more dissatisfied with their current compensation, more so because of

Table 8.1

Organizational Contexts of Two Sets of I-deals

	Lakeside Leadership Institute (LLI)	Feather River Science Systems (FRSS)
	Ineffective Use of I-deals	Effective Use of I-deals
Market	• Not competitive • Suburban location offered limited employment in challenging fields package designers	• Highly competitive for data-mining designers • Moderately competitive for statistical
Human Resources Practices	• Conflict between program managers and senior management • Limited standard benefits • Low base pay • I-deal only for mobile worker	• Supportive collaborative culture • Market-based standardized benefits • Position-based pay • I-deals for high contributor and recruits from new market
Management	• Weak director acted to avoid conflict—rewarded mobility, not contribution	• CEO acted strategically and in conjunction with another manager
Culture	• Secrecy conveys lack of legitimacy; i-deal violated equality norm within program manager workgroup • Two distinct cultures at top and bottom, with the program managers experiencing an "us versus them" relationship with management	• Consensus building to create and reinforce shared understanding that differential treatment was required by strategy and need to innovate

the inherent unfairness of paying a mobile worker more than her equally performing peers.[4]

LLI's current management had an adversarial relationship characterized by distrust and conflict avoidance. Under the previous director, Marie Dupont, the PMs had felt supported even though their compensation and benefits were not significantly different. With a supportive manager and relatively comparable treatment, the PMs largely accepted the deal they had been offered: interesting work close to home at relatively low pay. Jay enjoyed less respect and trust than Marie had, though neither exercised much formal power because the CEO made most key decisions. Jay's decision to make a secret deal with the one mobile PM brought the festering interpersonal conflict to a head. Not surprisingly, he quit within a year.

At FRSS, Carole and Nikil enjoyed the respect of staff and effectively exercised authority. Nikil's special promotion and enhanced employment arrangement were largely viewed as something earned by past accomplishment and appropriate to his role in leading the company's data-mining initiative.[5] Separating those hired into the data-mining unit from existing employees downplayed the salience of the different deals created to attract the new, valued workers. Though FRSS employees were aware that different packages were being offered these recruits, the symbolic as well as physical boundaries created by locating them in another unit eased day-to-day acceptance of the situation.[6] In contrast, at LLI, the deal Ellen—a good but not star performer—got because she threatened to quit challenged top management's claim that the PMs were paid what they were worth.

Finally, the processes used to create and implement the i-deals were drastically different. The openness at FRSS and the secrecy at LLI were consistent with the interpersonal styles of their respective managers and the cultural differences between the firms. FRSS's management was open and highly trusted, having built a collaborative environment focused on professional development and innovation. LLI had a less-supportive management style with an "us versus them" relationship between the PMs and LLI's leadership. Intragroup differences in rewards violated the equality norms within the PM work group. Indeed, even had Jay been more forthcoming about an i-deal for Ellen, it was unlikely to have been accepted. LLI's use of i-deals was out of sync with its human resource practices as a low-paying employer capitalizing on its location, resembling instead preferential treatment. What made FRSS a successive implementer of i-deals was the extent to which the deals fit into the firm's broader human resource practices and demands of its labor markets and business. FRSS's implementation process further reinforced both management's trustworthiness and the legitimacy of its practices.[7] In considering whether i-deals serve the interests of the employer, we need to pay attention to how well they fit in with the firm's other human resource practices, whether the employer has the management capability to implement them well, and the cultural implications of differential treatment among employees.[8]

Human Resource Practices

I-deals play a role in the firm's broader human resource practice and strategy. They are one element of the employer's menu of choices regarding how to allocate resources to workers—broadly to all, selectively to those with high status or value, or contingent on individual bargaining. The outcomes employers realize from granting i-deals result from their role in the entire resource package an employer provides and their fit with the firm's strategy. Examining the firm's HR practices sheds light on employer use of i-deals as supplements or substitutes for more standardized rewards, and the role i-deals play in rewarding high performance.

Employers distribute valued monetary and nonmonetary resources to workers in three ways: standardized, position-based, and idiosyncratic (Figure 8.1).[9] These three allocations together constitute the bundle of resources or rewards available in employer-worker exchanges. The resources involved can be mixed and matched in a virtually infinite array. Other things being equal, those employers best positioned to compete for, motivate, and retain talented workers, often termed "employers of choice," are those that make a broad array of valued resources available to workers generally.[10] FRSS tends toward an employer-of-choice strategy with its package of standardized and position-based benefits used to build a communal culture to retain a skilled, committed workforce. In contrast, firms that base their strategy on keeping labor costs low are inclined to offer more limited resources, as we saw in the case of LLI.[11] We can discern much about a firm's human resource strategy, and by implication at least some aspects of its business strategy, from the resources offered to its workforce.[12]

Standardized resources are available to all regular workers in a firm (e.g., sick leave, vacations, health-care benefits, health and safety supports, promotion from within, training). Standardized resources can be contingent— for instance, bonuses given for high performance—or automatic, as in the case of sick leave. When benefits are accessed as a group (e.g., health and retirement packages), employees commonly prefer benefit plans where they can choose from a set of alternatives. Standardized resources comprise what economists refer to as efficiency wages: workers are compensated in ways

Figure 8.1 **Bundle of Resources in Employment**

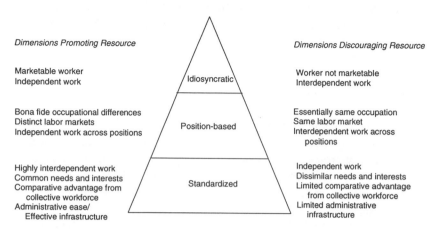

Dimensions Promoting Resource

Marketable worker
Independent work

Bona fide occupational differences
Distinct labor markets
Independent work across positions

Highly interdependent work
Common needs and interests
Comparative advantage from
   collective workforce
Administrative ease/
   Effective infrastructure

Dimensions Discouraging Resource

Worker not marketable
Interdependent work

Essentially same occupation
Same labor market
Interdependent work across
   positions

Independent work
Dissimilar needs and interests
Limited comparative advantage
   from collective workforce
Limited administrative
   infrastructure

Idiosyncratic

Position-based

Standardized

that make their jobs more valuable to them over time, enhancing worker willingness to contribute on the employer's behalf and to remain with the firm.[13] Such resources often are future-oriented when the employer seeks to promote retention, including the promise of promotion from within, development opportunities, seniority-based wages, and retirement support. Though individual workers can receive different amounts of standardized resources due to seniority or tenure requirements, all regular workers participate in the system through which these are allocated. The broader the array of standardized resources employees receive, and the lower the disparity between them, the stronger the reinforcement of the workforce's common identity or sense of "we."[14]

Position-based resources are available to certain groups of workers as a function of job classification, occupation, or formal role (e.g., specialized training opportunities, tuition reimbursement for managers only, wage rates for unionized workers, salaries for professionals). These resources often reflect the practices that characterize the particular market sectors from which groups of workers are drawn (e.g., the norm to provide stock options to executives but not necessarily to shop-floor workers).[15] Positional features offered to all members of a particular classification may or may not be contingent on performance. When bona fide job requirements necessitate certain hours or work locales, flexibility also can be position-based. Factory workers cannot readily bring work home, and customer service representatives need to be available during the hours when customer needs arise. Many knowledge workers, in contrast, can do their jobs in a distributed fashion using the Internet to work asynchronously with colleagues and clients. Labor-market factors (e.g., salary levels of computer science graduates compared to those of psychology majors) and bona fide job requirements (e.g., accounting graduates need support to study for the CPA exam) account for many position-based differences in rewards, which tend to be viewed as legitimate, especially by workers in market economies.[16] Other positional resources are attributable to the behavior of the organization's management and its culture, including the exercise of power in a hierarchical fashion (e.g., secure retirement funds for senior executives but not shop-floor workers). While positional differences can be legitimated by bona fide occupational distinctions, failure to legitimate positional differences can create a sense of inequity among those workers with less.[17] If position-based allocations are more salient than the standardized ones that workers share, they can reinforce subcultures at the expense of a common culture.[18]

Idiosyncratic resources—the subject of this book—are those resources allocated only to particular individuals. On certain issues, such as personal growth and development, where individuals differ in their preferences, workers may prefer to make arrangements with their employer as individuals, leaving standardized and positional allocations for those arrangements of collective interest or where little difference exists in preferences (e.g., health and safety, promotion and seniority systems).[19] Relatively speaking, however, the more resources that are provided through a standard employment package, the less individual workers need to bargain to obtain desirable conditions of employment. This is particularly the case when the level of resources (e.g., the *amount* of training) and their variety (e.g., the *types* of training) are sufficient to cover the array of worker interests and needs. As in settings with standardized resources, workers in jobs that offer a broad array of position-based rewards are likely to have less need to bargain to obtain valued resources. The functionality of i-deals depends on how compatible individual bargaining and differentiated deals are with the firm's broader HR strategy and its fit with market conditions.

A hot economy may drive an employer to entertain more i-deals than it might normally provide, and workers will read that behavior differently than the behavior of an employer that tends to be supportive of individual requests as a matter of course. Employers that grant i-deals when they are viewed as having a choice (a buyer's market) are likely to generate a more positive response from workers than firms that are viewed as having limited discretion (a seller's market).[20] How workers interpret their own i-deals also depends on whether the deals are bundled with positional and standardized resources, an issue to which we now turn.

The Relative Mix of Standardized, Positional, and Idiosyncratic Resources

Resources can be allocated to workers in various combinations of standardized, positional, and idiosyncratic conditions (referred to in compensation research as "bundles").[21] Understanding i-deals from an organizational perspective requires attention to the relative mix or proportions of these allocations the employer makes. Through these allocations, employers signal the kind of relationship they seek with their workforce, and what benefits, if any, workers can expect from remaining with the firm in the future. Employees tend to view their employer quite differently if they bargain for 90 percent of the employment contract as opposed to 10 percent. Rampant bargaining can create competition between workers. Some internal competition is reasonable, particularly in the case of promotion at higher levels.[22] However, when other basic resources such as equipment required to do the job well come only through bargaining, this overuse of i-deals creates dysfunctional competition among coworkers.[23] When workers get few desirable conditions of employment unless they demand them, they must bargain to secure the same employment conditions that might bind them to the employer if it were more supportive. Thus, an employer can overuse i-deals where standardized allocations would better motivate and support its workers. The point marking optimal use of i-deals is likely to vary with the HR practices and related supports the employer provides.

One firm might provide resources based on worker membership (standardized) and job level (position-based), with little variation between individual workers. This practice, which would affirm the notions of community and teamwork embedded in its corporate culture, is characteristic of firms with the high-involvement work systems used in worldwide automobile manufacturing, where competitive advantage is embedded in the collective knowledge and capabilities of the firm's workforce[24] (Figure 8.2). When abundant resources come automatically with employment itself, high ratios of standardized and positional (relative to idiosyncratic) conditions convey substantial employer contributions on the workers' behalf—an investment in workers that can give rise to a relational attachment between workers and employer. Such conditions can lead a worker to view the i-deal as a further reflection of the employer's supportiveness.[25]

In another employer, the bundle of employment conditions might vary considerably among its workers. If there are few standardized and positional rewards and many idiosyncratic ones, virtually the entire employment relationship is subject to bargaining (Figure 8.3). This allocation pattern suits firms in talent-based businesses such as modeling and entertainment,

Figure 8.2 **Resource Bundle in Egalitarian Organization**

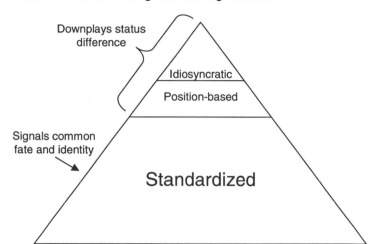

where workers make independent contributions often under intense market competition.[26] In this case, the employer signals its view that employment is fundamentally a business transaction, an economic exchange without a relational basis.

HR strategies account for variations in employer use of standardized, position-based, and idiosyncratic arrangements. The particular ways in which an employer provides resources to workers, from pay schemes and job assignments to developmental opportunities, constitute its human resource strategy. Whether by design or by the accumulation of ad hoc practices over time, HR strategy reflects the positioning of the firm's workforce to accomplish business objectives. When HR practices are aligned with an effective business strategy, employers are better able to create and keep commitments to their workers.[27] Consequently, the ways employers approach i-deals need to be informed by their broader human resource strategy. HR practices that reflect demands of the business are often easier to legitimize and create shared understandings around, particularly when organization members are widely informed regarding the firm's business strategy.[28]

When i-deals are created in the service of an HR strategy suited to the firm's business needs, it is easier to use them in a coherent fashion. Beginning in the late 1980s, for instance, many professional service firms recognized that their existing HR practices were based on majority-group men, while many of their critical new hires were minorities or women. I-deals made to women and minorities helped these firms adopt ad hoc practices such as job sharing and special career paths.[29] The business reasons moti-

Figure 8.3 **Resource Bundle in Non-egalitarian Organization**

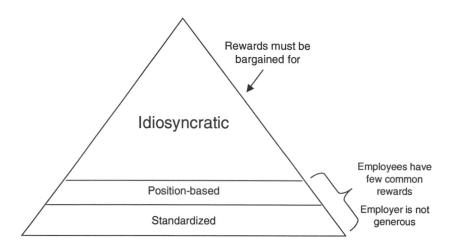

vating these i-deals—in particular, the increasing proportion of women and minorities graduating from college with technical skills (and the decline in the proportion of white men in the labor pool)—were widely understood. Over time, these ad hoc practices became institutionalized and available to men as well as women, and to majorities as well as minorities. More recently, for example, at Deloitte and Touche parental status has become irrelevant for workers seeking a flexible work arrangement. They need only demonstrate that they can meet their job requirements. To quote the national director of the company's Employer of Choice—Next Generation Initiatives, Stan Smith:

> We believe that a flexible environment that helps our people navigate their personal and professional responsibilities is part of a sound business practice. . . . Flexible arrangements are available to all of our people, whether they're married or single, parents or non-parents, provided they continue to meet the service needs of their clients and the arrangement makes business sense.[30]

This institutionalization of standard practices that began as i-deals reflects how innovative and sustainable HR practices can arise from i-deals made in response to the firm's need to adapt and evolve.

Employer decisions to use i-deals rather than more standardized practices are influenced by two factors: worker competitiveness in the external market and the interdependence among workers within the firm. Workers in highly competitive positions are likely to successfully negotiate i-deals more often than others, while highly interdependent workers are more likely to be rewarded in comparable fashion (via the standardized or position-based rewards in more generous quantities under competitive conditions).[31] In a sense, competitiveness and interdependence involve opposing forces. Competitiveness gives individual workers power to bargain on their own behalf, but employers risk conflict and dysfunctional workplace behavior when they rely on i-deals to attract, motivate, and retain those workers whose performance depends on close collaboration with their peers. Thus, as described in chapter 7, more selective use of i-deals is expected in firms in which workers are highly interdependent; in their place we expect broad use of standardized rewards to attract and retain a collective of qualified workers. The use employers make of i-deals depends on the interplay of competitiveness and interdependence. I predict that i-deals will be more broadly relied on for marketable workers doing independent work (e.g., fashion designers, creative writers), while somewhat less use will occur among marketable but interdependent employees (e.g., scientists in a pharmaceutical firm who work in teams). Employers in the latter case are more likely to increase the quality of their standardized and positional rewards to recruit, motivate, and retain in-demand, interdependent workers. I-deals will be used far less often for workers in noncompetitive positions performing tasks independently (e.g., retail salespeople, call center workers), with such workers receiving limited standardized benefits, which are easy to administer. On the other hand, less-marketable workers who are highly interdependent can receive more standardized rewards than their independently working counterparts because in this way their employers obtain the benefit of retaining a stable workforce able to work together effectively (e.g., semiskilled manufacturing workers).[32] I-deals play different roles for marketable workers and their employers, depending how interdependent their work is. They are the primary basis of the employment relationship for independent workers in high demand and supplement the more standardized and positional arrangements accorded to marketable workers whose jobs require that they work closely with others.

Rewarding High Performers

Employers face the challenge of how to motivate workers to perform well.[33] One method is to reward workers based on how they perform. All three allocations we have discussed can be made contingent on performance. Employee-of-the-month programs are a standardized resource available to all, even if only a few actually receive the award. Sales bonuses are positional rewards offered to sales personnel, though the size of the bonus depends on the performance of the individual or his or her unit. Nonetheless, many standardized and positional resources are not contingent on performance, including salary, retirement benefits, sick leave, and vacation time. Standardized contingent rewards are infrequent, often taking the form of prizes or bonus awards given to an outstanding employee. More commonly, position-based rewards, such as sales bonuses or promotion opportunities, are contingent on performance.[34] Promotion systems structured as tournaments are designed to reward performance but run the risk of creating too much competition unless they are offset by other practices that support cooperation.[35] I-deals, particularly performance-based ones, play a special role in rewarding performance.

Despite the widespread effort of employers to use them, performance-based rewards systems can be difficult to execute.[36] Performance metrics are seldom comprehensive enough to completely capture a worker's actual contributions to the firm. Not only is performance difficult to assess appropriately, but allocating rewards directly to workers based on their current performance poses other challenges in that there may be more good performers than there are formal rewards available. For example, only so many workers can be made employee of the month. In one Pittsburgh hospital, employees participating on a quality-of-work-life council decided to do away with the employee-of-the-month program. They objected to the implication that high-performing employees were the exception rather than the norm. For workers on teams, singling out one person can be at odds with both the team ethos and the reality of group performance. Team-based rewards can be problematic when resources aren't easily divisible (e.g., status or development opportunities).[37]

Where good performance is difficult to reward formally, performance-based i-deals can be very useful. Managers can use their judgment to identify when rewards are due, determine what type of reward is an appropriate incentive for a particular individual, and carry out existing personnel practices from performance reviews to job assignments in ways that are likely to be especially meaningful and effective in motivating an individual employee. As de La Bruyère said, "Liberality consists less in giving a great deal than in gifts well timed"; performance-based i-deals give managers the opportunity to target specially valued rewards to high performers in a timely manner.[38]

Evidence suggests that i-deals may be widely used to informally reward exceptional contributors. Scholars have observed that employers often overpay low performers and underpay high performers, giving the latter public recognition and status instead of pay equal to their monetary contribution to the firm.[39] Aside from the problem of determining a worker's actual contribution, full direct monetary compensation seldom occurs, because the top performers' high status garners them special benefits aside from pay. These stars are recognized publicly, gaining whatever psychological benefits are associated with high status, and they are more likely to use their power to bargain for idiosyncratic arrangements that entail flexibility and nonfinancial perks.[40] The availability of perks for high performers can generate a sense of injustice in the eyes of coworkers who pressure the employer to reduce pay variations. In effect, as Robert Frank has argued, a "fair" wage compensates people not only for their performance but also for where they stand in their respective status hierarchies.[41]

Through nonmonetary i-deals and pay more in line with that of their peers, star performers can be compensated in ways their coworkers endorse.[42] Such adjustments are an attempt to balance the firm's interests in rewarding individual merit while sustaining cooperation and goodwill among peers, as discussed in chapter 7. Moreover, nonmonetary compensation in the form of i-deals can be used to offset constraints on salaries (e.g., tight budgets, legal or contractual limitations on raises). In effect, i-deals for high performers in the form of extra, nonmonetary compensation may be *necessary* to promote fairness in the workplace.

Implications

I-deals serve the interests of the employer when they complement its broader mix of standardized and position-based human resource practices. In virtually any firm, performance-based i-deals can target appropriate rewards to high performers in a timely way, offsetting some of the difficulty employers have in providing contingent rewards. Standardized and position-based allocations are likely to play a greater role when effective performance depends on cooperation among workers. In such settings, i-deals may play a proportionately smaller role, suited for workers performing more independent tasks, or in providing nonmonetary rewards to motivate and retain star performers while maintaining coworker goodwill. I-deals can also provide customized arrangements for workers with needs not anticipated by the firm's HR practices, a potential source of innovation as the firm seeks to adapt to changing workforce demands. In contrast, idiosyncratic arrangements tend to dominate standardized ones in talent-oriented businesses where how workers perform is a direct result of individual assets and capabilities.

The Manager's Role in I-deals

The notion of an employer with whom a worker negotiates is often an anthropomorphism, because the employer in most work settings is a legal abstraction rather than an individual person. In small businesses and start-ups, the employer actually is a person with whom workers deal directly.[43]

In most i-deal negotiations, however, a worker's prospective or immediate superior represents the employer.[44] Managers are not monolithic. Though agency theory maintains that managers in the same firm have little variation in the way they implement employee relations, this perspective is unrealistic in the face of differences among managers as individuals and as enactors of their own organizational roles.[45]

I-deals give rise to problems when individual managers in the same firm use them differently. Some managers may be more willing than others to entertain special requests, creating issues of equity particularly when i-deals used to reward high performance are concerned. The same contribution made by two different workers may not lead to comparable recognition or reward. A company's managers need not implement its established practices consistently, as is often the case with performance appraisals, which some managers do regularly and others use sporadically.[46] If managers are inconsistent in their use of established practices, the actions they take regarding i-deals are likely to be even more variable. Inconsistency in the use of i-deals can have adverse consequences on how employees believe themselves to be treated by their employer. It also leads to overuse in some circumstances and underuse in others, depriving the employer of a coherent role for i-deals in its system of personnel practices.

The centrality of the individual manager is evident in the numerous accounts of how workers have negotiated i-deals.[47] As managers impact the creation of worker roles, duties, and responsibilities—a phenomenon referred to as "role negotiability"—it is no surprise that they play a predominant role in negotiating i-deals, too. Consider the items organizational researchers have used to study role negotiability (emphasis added):[48]

- My *manager* is unwilling to consider my requests to change my work role.
- My *manager* is personally inclined to help me adjust my role to best suit my talents and needs.
- I have been influential in shaping the way my *manager* views my role.

In firms, the manager is central to how negotiable an individual's work role might be. A manager's willingness to entertain a special arrangement for an individual worker often makes or breaks the deal.

Managers Use I-deals to Enable HR Practices

Managers broker their organization's HR practices. Faced with individuals who differ in what they value and have to offer, managers can use i-deals as a means of making a firm's more routinized HR practices work better.[49] I-deals that arise from a performance appraisal, for instance, can help a manager reward a high performer. Laurie Levesque describes such an instance in a high-tech firm, quoting Chandler, a cofounder of a software firm:

> In a candid moment, later, after the review was over, [an IT professional] shared that he really hated his job. He had a broad range of responsibilities, but the focus was tech support. And I said, "What would you rather do?" And he said he would rather focus on web development. And that was one of his job descriptions, but wasn't the major focus of his being here. . . . We restructured his job around that desire, and he is actually much better at that than he ever was at tech support.[50]

As in this case, managers are often well positioned to offer workers the things they value in a timely manner. A well-timed i-deal, when a worker expresses a need or makes a special effort, can reinforce the worker's relationship with both the manager and the broader organization.

I-deals can enable a firm's HR practices by making it possible for managers to provide a particularly suitable reward at the time of a performance review, completion of training, or promotion opportunity. They provide managers a means of customizing rewards and support. I-deals can add custom features to existing practices for workers whose needs are not otherwise met (e.g., special training to support a promotion, flexible hours to augment a competitive salary). I-deals also can act as powerful inducements when the manager lacks authority to force compliance or the undertaking requires the worker to be particularly motivated to be successful.

Power to Grant and Sustain an I-deal

Managers differ in the power they have to make and maintain the i-deals subordinates seek. A manager who has more upward influence or idiosyncrasy credits, for example, is positioned to create i-deals with less likelihood of challenge from a superior, peers, or the larger firm.[51] Organizational decentralization also renders greater power to individual managers.[52] When their divisions and departments are geographically distant from headquarters, for example, field managers can enjoy particularly wide latitude in relations with their staff due to limited external monitoring or control. In such settings, managers face fewer constraints and can be freer to grant i-deals.

When managers lack the power to live up to an i-deal they have already made, the consequences can be worse than providing no deal at all. Kim Collins, a manager who decided to remain with his employer after negotiating support to enroll in a Friday–Saturday executive MBA program, was upset to learn that the boss who agreed to the i-deal now needed him to make an international trip that conflicted with the program's schedule. His manager told him that his own boss insisted on it because of a problem in an overseas facility. Employers who fail to honor i-deals that they have granted engender anger and a sense of contract violation. Kim had forgone other opportunities that could have provided him the flexibility needed to advance his education because he believed that his employer would be supportive. Making the situation worse, the poor grades he earned in this MBA program due to his absences made it difficult for him to fulfill its requirements or be admitted to another program at a more convenient time. This suggests that managers need to exercise care and ensure that they grant only those i-deals they are in a position to sustain.

Leadership Style

When a firm's managers differ widely in their leadership styles, i-deals may be granted inconsistently. Managers vary in the consideration and support they show subordinates. A supportive manager who tends to trust his or her staff might provide many opportunities for flexibility and customization in order to develop and motivate them, while a less-supportive counterpart might prefer a one-size-fits-all approach that is more easily administered. Recall the role-negotiation items described above. The managerial behaviors they reflect are consistent with what has been termed "individualized consideration," a facet of leadership behavior represented by actions taken to provide workers with personal support, well-timed encouragement, and appropriate developmental experiences. Such behaviors characterize leaders who delegate significant responsibility to those they oversee and eliminate unnecessary bureaucratic constraints.[53] Supportive managers can view negotiating with subordinates as part of delegating. Subordinates tend to be more willing to negotiate with a manager they see as supportive. In contrast, when a manager is less supportive, only the most assertive subordinates are likely to get such opportunities.

Managers also differ in how they assert their power in relation to workers.[54] Some share power *with* workers, while others exert power *over* workers. Whether workers directly communicate their interests to a manager is a function of the use of power in their relationship. Highly autocratic leaders, in particular, can constrain the amount of information shared. In contrast, subordinates of more participative managers can find it easier to exert influence in shaping the conditions of their employment.

Managerial differences in willingness to experiment with workplace arrangements culminate in an array of responses to requests for i-deals. Managers inclined to build high-quality relations with their subordinates tend to be more flexible.[55] Flexible managers can be proactive as well as reactive by anticipating worker preferences when deciding which practices to engage in and by asking workers to state their preferences before initiating change. In contrast, less-flexible managers can treat existing practices as the standard and push for compliance with them. When a young father tried to negotiate a four-day workweek, his boss told him, "You're not old enough!" Had he been approaching retirement, the boss indicated, she might have been willing to consider the reduced schedule since the company historically permitted preretirement wind downs. An inflexible manager, like this one, may not appreciate that workweek reductions can be given to younger workers, too. Managerial style also influences whether coworkers readily accept the legitimacy of the i-deals that are granted to others. Managers with a history of supporting subordinates and those who command sufficient respect or authority to promote subordinate acceptance may be better positioned to grant and sustain an i-deal.[56]

Demographic Similarity

I-deals may be more readily negotiated between managers and workers who share a common background. Common background (e.g., gender, education, industry experience) increases the likelihood that manager and worker have similar information in common, are familiar with each other's circumstances, and share values and frames of reference.[57] It increases the likelihood that they will make additional disclosures while bargaining. Dissimilarity between worker and manager, in turn, can inhibit both trust and information sharing. Large social differences between the two parties tend to reduce shared understanding due to limited opportunities for interaction and the absence of common frames of reference.[58] Not surprisingly, when members of different cultural and societal backgrounds negotiate (in contrast to members of the same group), there is an increased incidence of mistrust, more negative stereotyping regarding intentions, and greater use of threats relative to promises.[59]

Effects from demographic similarity contribute to three downsides of i-deals: inequity, appearance of favoritism, and inconsistency. It is inequitable to grant an i-deal to one high contributor but not another based on background. Such i-deals fall in the grey area where they resemble preferential treatment (chapter 3), even if given to an otherwise deserving high contributor. Managers whose demographic similarity with would-be i-dealers influences their response cannot avoid behaving inconsistently in the eyes of third parties.

Managerial Experience with I-deals

As in any complex behavior, there is a learning curve in making and sustaining i-deals.[60] Just as individual workers learn to negotiate with their
employers, managers benefit from experience with i-deals in order to learn
what works and what can go wrong. Experience comes in two forms: whether
the manager has been granted i-deals by his or her own bosses and what has
been learned from i-deals he or she has made with others. Managers whose
own bosses have created effective i-deals can view them as indicating the
legitimacy and appropriateness of i-deals.[61] These experiences affect whether
individual managers see i-deals as normative and appropriate.

Don Loftus, a research and development head, suggested to a mid-level
scientist that he take the outside offer that would have doubled his salary.
Don knew only too well that trying to match such a deal would be difficult
to justify. By keeping track of accommodations that were provided in the
past, Don knew the sort of arrangements he could afford to make and still
maintain a sense of fairness among the other scientists. He regularly legiti-
mized these arrangements by communicating them to the department's business manager, who would remain in place even if Don changed roles or left
the firm. Subsequently, a subordinate, Carrie Anderson, was promoted into
Don's position on his retirement. It was easy for Carrie to use Don as a
model in the approach she adopted to i-deals. Carrie was aided by the fact
that she followed Don's practice of logging i-deals in with the business
manager. Managerial experience can help managers grant appropriate i-
deals and implement them well.

When an Employee Has Many Managers

Employees who do not have a clear reporting link to a superior, as in matrix
organizations or firms undergoing restructurings or other transitions, can
have a difficult time negotiating an i-deal because no manager is specifically responsible for their relationship with the firm. When they report to
many different people, as often occurs with project work in consulting firms
or for clerical staff in a law office, workers may negotiate their employment
terms with an HR manager.

Proponents of workplace flexibility, Friedman, Christensen, and DeGroot
describe the case of Jane, an aspiring novelist working for an accounting
firm.[62] Because her work was project-based and her managers were always changing, Jane approached the HR manager who was responsible
for her department with a request to reduce her workload from twelve to
eight clients. The HR manager sat down with Jane and worked out, client

by client, which ones she should keep and which could be passed on to other associates. As issues arose in implementing this arrangement, the HR manager invited another HR staff member to help figure out how to make it work. After three years, Jane—still pursuing her avocation as a novelist on her alternative schedule—was promoted to manager along with others in her cohort. The HR manager and Jane subsequently served together on task forces looking for ways to innovate based on her experience (such as creating project databases that make it easier to anticipate workload). In this firm, the employer's established policies of flexible arrangements for new parents and others with special needs were expanded to provide creative ways of capitalizing on the seasonal nature of the accounting business.

Workers with many managers often find it more difficult to negotiate an i-deal unless a senior manager or HR representative is sympathetic to their concerns. Such circumstances require more effort on the part of workers to prepare the business case that promotes acceptance of their i-deal, because the relationships involved are complex.

Managers as Principals and Agents

Managers are expected to make i-deals when they believe doing so is in the firm's best interest, as conscientious agents on behalf of the firm, and there is ample evidence that managers attempt to do just that.[63] Managers have granted part-time status to valued employees they really prefer to work full-time and created promotion opportunities for workers they would prefer to continue to work for them. But the motives underlying managerial behavior regarding i-deals are not well understood, in particular, why managers might negotiate an i-deal when they themselves may not receive its benefits.

Managers have been observed to view an i-deal as a "gift exchange," a display of commitment to the worker in order to evoke a sense of future obligation.[64] As one manager in Clark's study of part-time professionals said, "We preferred the route of staying a little bit tighter with him in terms of keeping him as an OilCo employee. Taking care of him, and hopefully he will see that as a value and appreciate it later. . . ."[65] Another reason managers agree to i-deals is to recognize specific individual workers' potential or past contributions. Managers are known to cultivate relationships with those employees who facilitate the manager's own performance.[66]

Managers can act as the principal, as well as an agent of the employer, in creating i-deals for those workers who help them do their own jobs better.[67] Evidence that self-serving biases operate in workplace decisions suggests that managers may at times extrapolate to the firm the benefits i-deals bring themselves.[68] How effectively managers act as agents of the firm with regard to i-deals is an open question. It may be easier to do so in some firms than in others. If a firm's business strategy and resultant human resource needs are widely understood, individual managers can find it easier to make i-deals aligned with the employer's interests. Similarly, it may be easier when there is shared understanding regarding when it is appropriate to grant an i-deal to some workers and not others.

Implications

I-deals are most effective in serving the employer's interest when their use is consistent with the firm's strategy and HR system. Yet individual managers typically represent the firm in bargaining for i-deals, and their responses are influenced by their interpersonal style, use of power, and shared background with subordinates, among other factors. Managers' differences in their responsiveness to requests for i-deals can create inconsistencies that lead subordinates to view the firm's approach to i-deals as unfair. When their responses to requests for i-deals are informed by the firm's broader strategic and human resource concerns, individual managers are better able to respond appropriately to requests for i-deals. When managers make performance-based i-deals, the quality of the firm's performance appraisal process can be critical to effective use of i-deals in appropriately targeting rewards to high performers.

Challenges for the Organization's Culture

While HR practices and managerial action provide organization members with information regarding i-deals, the culture of the organization shapes how members interpret them. Culture is the shared beliefs, values, and behaviors that characterize a group or collective.[69] A particularly important aspect of culture is the values members hold. Values provide a basis for gauging the legitimacy of actions, whether management effectively authorizes i-deals as legitimate and workers endorse this belief among themselves. Culture patterns vary from one firm to another, some characterized by a homogeneous culture in which all share, others by an array of subcultures loosely intertwined, and a few by isolated or even antagonistic subgroups.[70] Whether the cultural patterns within a firm unite, divide, or isolate members, they shape the assumptions and beliefs members use in interpreting i-deals.

The differential availability of i-deals across positions can reveal fault lines in the organization's culture. In some settings, only workers with higher status can successfully negotiate i-deals, as in Hochschild's Amerco. Such practices can be more readily legitimated when there are bona fide job requirements making flexibility easier for higher-status workers than for others in lower-level jobs (e.g., engineers may be able to work from home on occasion, but paint-shop workers need to come to the factory). On the other hand, double standards do exist, as Hochschild described: "The only people I ever hear of getting part-time jobs are the women managers," never secretaries.[71] She reports a secretary's unsuccessful attempts to cut back her work hours in exchange for a voluntary pay cut, which—though supported by formal company policy—was not permitted by her supervisor. Certain i-deals can be incompatible with bona fide job requirements: Assembly-line workers and surgeons, for instance, cannot negotiate to work at home. Nonetheless, when not justified by job requirements, disparities in the availability of such i-deals can lead those in lower-status and less-powerful positions to see themselves as an out-group, reifying cultural barriers that erode trust, and leading to the belief in an unjustifiable double standard where i-deals are concerned.

Despite their often exceptional nature, an indicator that i-deals are in line with the employer's interest is the degree to which those granted are consistent with the fundamental priorities that organization members share. In effect, an i-deal should pass a "values test." Giving someone a flexible schedule or a better office merely because he or she complains the most has no apparent underlying value proposition. In contrast, responding positively to a valued worker's request for greater control over assignments can signal that the firm places a priority on developing and rewarding its people. One experienced manager regularly responded to worker requests for special arrangements with the demand "Tell me why it is legitimate." Many had no reply; others learned to do their homework to prepare their case. In general, the acid test is whether the reason for the accommodation is one that managers and i-dealing workers can comfortably publicize.

Arrangements that are consistent with employer values are more readily shared than those that are not. The i-deal Ellen negotiated in the Lakeside Leadership Institute was at odds with the organization's formal policy, violated the equal-pay-for-equal-work principle, and was in effect unshareable. In contrast, Carole's public acknowledgment of the need to offer special arrangements to new recruits gave FRSS a way of vetting i-deals and building support for the firm's new strategy. An i-deal's shareability is important for creating institutional knowledge for the firm regarding how i-deals that meet standards for fairness might be made. If the reasons behind a special arrangement are confidential (due to illness or sensitive personal matters, for example), the practice is better formulated as a general policy in which the confidentiality of individual workers is guaranteed (e.g., medical leaves).

Workers doing similar work equally well have reason to expect the same access to flexibility.[72] Obvious disparities among workers making comparable contributions create resentment and potential backlash against i-deals. Consider the common occurrence in professional-service firms in which women lawyers or accountants take family leave with fewer adverse career consequences than their male counterparts. This situation is motivated by political correctness, showing that an employer is not hostile to women, while underlying forces in the firm's culture make it more difficult for men to enjoy this benefit. It fails to reflect a deeper, broadly shared value, of equality, equity, or family supportiveness.[73] A similar failure to reflect broadly shared values is behind the common finding that mobility-based rewards are seen as less fair than performance-based rewards.[74] Although worker mobility is highly correlated with competence, many highly competent people remain with their employer because they are highly committed or have dual-career constraints. To reward workers for mobility reflects not a shared value but rather an opportunity for the employer to get by with providing less to comparable workers who are otherwise unwilling or unable to quit.

Creating a shared understanding is an important culture-based mechanism for overcoming the inconsistency plaguing the use of i-deals in many firms. Without a shared understanding regarding eligibility, managers are likely to deploy i-deals differently, eroding the message of employer support such arrangements might otherwise send to the broader workforce. In contrast, when managers in the same firm share an understanding of the basis on which i-deals should be granted (e.g., a clear business case, rewards for exceptional contributions, a personal emergency on the part of a long-standing employee), they are more likely to be consistent in their use of i-deals. In effect, widespread agreement can be the basis of a meta-contract that guides managers throughout the organization in establishing and maintaining strategically appropriate relations with workers.[75]

Implications

Use of i-deals as an effective personnel management device is aided by a shared understanding regarding the conditions under which i-deals are appropriate. Shared understanding may need to cut across the firm's subcultures (e.g., hierarchical levels, such as managers and lower-level workers; functional areas, such as marketing and engineering). It can take the form of a meta-contract, an articulation of the broad principles with which the firm conducts itself in relation to its workforce. Cultural factors within the firm can give some workers more opportunity to bargain, as in the case of workplace flexibility afforded high-level staff but not lower-level workers. When there are no bona fide work or market factors constraining flexibility, its availability only to members in some positions may challenge the legitimacy of the practice and reinforce negative attitudes toward idiosyncratic arrangements generally.

Conclusion

I-deals arise at the intersection of market pressures, human resource needs, and the capacity of individual managers to effectively motivate employees. The field of human resource management emerged out of recognition that systematic, consistent treatment of the workforce is critical to promote fairness, cooperation, and efficiency.[76] Standardized resources increase the value workers attach to their jobs and motivate them to stay with the employer. They reflect interests workers hold in common and reduce the need for workers to bargain for employment conditions they generally prefer. Standardized resources provide employers a means for signaling their quality as an employer and for future opportunities, and are particularly important when productivity depends on cooperation among workers.

I-deals pose a dilemma for both managers and HR professionals. Though consistency is an important element in a procedurally fair HR system, some degree of local flexibility is needed to adapt to changing circumstances. Local managers able to choose from a broad repertoire of means to motivate their workers are likely to be more successful than those who are overburdened by rules. Nonetheless, inconsistent HR practices can erode trust and motivation. This tension between consistency and flexibility is not a problem to solve but a fact to be managed—and shared understandings are an important means to do so.

Despite the value workers place on resources that come automatically with the job and the needs employers have to treat interdependent workers similarly, fewer and fewer conditions of employment are preset. Trends toward standardized treatment across workers in the early twentieth century coincided with concerns over social justice, giving rise to social security benefits in the United States and broad-scale social welfare benefits in many northern European countries (e.g., Belgium, the Netherlands, Germany). The more recent decline of unionism and weakening of labor laws continuing into the early twenty-first century in many developed nations create a greater potential for variation in individual workers' conditions of employment—variation that is often at odds with well-functioning i-deals.[77] More research is needed into employer interests in creating i-deals and how these interests change with market conditions, with types of workers, and over time.

— 9 —

Cross-National Factors and Idiosyncratic Deals

And in many societies . . . the sort of compensation dispersion
observed in U.S. firms is viewed as more than illegitimate; a
commonly heard word is *obscene.*
—*James Baron and David Kreps*[1]

This chapter adds a codicil to our treatment of idiosyncratic arrangements at work by reflecting on their cross-national implications. It offers a guide for future research on i-deals across nations and a way of thinking about how society affects the nature and dynamics of i-deals.

Though to date there has been little research on i-deals across countries, we can gain some insight from related work on the psychological contract. Rene Schalk and I worked with a team of international scholars to examine society's role in the formation of psychological contracts in employment.[2] We observed ways in which a country's institutions shape the negotiability of employment conditions available to its workers and employers. Each society we examined put certain limits on what is negotiable in employment. Just as the average citizen cannot negotiate with the power company regarding the price to pay for household electricity, neither worker nor employer can negotiate away the legal protections of their country's labor laws. In particular, all developed nations guarantee workers some a priori employment conditions—though the specific guarantees vary substantially by country (from worker and employer rights to terminate employment at will to safety and wage protections). Some varia-

194

tion among individual workers doing similar jobs for an employer may be allowed, but the variation's content and scope depend on the country in which the negotiations take place.

Consider the case of Heinze Schulte, a German engineer who became "Americanized." Heinze was a mechanical engineer employed by a heavy-manufacturing firm. At home in Germany where the firm was headquartered, his pay, hours, and career opportunities were comparable to those of peers with the same qualifications and years with the company. For several years, Heinze tried unsuccessfully to be assigned to a more entrepreneurial setting within the firm. Hoping to gain more opportunity to pursue his preferred career path, he ultimately expatriated to the United States in an advisory role within the manufacturer's North American subsidiary, with the comparable rank and compensation as his German peers plus an adjustment expatriates received for their moving costs, costs of living, and children's education. Three years later, when the American assignment ended, he asked to be posted to the firm's South American operations. This time, however, his request had one significant difference from his last arrangement: Heinze asked the American subsidiary, rather than the German headquarters, to send him on the assignment and also asked that he be sent "as an American." By expatriating to South America as an American, Heinze would be able to bargain more readily for a customized pay package, and his American boss could facilitate a negotiation with the subsidiary to ensure that his next position would have a broad scope and greater accountability. His request was ultimately granted. In this case, negotiability resulted not only from the worker's relationship and value to the organization, but also from the negotiability that is more characteristic of one society (America) than another (Germany). Heinze's bargaining success resulted from the more flexible human resource practices that characterize American firms. As a German who made use of the American system in negotiating his new assignment, Heinze commented, "'The deal' an expat gets depends on the country he comes from."

Societies differ considerably in the range of employment conditions individual workers and employers can negotiate.[3] As the Heinze Schulte case illustrates, American workers commonly negotiate special educational or career development opportunities as part of their employment packages, while their German counterparts have fewer options for treatment that differs from that of their peers. Insofar as individual Americans and Germans seek out such arrangements, they probably can anticipate somewhat different reactions on the part of their employers and peers.

Further international differences are evident in that workers in some countries have to negotiate for things their counterparts elsewhere take for granted. American workers often have to assert themselves to avoid having coworkers call them at home if a problem arises at work, while the bosses and coworkers of their continental European counterparts would be more reluctant to call a worker at home since personal time is more sacrosanct.[4] In societies with strong normative beliefs regarding the boundaries between work and nonwork life, balancing work and personal life may be more highly valued, and no such separations need be negotiated in the first place.

This chapter examines societal impacts on workers' opportunities to negotiate employment conditions. It does so by considering three prerogatives workers require to successfully negotiate an i-deal and by exploring the forms these prerogatives take in other countries compared with the United States. These three prerogatives impact i-deals via their effect on an individual's legal, normative, or moral claim to idiosyncratic employment conditions:

1. *the prerogative to ask:* whether it is acceptable for individuals to assert their preferences regarding conditions of employment
2. *the prerogative to be different:* whether individuals are permitted to negotiate employment conditions that differ from those of their coworkers
3. *the prerogative to realize particular preferences:* whether flexibility exists regarding specific conditions of employment; laws and customs can take certain conditions completely off the table; the broader the array of work conditions that can be negotiated, the more flexibility is available

To Ask: Can Individuals Influence Their Own Employment Conditions?

Workers have long desired to participate more actively in determining their employment arrangements.[5] A variety of forces shape whether this participation is manifest in a society, or takes the form of collective action, individual voice, or some combination of the latter two. These forces include societal institutions, social norms pertaining to individual self-expression, and the composition of firms and workers that gives rise to the employment patterns within a society.

Idiosyncratic arrangements negotiated between workers and employers constitute one form of workplace participation. The desire to have a voice when one's interests are involved is particularly high in the United States, where private employers have more influence over employment conditions and a greater zone of negotiability exists than elsewhere in the world.[6] In contrast, in nations where industrial relations systems based on representational bargaining are more prevalent, such as France and Belgium, an individual employee's voice is channeled through collective processes such as unions or government-sponsored mechanisms.[7] If society mandates a broad array of employment conditions (e.g., required benefits; mandatory sick, vacation, or family leave), it can reduce the need for negotiation and mitigate the practice of individual bargaining. In contrast, when few conditions of employment are prespecified, workers must bargain to get the things that make their jobs valuable to them. Note that while it is conceivable that societies might be characterized by high standardization and high bargaining, and low standardization and low bargaining, I speculate that these combinations are less likely to appear as a broad societal condition.[8] They might, however, characterize local labor-market segments within a society (as in the case of the low standardization and low bargaining that is characteristic of migrant workers with relatively little bargaining power).

To actually bargain for what he or she wants in a job, a worker must first believe that he or she *can*. Though it may seem minor, being able to ask is no small thing. Workers often are, or believe themselves to be, relatively powerless. In some settings, directly asking an employer to provide nonstandard conditions violates social norms regarding respect for authority. In the centralized employment systems that once existed in Communist China and the former Soviet Union, for example, worker preferences were discounted out-of-hand by the very structure of the employment system. The only person-specific deals available in such systems may be those obtained through bribery or special relationships.[9]

Societal Forces

National law, culture, and other institutional forces impact an individual's right to ask for preferred employment arrangements: In France, for instance, labor statutes and union-management agreements that the government helps broker specify an array of employment conditions at the national level that reduces local bargaining.[10] While such practices reduce the need for workers to ask, by guaranteeing them desirable employment conditions, they can create a tendency toward standardization that makes individual negotiation less frequent and potentially counternormative.

Cultural factors can also hamper individual bargaining, especially when asking constitutes a disrespectful challenge to authority or a brash assertion of individuality. In Singapore, for example, directly asking for preferred employment conditions is widely considered to be disrespectful.[11] Singaporean recruits, particularly when younger than the people hiring them, commonly accept employment terms the company offers without attempting to bargain. In China, workers often are expected to "inspire their supervisor" over time to know their needs and provide them with special accommodations without workers ever asking directly.[12] In Hong Kong, employers offer a limited set of commitments while workers report a wide-ranging sense of obligation on their part.[13] Overt individual demands for reciprocity are seen as inappropriate in such societies, where employers and the managers representing them are viewed as having greater authority and status than the workers they employ.

Despite the cultural and legal limitations that exist, the expansion of market-oriented thinking into many employment sectors throughout the world has increased the popularity of individual negotiation, even when the larger society is less supportive of individual bargaining. Witness the recent array of books aimed at workers in western Europe and New Zealand who hope to bargain more effectively with their employers.[14] Insofar as employment terms in the United States often are decided at the individual worker-employer level, market factors in America play a larger role, and preset factors a smaller role, than in many other countries in shaping what employers offer workers and what workers can negotiate. The result is likely to be more idiosyncratic arrangements in the United States than are found in other nations.[15]

The prerogative to ask is shaped by the nature of worker power, a factor that may be changing—eroding for some workers while expanding for others—across societies. The traditional basis of worker power in employment resided in collective bargaining agreements and legally supported job property rights. Job property rights entitle an individual to retain a position within an employing firm, even if the employer or its agents prefer otherwise. The weakening or elimination of job property rights often has coincided with the erosion of organized labor, giving employers in many nations a greater ability to fire workers. For example, New Zealand in the 1990s radically reshaped its employment relations, reducing the number of laws constraining employer termination decisions and creating a more market-oriented society with fewer prespecified employment conditions. After a rough transition that challenged many cultural beliefs about the society itself, the result has been an explosion of entrepreneurship and free agency among workers.[16] Those workers who have benefited from this transition are those who have found effective ways of controlling their own labor, through starting their own firms or pursuing employment arrangements that build sought-after distinctive skills and capabilities. I-deals are both a cause and an outcome of the changes occurring to worker power worldwide. To use something as a bargaining chip, a person must have control over it. The essential point here is that the control workers' exercise individually over their own employment is generally increasing among those with high-demand skills.

Timing: When Can a Worker Ask?

Timing affects when workers can legitimately ask for an i-deal. This means, for example, that *ex ante* deals may not be culturally acceptable, but *ex post* ones are a different matter. This observation became apparent to me while teaching in Singapore. We were discussing how knowledge workers recruited by American employers were bargaining for preferred assignments, career opportunities, working hours, stock options, and other benefits. To draw on the students' own experiences, I asked them to give examples of how they personally had bargained with prospective employers. First, there was silence. Then, one by one, the participants spoke:

"We don't negotiate; it's just not done."
"It's rude and the company won't hire you."
"We wait 'til we're on the job a while, and then we can bring up what we want."

Ultimately I came to understand that my students were saying this: Asking for what you want has a different meaning in the middle of a relationship than at the beginning of one.

The point in time when a worker negotiates with an employer varies according to the basis of a worker's power and the society's norms. Employment negotiations that occur before an employer hires a worker (*ex ante* negotiations) differ from those that occur once the individual is on the job and has built a relationship and performance record with that employer (*ex post* negotiations). In some societies like Singapore, directly asking a potential future employer for the benefits one wants can be construed as a sign of selfishness or disrespect.

Ex ante bargaining allows workers to propose, accept, and reject terms of employment at the relationship's outset. It characterizes settings in which individuals have power and in which asserting their own preferences reflects the legitimacy of the market, rather than the power of those in positions of authority in setting conditions of employment. Societies where individualism coupled with market ideologies dominate in employment, such as the United States, are more accepting of *ex ante* bargaining.[17]

When *ex ante* bargaining is not the norm, i-deals can still arise, but they do so later in the employment relationship, once trust and mutual interdependence have arisen.

I postulate that *ex post* negotiation in employment is far more common around the world than *ex ante* negotiation. Let's consider the case of Singaporean workers reluctant to ask explicitly for job conditions that match their preferences. The dominant ethnic group in Singapore is Chinese, with strong notions of hierarchy and status-appropriate behavior. Bargaining with a would-be employer risks conflict and disagreement, may be construed as rude, and may create a winner and loser rather than mutual beneficiaries of a deal, resulting in a loss of face to the loser. Moreover, the highly bureaucratic personnel systems of many Singaporean firms do not readily permit overtly inconsistent treatment of workers who hold the same positions. However, in Singapore's hot labor market in the late 1990s, a worker who was dissatisfied with one employer could find another job fairly easily.[18] As a result, managers who responded to cues from employees were more likely to retain them.

Ex post bargaining, though often in highly polite forms, characterizes idiosyncratic negotiation in Singapore and other culturally Chinese job settings. Expectations of reciprocity underlie employment relationships, particularly between workers and supervisors.[19] Both workers and their managers tend to exercise control via interpersonal relations.[20] Bargaining in China is done in the shadow of other ties people have, such that people build relationships with others who they believe are well placed in the social setting. Indeed, relational issues complicate the identification of workers with talent in China because firms and their managers are oriented to viewing people in the context of the social ties they bring with them.[21] In this context, it is interesting that rules tend to be seen as less binding; as one Chinese manager told a new recruit, "There are always exceptions."[22] A Chinese management professor describes his efforts to get his wife's employer, a state enterprise, to let her complete her doctoral studies: "I went to the bureau manager with bottles of whiskey and talked to him about [my wife's] desire to finish her dissertation. I did not ask him directly, but told him how important this was to my family. He never said anything to me one way or another about what he would do. He didn't let her go, I think because he doesn't get along with the bureau chief." People in this culture approach negotiations thinking not only of the principals but also of those people to whom the principals are tied.

Chinese workers tend to conceptualize their employment more strongly in terms of relationships with individuals, particularly their managers, and with the people to whom that manager is tied. This raises the notion that what looks like an i-deal to a Westerner may be preferential treatment as represented by the Chinese concept of *guanxi*. Literally referring to "connections" or "relationships," *guanxi* characterizes close personal relationships comprising both personal sentiment and obligation.[23] Such relationships may vary in the meaning less-traditional workers ascribe to them, and any broad generalizations would be risky here. Still, this difference illustrates how the basis on which workers are valued by the employer may differ across societies, from behavioral factors such as moral character, loyalty, and diligence to more outcome-oriented indicators of individual performance and results.[24]

Workers as Resources on Which Firms Depend

Societies are composed of different mixes of firms and industries. A nation's business context shapes employer responsiveness to worker requests. A country comprised of more staid industries or high levels of government employment can be expected to be less responsive to individual worker bargaining than a society with a more dynamic private sector. Firms located in dynamic industries where new businesses start up every day and old ones continually transform tend to be more flexible about their employment relationships. Same-sex partner benefits, for example, are not widely available yet in the United States but are becoming more common in entertainment, fashion, and arts, which recruit from labor markets with greater proportions of gay and lesbian workers.[25] In contrast, firms that operate in environments where the labor force is relatively homogeneous and generally more conservative may receive fewer idiosyncratic requests and, therefore, may have a greater tendency to view such accommodations as inappropriate or otherwise off the table.

The presence of women in the labor force, especially in the more powerful ranks of managers and knowledge workers, can legitimate greater individualization and accommodations that are enjoyed by both male and female workers. For example, those employers who most depended on a female-dominated workforce sought ways to accommodate the child-rearing responsibilities traditionally performed by women and thus led the way in adopting flextime and other flexible, family-friendly work arrangements. Interestingly, these practices now have been extended to women—and some men—in largely male-dominated firms, though it appears that women still may be more adept in negotiating flexible work schedules (or are responded to more positively) than are their male counterparts.[26] Accommodations that start out as individual-specific can ultimately become normative in labor markets where such features are particularly valued.

When government employment dominates a country's labor market, more bureaucratic employment practices are likely to constrain idiosyncratic arrangements. These strong behavior-regulating situations are characterized by established structures, explicit and enforced rules and regulations, and elaborate behavior monitoring and controls. The archetypal example is a high-reliability organization such as a nuclear power plant or air traffic control facility, in which deviations from standard practices can cause tremendous harm and are therefore severely sanctioned, and any non-task-related behavior is restrained to avoid distractions. These are often long-established work settings in which technology and external monitors regulate behavior. Workers tend to be highly interdependent, and individualistic behavior is constrained in favor of manageable, predictable routines. Insofar as such work settings regulate behavior to a greater degree, they reduce the latitude both workers and managers have to create idiosyncratic arrangements.[27]

In contrast, a predominance of small businesses, start-ups, and self-employment promotes more idiosyncratic practices (as might be expected in the nations with the largest proportion of start-up firms, including the United States, Finland, and Israel). Such settings have few established norms, explicit rules, or standard practices. Researchers have found that in these flexible settings, "the people make the place."[28] Individuals shape their own work practices in line with their predispositions and preferences, with wide latitude in how they do their job (whether they elect to work five eight-hour days a week or twenty hours straight and then take the next two days off). In these settings, an individual's favored work styles and preferred ways of relating to coworkers and managers are more likely to be evident. Managers in weak settings are more likely to be indifferent to *how* work is accomplished, as long as the desired results are achieved. In societies where firms tend to be smaller, opportunities for individual flexibility can be easier to come by.

Implications

Several societal factors influence a worker's prerogative to ask for idiosyncratic employment features. The first is the social norms associated with assertion of individual preferences, particularly whether asking is viewed as rude or inappropriately emphasizing the individual over the collective. The second is a societal tendency toward standardization, in which widespread pre-specification of employment conditions can make individual bargaining both less necessary and less normative. The third is the opportunity individuals have to assert their preferences, because countries differ in their workforce composition, mix of industries, and employment concentration across sectors. I-deals may be more common where start-ups and small businesses predominate, and more difficult where substantial proportions of workers are employed in governmental organizations that typically rely on standardized and bureaucratic employment practices. Idiosyncratic arrangements may be more readily achieved when characteristics of the workforce make workers' voicing their individual demands more legitimate (e.g., women seeking flexibility, high-demand knowledge workers seeking development opportunities).

To Be Different: Is Difference in Treatment Tolerated?

Arrangements that give some workers different perks and benefits than their peers can generate an array of reactions among colleagues, from indifference, to protest, to the desire to get themselves an even better deal. Although performance-based incentive systems are increasingly popular, rewarding members of the same group differently appears to go against the common grain of work-group dynamics. As Robert Frank has cogently argued, we may be programmed in an evolutionary sense to "'feel bad' when we are not as well-off as our peers."[29] How people react to differential treatment is tied to societal norms regarding equality and difference.

Society's Role in Standardizing Employment Conditions

The standardized social guarantees societies provide workers can reduce the need for i-deals. Job property rights in France, Germany, and Belgium guarantee job security, though they provide varying benefits and pension supports. In contrast, American employers generally have little if any obligation to provide job security, but they are obligated to contribute to their workers' retirement through the federal social security system (except in the case of government employees).[30] Fewer guarantees create more need for individual workers to assert their personal interests in an employment relationship. Lack of societal guarantees tends to co-occur with greater tolerance of differential treatment.

Societal standardization of worker benefits reflects an effort to create greater equality and mitigate power differences between workers and firms. Greater standardization within a country is suggestive of societal intolerance for inequality. Concern over the relatively low power some workers have in relation to their employers as well as to other workers increases societal reliance on combinations of collective agreements and regulations to standardize employment conditions. In explaining how the French government plays a powerful role in shaping the employment relationship, Cadin describes the French preference for the "rule" as opposed to contracts as a building block of society and, in particular, of work relations:

> Statutes create "social public order" by introducing a legal hierarchy with law at the top, collective bargaining next, and individual contracts last. Individual contracts cannot depart from legal rules and collective conventions. . . . At the heart of the French employment relationship is the assumption that the state is supposed to compensate for any imbalances in this relationship.[31]

The extent to which a society tolerates difference is indicative of its acceptance of unequal or dissimilar outcomes for individuals measured in terms of work conditions, perks, and benefits. People interpret such differences through the lenses their society provides. Socially acceptable motives for differential treatment can include merit, employer responsiveness to individual worker needs, or respect for diversity. This acceptance is conveyed by an MBA from India working in technical marketing who accepted the fact that he received less than his peers: "I was paid less than my fellow employees because I had less experience." Similarly, an American manager at a manufacturing firm known for its family-friendly benefits describes the reaction of workers who have no family, and thus receive no special perks themselves: "They like that [the company] really cares about people . . . they feel good to be part of a good company."[32]

Observed differences are less socially acceptable when others believe that they are unearned, signify favoritism, or indicate that an individual has asserted his or her personal interests over those of the work group. Coworker sensitivity to differential treatment has been observed even in the case of accommodations made for workers with disabilities. Adrienne Collela and her colleagues report that in the merit-focused United States, coworkers can be sensitive to accommodations that permit workers with disabilities to reduce their contributions to the firm (e.g., flexible hours not available to others, lighter workloads), particularly when the person with the disability appears to be better positioned for success than his or her coworkers as a result of the accommodation.[33] The norm of being kind seems to disappear in many competitive situations.[34]

Social norms regarding the allocation of rewards and benefits are intrinsically tied to the explanations, or social accounts, people offer regarding why differences in these allocations occur. Differential treatment that is understood to reflect hard work or legitimate need based on an obvious disability (e.g., blindness) is more likely to be seen as deserved than as special treatment based on favoritism or needs construed to reflect personal failings (e.g., substance abuse). In contrast, differential treatment for workers with disabilities is more acceptable in societies with stronger norms of communal support and solidarity.

Norms Promoting Equality

When society's norms promote equality and downplay differences, workers will accept fewer legitimate reasons for differences in employment conditions. As described by Australian social scientist Sol Encel,

> The conception of equality which prevails in Australia is one which places great stress on the enforcement of high minimum standards of material well-being, on the outward show of equality and the minimization of privileges due to formal rank; and almost by implication restricts the scope for the unusual, eccentric, or dissenting individual.[35]

In Australia, overt signs of privilege are not socially acceptable. In their place are preferences for equal outcomes and a distrust of unequal wealth. Greater attention is paid to enforcing minimum standards of well-being in the workplace and in the larger society, while outwardly promoting equality and minimizing special treatment. Further, Australians tend to identify strongly with their work groups and feel solidarity with their peers, creating a general distaste for differential treatment. Similarly, Japan's intensive collectivism pressures individuals to downplay their differences in favor of strong group identification. Such pressures are reinforced by the tendency of training in Japanese firms to emphasize all-around competence rather than specialization, and participation in consensus-based rather than individualized decision making.[36] The consequences that face Japanese workers who behave and benefit differently from others is aptly summed up as "the nail that sticks up gets hit." Perhaps not surprisingly, only a limited number of job categories in Japan permit the use of flexible or temporary workers. In the Netherlands, as well, cultural norms reward individuals for "being normal," acting as others do in the work group, as opposed to setting themselves above or outside the group. As Schalk and Freese describe the Dutch predilection for equality in treatment,

> The Dutch taste for equality trends to lower aspirations for rewards differing from peers'. Employees want to be recognized for their performance, but outstanding performers are also vulnerable to social sanction and must strive to be better than others in an inconspicuous manner. . . . "Acting normal" is very important in the Netherlands, and the biggest compliment a successful manager, politician, actor, or scientist can get is to be considered down-to-earth despite his or her success.[37]

In settings where collectivistic orientations predominate, workers are inclined to view representative participation, where arrangements are negotiated on behalf of a group, as fairer than individual workers negotiating for themselves.

Norms promoting equality often are bundled with human resource practices that further reinforce the concept. In the case of Japan, and in Korea to a lesser extent, hiring tends to focus on building a cohort of workers who will move through the organization's hierarchy at the same time. Cohort hiring permits firms to evaluate workers against those with the same tenure and development opportunities. Similarly, skill-grade pay systems tie pay increases and promotions to the acquisition of skills, where the same set of skills is expected of all in the cohort.[38] In these employment situations, idiosyncratic arrangements would constitute a powerful signal of difference justified in only the rarest of circumstances.

Even in societies that accept some degree of *ex post* bargaining, empathy among peers and the desire to be accepted by a work group can make it personally intolerable to have a different deal from one's peers if the situation becomes too public. I interviewed a twenty-five-year-old ethnic Chinese man who had worked full-time for Federal Express in Singapore. He asked his boss whether he could leave two hours early several days a week to take evening courses. The boss granted this request because the man was a good candidate for promotion to management. A year into this arrangement, however, the employee quit to become a full-time student: "I felt uncomfortable leaving early while my coworkers kept working," he said. Similar patterns have been reported in Mexico among high performers who receive recognition and a pay raise. After being singled out as high performers, workers report feeling ostracized by colleagues, who see them as "management's favorite." Turnover among such high performers is common in Mexico.[39] Employers in Mexico who are particularly effective at motivating and retaining workers often go out of their way to play up communal solidarity and downplay social distance.[40] Norms that suppress differences, as in Japan and Australia, reduce the variation in employment arrangements from one worker to the next. In these societies, i-deals can be viewed as selfish, egotistical, political, and devaluing of the work group.

Norms Tolerating Inequality

Idiosyncratic employment arrangements are more common when social norms make different outcomes acceptable. Societies that accept some degree of self-interested behavior tend to support allocation of rewards and perks based on individuals' contributions and achievements (i.e., distributive fairness, as described in chapter 3). Insofar as unequal outcomes are tolerated to a greater extent in the United States than in most other industrialized nations,[41] differences tend to be justified by beliefs in equal opportunities, the idea that any two people could have the same outcomes if they worked as hard, as long, or as well. Explanations for differences include merit (i.e., results, hard work, paying dues) and the labor market (i.e., experience, skill levels, and demand), along with positional differences based on earned credentials (i.e., professionals versus nonprofessionals, faculty versus staff, permanent versus temporary workers). Unequal outcomes are seen as legitimate when they are earned through hard work, education, or contributions over time.

Seniority, if not necessarily age per se, appears to draw widespread respect across societies. Greater allocations to high-tenure workers are acceptable in individualistic societies as well as collectivistic ones. In the former, senior workers need to sustain their performance, or at least be seen as valued contributors.[42] Nonetheless, many societies are likely to accept rewards for long-standing contributors, as seniority can be viewed as either an ascribed (status-based) difference in treatment, or an earned or merited one, from which all workers might eventually benefit.

Implications

Social forces can act to both suppress differences and promote equality. Against a backdrop of pressure for similarity, idiosyncrasy is more likely to be tolerated under conditions that legitimate difference, such as positive social attributions for differential outcomes (e.g., merit, market value). The ethos of merit often is seen in societies where market-based thinking dominates. Another attribution that makes differences acceptable is responsiveness to personal need, particularly where the needs are visible and generated by factors beyond the individual's control, such as disability. Seniority also appears to be an acceptable basis for greater reward allocation, and potentially more idiosyncratic arrangements, across many societies. However, the extent to which senior workers must sustain their contributions to continue meriting such special treatment depends on the societal context.

**To Ask for Certain Kinds of Preferences: What's Available?
What's Taboo?**

As the song goes, "You can't always get what you want." Even when individuals have the right to ask and work in settings where outcome differences are socially acceptable, certain preferences might still be unavailable or seen as illegitimate. There always are constraints on what can be obtained, earned, or bargained for in employment. Even the most liberal society can view some employment conditions as unacceptable. A Swiss or Israeli army reservist is permitted to carry his weapon into work, while his American counterpart probably is not; Bible-study groups are a common occurrence in Singaporean workplaces during the lunch hour, but less so in Western Europe or North America. Institutional factors such as culture, laws, and established organizational practices take certain employment conditions off the table and focus special attention on others. In doing so, these forces shape the zone of negotiability. Market pressures and changing cultural norms can cause employers to expand what they are willing to offer employees.[43] Workers and their managers also encounter opportunities for experimentation that allow each to take advantage of conditions that make otherwise unavailable employment conditions feasible.

Employers will not usually provide accommodations that are otherwise illegal or impractical, or violate cultural or societal norms. Offering the service of prostitutes to managers is illegal in the United States, for instance, but has traditionally been somewhat more acceptable in Japan. Many German workers are legally barred from owning stock in their firms, while American workers often have substantial portions of their retirement funds automatically invested in their employers' stock. Pilots for United Airlines cannot negotiate individually to avoid working weekends because their union contract states that seniority and air traffic demands determine pilot schedules. Conventional money-based employment relationships may be difficult to create in a transitional economy. An employer in a cash-strapped Ukrainian T-shirt firm paid his workers in T-shirts because he lacked ready access to foreign buyers and could not afford to issue paychecks. While workers could not negotiate for payment in cash, they were able to barter the shirts for other necessary goods on the local market.

Local economic forces act on firms as well, affecting their willingness to provide certain employment conditions. In contemporary India and Singapore, for instance, employers are often reluctant to provide training to workers for fear that trained workers will quit and take a job with another employer.[44] Bargaining for development may be easier where employers view it as a means of adding value to their collective workforce, or where they cannot attract or retain good workers without doing so. As local economic circumstances change, a firm's willingness to put certain features of employment on the bargaining table increases if it grows more dependent on workers who particularly value these conditions. Greater employer dependence on women workers in Western Europe, for example, has made firms more flexible in the conditions offered to women.[45]

Implications

Societal characteristics, including law and custom, can put some potential i-deals off the table by making them illegal, impractical, or taboo. Work settings that permit one type of accommodation still can limit others. Nonetheless, changing market demands can bring formerly off-limits idiosyncratic conditions into the zone of negotiability.

Conclusion

As the biologist Ursula Goodenough said regarding evolution, "The ongoing, underlying fact is that the process is totally dependent on context."[46] Societal context has a direct impact on the extent to which individual workers can negotiate for themselves. This negotiability is shaped by three dimensions: (1) whether a worker can assert his or her own interests and negotiate with an employer to achieve them; (2) whether organization members will tolerate another's differential treatment; and (3) whether the arrangements preferred are culturally and legally sanctioned. To the degree that these dimensions are present, individuals can engage in greater self-determination at work by bargaining more effectively on their own behalf.

The traditional assumption in many societies, particularly those where industrial relations systems have dominated employment, is that workers cannot bargain as individuals. Indeed, for many workers, their power to bargain is quite limited. Nonetheless, globalization is motivating economic overhaul in the employment regulations of developed nations, reducing the conditions of employment workers can enjoy without bargaining.[47] Further, globalization has contributed to a shift in the balance of power for many knowledge workers and promoted the market mentality characteristic of highly mobile boundaryless career workers. These sectors exist across many societies; as they grow, they provide fertile ground for the evolution of i-deals.

One caveat is in order, however. Ng and Ang point out the danger of assuming that human resource practices that *appear* similar across countries actually are similar.[48] The performance appraisal systems of North America and East Asia may go by comparable names, but the latter place greater emphasis on the character of the whole person and his or her contribution to the group, while the former emphasize individual effort and results. As such, idiosyncratic arrangements may have different content, symbolic value, and social significance in work settings located in different countries—a topic for future cross-national research on i-deals.

— 10 —

Learning from I-deals

What is a weed?
A plant whose virtues have not yet been discovered.
—*Ralph Waldo Emerson*[1]

The unpredictable, the free will, the chaotic creates novelty,
and novelty is the author of new order.
—*Ross Marion*[2]

Looking at employment through the lens of i-deals allows us to appreciate the myriad details and nuances that the individuality of workers brings to the employment relationship. This reality is at odds with the top-down view of firms espoused by many practitioners and organizational scholars. Note that i-deals are not a bottom-up phenomenon either. Rather, they are interactive, emerging from individuals in work groups interacting with firm-representing managers, the multiplex wellsprings of the employment relationship. This interplay compels a more complex view of employment than standard theory and management practice tend to acknowledge.

By recognizing the existence of i-deals and the broader array of idiosyncrasy permeating employment, we can become more mindful of the fundamental ways individual employees shape their own working conditions, current perks, and future opportunities. I-deals are a fact, not necessarily a problem or a panacea. Through them valued workers get conditions they prefer and employers have a way to attract, motivate, and retain them. Nonetheless, i-deals are no substitute for standard arrangements that bind workers to their employer and one another, particularly when productivity requires effective cooperation and interdependent action. All employment agreements can't be i-deals. The architecture of employment requires standardized and positional conditions, too, because some signals and incentives are meaningful only when many workers share them (e.g., competitive promotions) or are too costly to administer piecemeal (e.g., health-care benefits). Organizations simply cannot standardize everything.

I-deals are at once useful and difficult. Their widespread presence is evidence that i-deals are a situational response to needs that standard practices don't meet. Human resource innovations, which give workers and employers new ways to solve problems, often have roots in i-deals. Yet their often covert use indicates that conflicting interests can go unresolved when an i-deal is executed. Taking the form of secrets and workarounds, i-deals go against the grain of acknowledged organizational practice, managerial rhetoric, and existing theories of employment. To acknowledge them would require that we challenge our assumptions regarding workplace justice and employment relations. Though management theories treat the lack of perfect information about worker competencies and employer intentions as inherent in the structure of employment, i-deals are evidence that workers and managers also purposefully withhold information from coworkers and the broader firm.[3]

Information asymmetry arises in part because organization members take actions that make it so. Pay secrecy and hidden side deals are a fact of organizational life. Covert acts are justified because there seems to be no other way to keep coworkers from feeling unfairly treated. Yet it is because i-deals largely have existed underground that we generally lack the shared experience to know how to do otherwise. To make more broadly beneficial i-deals with fewer downside risks requires managers, employers, workers, and social science to have competencies we do not *yet* possess. With an accent on "yet," this chapter addresses what we might learn from i-deals. It focuses on necessary learning regarding workplace justice, innovation in human resource practice, and competencies required to understand and capture the full value i-deals offer.

Justice Is More Than "Perceived Fairness"

If i-deals are to benefit workers and employers, creating positive externalities and eliminating negative ones, we need a concept of workplace justice tuned more finely than evident in current conventions. These conventions center around two forms. With slight exaggeration we can describe them as the hedonic treadmill of insatiable freedom and diversity characterizing anything-goes bargaining on one extreme and the standardized one-size-fits-all dispensations of mindless bureaucracy on the other. Free agents and contractors bargain as individuals, and standard theory and practice apply. However, when individual employees bargain, it takes practitioners and social scientists into uncharted territory—the dynamic triangle of worker-employer-coworker relationships. The embeddedness of employees in a collective workforce can make i-deals unsettling for all parties. Though even contemporary unionists assert that employees and their managers seem to prefer individual representation, this belief is at odds with evidence of worker preferences for employers of choice, that is, those firms providing standardized compensation and benefits with no negotiation required.[4] Yet standardization often rules out flexibility when workers are treated as interchangeable. Somewhere between anything-goes bargaining and regimented standardization, work settings and the scholars who study them have the potential to realize and balance both individual agency and community interests.

Justice research to date has not explored the terrain between the extremes of agency and community. It gives little attention to conditions under which differentiating between coworkers is beneficial, satisfying, and just. In its focus on employer and managerial action, it has ignored workers' individual efforts to realize their personal preferences while maintaining good relations with peers. Studies of workplace justice focus on the narrow locale in which employers provide resources to workers who passively receive them. The only action on the part of workers that justice researchers acknowledge, except for an occasional complaint or adjustment of their performance to feel better about their compensation, is limited to judging the fairness of their treatment.

Despite evidence that workers have a hand in determining what employers offer, justice research frames this exchange as an employer decision. Insofar as the focus on the employer as actor limits our view, the dynamics of workplace justice are further obscured by the traditional emphasis on how recipients react. Nonrecipients are assumed to be irrelevant nonparticipants, with no involvement in the processes by which this exchange occurs, even though their interests often are undeniably affected. Justice research looks at the employer-worker dyad, not the worker-employer-coworker triad so critical to the functionality of i-deals and to the employment relationship generally.

Consistency with respect to rules is the dominant concept of procedural fairness. Since i-deals are by their nature nonstandard, we need to explore how consistent principles can be applied when consistent procedures aren't readily achievable. Some rules may be workable, for instance, requiring notice before taking time off, and these embody important principles, such as the obligation to respect others while exercising personal freedom. Other facets of procedural justice, underplayed in conventional justice research, may be even more useful. Voice is a critical element in procedural justice. It can turn nonrecipients into participants by involving an i-deal's constituents in the process of creating and sustaining the deal. When exceptional circumstances make rules unworkable, interactive fairness becomes a critical aspect of justice; in this way, respect is accorded nonrecipients of i-deals through the quality of interpersonal treatment and communication provided by both employer and i-dealer. In the workplace, justice is not merely individual or dyadic; it is collective, too.

I-deals raise issues that traditional research on justice and fairness in the workplace has not addressed. First, allocations of resources via i-deals often involve asymmetry of information. Managers may swear an i-dealer to secrecy, and many i-dealers themselves may be reluctant to fully disclose their arrangements to avoid conflict with coworkers. If coworkers feel fairly treated because they are unaware that an i-deal exists or know only parts of it, is this justice? The restriction and distortion of information regarding i-deals occurs in the pursuit of "perceived fairness," manipulating the sentiments of coworkers through inaccurate information. Rectifying information asymmetry rather than exploiting it is the way forward. I have no illusions that if i-deals are disclosed everyone will be happy, and most certainly not immediately. But disclosure motivates conversation, action, and perspective taking, which increase the odds that more mutually beneficial arrangements ultimately can arise. The positive externalities of i-deals may take time to foster, but they do exist, in the form of greater transparency and a trustworthy workplace. A second consideration justice research has ignored is the effect of resource allocations over time. I-deals can alter the *future* relative standing of work-group members. Workers bargaining for flexibility can subsequently find that their nonconforming work practices disadvantage them for promotions and bonuses. On the other hand, i-deals that give workers more visibility in the organization or the opportunity to develop valued skills can subsequently provide them with an advantage over coworkers with respect to those same promotions and bonuses. By viewing fairness as a one-time postallocation judgment, the full significance of the i-deal to workplace justice is overlooked. If the goal is justice, it may be that one-time informant reports of subjective fairness are too low a standard.

The dynamics of i-deals beg a more positive, constructive approach to justice, simultaneously attending to the interests of multiple parties. John Rawls characterizes justice in terms of two principles.[5] The first is that each individual has a right to the most extensive basic liberty compatible with the same liberty for others. The second principle is that inequalities, social or economic, are just only to the extent that they serve to promote the well-being of the least advantaged. The first core idea here is that greater flexibility is more just for individuals than is less flexibility, a view consistent with individual agency, where workers strive to fulfill their own particular preferences. The second is that any differences in treatment arising from this greater flexibility need to create net benefits even for those in lower-status or less-privileged positions. Thus, the worker who bargains for a more challenging assignment, flexible hours, or an at-home work arrangement, and the employer who grants this request, should do so to the broader benefit of coworkers and the organizational community (e.g., by clarifying what performance is valued and what flexibilities are possible, or by increasing awareness of the company's support for its employees).

In contrast to justice research's focus on fairness, Rawls's view of justice is a positive—a net benefit rather than a neutral (the absence of perceived unfairness doesn't cut it). Benefits are tangible as well as subjective, not the result of manipulated information. What we seek in each work setting are the arrangements that permit individuals to bargain on their own behalf while improving working conditions even for coworkers less able to bargain. In effect, workplaces need processes that allow all participants to enjoy a certain satisfaction from both tangible and socioemotional benefits.

Let's push justice a little further. An even higher standard is a guarantee of certain outcomes that meet the criterion of "envy-free." Envy-free divisions, defined by Steven Brams and Alan Taylor, arise when every person to whom an allocation pertains thinks he or she received the most valuable portion, based on his or her own valuation, and hence does not envy anyone else.[6] Resources can be divided, allowing entitlements to be reflected in the allocation, as in the case of star employees who have greater a priori claims than others. Envy-free divisions involve two things: shared information about entitlements and alternatives plus the opportunity to choose. The simplest example of envy-free division is the way a wise parent has two kids divide a piece of cake: one cuts and the other chooses.

To arrive at conditions that give individuals maximum flexibility while protecting those who are least advantaged, Rawls argues that what is needed are preestablished allocation rules that members agree to live by *before* they know what their own allocation will be. Evoking the notion of the veil of ignorance, Rawls proposes that each person must select rules to live by without knowing whether he or she will be prosperous or destitute in a setting governed by those rules. He calls this the "original position." Individuals in the original position will choose the arrangement such that the worst possible position, which for all they know will be theirs, is better than the worst possible position in any other system. From the perspective of i-deals, following Rawls's advice would lead us to create a meta-contract specifying how individualized arrangements can be created that meet the needs of individuals while benefiting the interests of coworkers and employer, a matter to which we now turn.

Innovation and Openness to Experimentation

Workplace innovations often begin as i-deals; the flexible schedules in widespread use today are a case in point. Workforce and market pressures lead employers to adapt and alter their HR practices. Workers, managers, and firms have a lot to learn about how to make such flexibility work well for all parties. In a rapidly changing environment, employers are challenged to find new ways to increase efficiency and productivity. Many work practices are outdated legacies in today's job market, such as the notion of starting at eight and ending at five, reflecting industrial norms that specified that workers needed to be physically present during normal work hours. Everyday workplace flexibility can be more important than the more publicized formal practices such as mommy or daddy tracks. Managers and scholars seeking to develop sources of future innovation and policy change would do well to observe the informal accommodations workers make and to keep track of i-deals for adoption more broadly.

Human resource innovations often are too complex to introduce all at once and may fail unless begun as experiments to learn what works and what doesn't. A consulting firm with high burnout rates, particularly among professional women with high family demands, brought its female consultants together to explore these challenges. By creating a network among women consultants and utilizing focus groups to identify what approaches had been tried and what the outcomes were, the idiosyncratic practices women had developed became a source of the firm's new HR policies. The i-deals they identified had limited travel or had given workers schedule flexibility via use of videophones and part-time partnerships. As a source of organizational learning, i-deals constitute a way in which HR policies originate in firms when successful local practices are adopted for workers in general. Wherever i-deals exist, innovative HR practices can be in the making. But treating i-deals as something to hide is no way to learn.

For i-deals to be a source of learning and innovation, it is necessary to evaluate how well they work over time, and then to redesign or terminate them if needed. Insofar as they are experiments, some i-deals may not work out well for either the firm or the worker. Building milestones into the assessment of i-deals—what negotiation researchers refer to as contingent negotiations—lets a deal's progress and consequences be evaluated.[7] Workers who negotiate shortened workweeks or work-at-home arrangements might review the arrangements regularly with key stakeholders (coworkers, clients) to assess their impact. Framing a deal as "experimental" can make adjusting the deal later on easier by cuing the parties involved that its conditions are not written in stone. By their capacity also to reshape how standardized employment conditions are allocated, i-deals create a basis for ongoing learning. In doing so, i-deals can also challenge the conventional notion that "standardized" means "fixed."

Because even standardized practices are subject to interpretation and adjustment, i-deals shine a light on the realities of standardization. Routines, including standardized human resource practices, are at times quite flexible. Though routines provide a basis for stability and consistency, their actual execution by specific people, at specific times and in specific places, involves individual action or agency.[8] Agency involves the ability to remember the past, imagine the future, and respond to present circumstances.[9] A person performing a routine may need to adapt it based on present or anticipated conditions. Managers who decide to redefine educational leaves to include sabbaticals that let valued workers pursue a hobby can morph such routines into new standard practices legitimated by the precedent just set. This notion of agency acknowledges the power residing not only in those people who create routines but also in those who perform them.

By their often developmental and emergent nature, i-deals demand recognition of the role of local variation, adaptation, and exceptions in everyday life, many of which can be a net benefit to all parties, and are therefore just. I-deals are a way small changes can create large outcomes. As means of responding to competitive labor markets and diverse worker needs and preferences, i-deals are useful as one-time fixes, yet potentially even more beneficial as experiments directed toward more systematic future adoption.

The dysfunctional consequences of pay secrecy and other covert employment practices underscore the need to learn how to make i-deals acceptable to coworkers while meeting the needs of the individual worker and his or her employer. A wise personnel manager once said, "Make no compensation decisions you wouldn't post on the employee bulletin board." Managers and workers are likely to be more willing to publicly acknowledge those i-deals based on values widely shared in the organization (e.g., merit-based rewards, support for serious personal needs, an opportunity for innovation).

We need to learn more about how individual employee choice can be implemented effectively and fairly. One issue is how organizations might develop practices to facilitate customization. Cafeteria-style benefit plans are a structured opportunity for employee choice, and help us conceptualize what a standardized vehicle for creating customized employment terms might look like. Employees are allowed to choose from a variety of benefit arrangements valued up to a certain dollar amount. That amount is the same for all members of the employee group, thus permitting similarly situated individuals to make personal choices within a defined framework. The procedure may be considered distributively fair insofar as it treats equals as equals; the organization cuts deals that are no more attractive for one person than for another. Cafeteria-style pay plans also may be considered procedurally fair because they apply decision criteria consistently to all employees and give these employees a voice in determining their own outcomes. Finally, such arrangements may be considered interactionally just insofar as they communicate the organization's commitment to satisfying employees' needs in a dignified manner. Cafeteria plans promote a sense of fairness based on their consistent availability to all and because they permit individuals to choose independently of the choices others make. Strictly speaking, however, the standardized nature of cafeteria-style pay plans does not allow them to be considered i-deals, which by their nature are exceptional.[10]

The Harvard Business School has its own sort of cafeteria-type flexibility, but it revolves around workloads. Faculty can negotiate their teaching and service contributions within a framework in which each activity is assigned units. A full load is twenty-two to twenty-five units, depending on contract and tenure, and can be customized to a fair degree. This structure replaced the rampant bargaining that had existed under an earlier system, which generated widespread mistrust among faculty. At the Harvard Business School, idiosyncratic arrangements still arise when faculty perform extra work up front in exchange for release time later or when they first take time off and subsequently "pay it back" by working more units. By establishing this framework for flexibility, the system counteracts the pressure to create separate deals, reducing coworkers' vigilance about what each faculty member contributes relative to his or her peers. This practice is similar to the time-off banks many firms use that allow workers to combine vacation, holiday, and sick days into a pool to be used as they please, with no questions asked.[11]

An advantage of standardized flexibility is that it offers choice within a framework, but not infinite choice. By creating a structure within which choice can occur, it reduces the burden of wondering whether one might have gotten a better deal by bargaining harder, making coworkers happier with what they have and less vigilant about what others receive. Though it sounds great, unlimited choice can actually be a burden, whether it involves thirty varieties of jam on a grocer's shelves or ten different health benefit packages offered by an employer. Such broad choices often are accompanied by incomplete information regarding the features and desirability of the various options. Research demonstrates that consumers are often less happy with their purchases when choosing from a broad selection rather than a moderate array of options.[12] Similarly, in employment situations—particularly where many workers have different but not necessarily unique interests—standardized flexibility may be more a desirable approach than infinite variation to providing choice.

When workers have more varied interests across the broad spectrum of resources, from development to personal schedules, standardized flexibility is less of an option. Instead, issues of choice are best addressed by a priori identifying and articulating the circumstances under which i-deals will be entertained. Consultation with coworkers during the process of negotiating an i-deal for another worker can alert all employees to the ways in which their work conditions are flexible. Employers also can publicize opportunities in which flexibility is possible (or even preferred).

Experience and the Development of Competency with I-deals

To reiterate an important point, i-deals are useful but difficult. The difficulty may not be inherent in i-deals per se, but rather in the conditions under which they have been typically implemented, conditions that can change with experience. I recall as a doctoral student taking a business school course on organizational design when the subject came up regarding matrix organizations (in which managers report to multiple bosses in the effort to balance functional, geographic, and market segment concerns).[13] The professor described how difficult it was for managers to balance the conflicts and competing demands inherent in these firms, and quoted one of the gurus of matrix organizations who claimed, "Matrix organizations haven't failed. It's people who have failed matrixes." At the time, the mid-1970s, matrix organizations were a relatively new form with widespread reports of how difficult they were to implement. In the intervening years, this organizational form and its variants have come to characterize many multinationals, and though conflicts are built into the matrix of reporting relationships, people are a lot more experienced with them.[14] So, in the case of i-deals, as with complex organizational forms, experience over time can lessen the difficulties faced—if effort is made to learn.

Experiences that build competence make a difference, in this case, the competence of the worker, manager, and firm to create and sustain i-deals. This book has addressed other contextual factors that influence the ease and sustainability of i-deals, including the degree of flexibility in the work setting (chapter 2), the acceptance of i-deals made possible by quality employment relationships (chapter 7), and the organizational conditions that legitimate their use (chapter 8). In chapter 8 we also described the effect of prior experience on the effectiveness of managers in making i-deals. Key learnings that managers need to develop include recognizing the importance of legitimating i-deals, often putting the burden on the would-be i-dealer to do so, and processes for making the i-deal sustainable over time. There are learnings to be developed on the part of workers and the firm, too.

Individual workers differ in their experience with i-deals, as they do in their experience with employment negotiation generally. Some workers are experienced negotiators (e.g., managerial employees, workers with boundaryless careers who cycle from employer to employer), while many others are not. Training in negotiation can be very advantageous for workers inexperienced at it. Research demonstrates that training can give workers a greater sense of control over the negotiation process and help them anticipate stumbling blocks and solve problems more effectively.[15] For many workers this means overcoming the socialization that taught them to defer to authority or wait for others to recognize what they need. It can mean recognizing that work arrangements are seldom as fixed as they seem, particularly to women and minorities, who often attribute the locus of control in the work situation to the organization to a greater extent than do majority-group men.[16] Competency can also mean perspective taking, whereby a potential i-dealer decides not to request certain arrangements because doing so, though possible, might not have desirable consequences for the i-dealer, coworker, or employer. Employee competence means more than becoming a good bargainer. Learning how to anticipate and solve problems and to manage relations with clients and coworkers when one's work arrangements are nonconforming is every bit as important.

Employees are also coworkers, third parties to another worker's i-deal. Because of the status implications i-deals raise as well as the tangible burdens they can impose, coworkers have reason to be wary. Experience with i-deals can alter or broaden an individual's perspective. Two aspects of perspective are particularly important: the capacity to put oneself in the place of others and empathize with their experiences, and the adoption of a longer view regarding the time frame of one's relationship with the employer. Perspective taking is a cognitively complex process and can take time and effort to understand and integrate into one's thinking and decision making.[17] Viewing relationships in a shorter time frame tends to couch differences in competitive terms, even though those differences can even out over time. Sustainable i-deals are adaptive, increasing benefits and reducing burdens. In particular, the participation of coworkers in the process of redesign can create new perspectives and substantive payoffs for all parties to an i-deal.

Firms can develop cultural competencies and managerial practices that let them capture the benefits i-deals can bring without eroding trust and cooperation. The firm's challenge is to develop shared understanding regarding when i-deals are appropriate, and to avoid misuse (i-deals that shouldn't be made) and poor implementation (appropriate i-deals that aren't executed well). Supportive changes in a firm's culture and management practices can mean that i-deals, though still exceptional, may be made in a more effective and just fashion. A firm with a well-developed performance appraisal process, for example, can support effective i-deals by providing a valid basis for performance-based arrangements. Explicating performance standards makes it easier for workers with nonconforming arrangements to monitor their performance accordingly. HR systems assume varying degrees of employee assertiveness or passivity. A system that generates effective activity on the part of workers provides them with clear opportunities to give input, evoking participation and exercise of choice.

Conclusions

I-deals are evidence that the different work experiences group members report are neither merely subjective bias nor the result of politicking and favoritism. Systematic processes are at work whereby workers differ in the terms they craft into their employment relationship. Organizational research to date has downplayed heterogeneity in the value and meanings individuals within a work group associate with their employment. The conceptualization of i-deals developed here invites investigation of how the differences in resources that employees in the same group enjoy can be legitimate and acceptable, making workers and their employer better off because flexibility and justice are in balance.[18]

I-deals that promote functional organizational practice arise under the same conditions that make for good relationships and business agreements in the first place. These include employees and employers that trust each other, respond to each other's needs, possess good information about each other's interests, and respect how their dealings impact coworkers, and settings where there are sanctions for opportunism. Individual agency is everywhere in the workplace; justice demands that we both nurture and balance it. As Rawls has argued, "The general concept of justice imposes no restrictions on what sort of inequalities are permissible; it only requires that everyone's position be improved."[19] As we learn from i-deals emerging in the workplace, we can push the envelope of justice farther to build the positive and reduce the negative externalities of individual bargaining in pursuit of greater flexibility with fairness.

Notes

Notes to Preface

1. Each of the following studies found that workers in the same departments, working for the same manager, had different psychological contracts (as indicated by substantial within-unit variance on psychological contract measures). D.M. Rousseau and S. Tijoriwala, "What's a good reason to change? Motivated reasoning and social accounts in promoting organizational change," *Journal of Applied Psychology* 84 (1999): 514–28; G.E. Dabos and D.M. Rousseau, "Mutuality and reciprocity in the psychological contracts of employee and employer," *Journal of Applied Psychology* 89 (2004): 52–72; G.E Dabos and D.M. Rousseau, "Social interaction patterns shaping employee psychological contracts: Network-wide and local effects," in *Best Paper Proceedings of the Academy of Management Meetings,* ed. K. M. Weaver (Briarcliff Manor, NY: Academy of Management, 2004).

2. F.W. Taylor, *The Principles of Scientific Management* (New York: Harper, 1929).

3. M.B. Arthur, K. Inkson, and J.K. Pringle, *The New Careers: Individual Action and Economic Change* (London: Sage, 1999), p. 43.

4. G.S. Leventhal, "The distribution of rewards and resources in groups and organizations," in *Advances in Experimental Social Psychology,* ed. L. Berkowitz and E. Walster, vol. 9, pp. 91–131 (New York: Academic Press, 1976).

5. R.B. Freeman and J. Rogers, *What Workers Want* (Ithaca: ILR Press, 1999).

6. R.N. Block, P. Berg, and D. Belman, "The economic dimension of the employment relationship," in *The Employment Relationship: Examining Psychological and Contextual Perspectives,* ed. J.A.-M. Coyle-Shapiro, L.M. Shore, M.S. Taylor, and L.E. Tetrick, pp. 94-118 (New York: Oxford University Press, 2004).

7. In effect, knowledge work is more industry- than company-specific, as described in the following: D.M. Rousseau and Z. Shperling, "Ownership and the changing employment relationship: Why stylized notions of labor no longer generally apply. A reply to Zardkoohi and Paetzgold," *Academy of Management Review, 29* (2004): 562–569; H.S. Farber, "Trends in long term employment in the United States, 1979–96." (Working paper 384, Industrial Relations Section, Princeton University, July 1997); H.S. Farber,

"Mobility and stability: The dynamics of job change in labor markets" (Working paper 400, Industrial Relations Section, Princeton University, June 1998); R.G. Rajan and L. Zingales, *Saving Capitalism from the Capitalists* (New York: Random House Business Books, 2003).

8. John Mitchell, 1903, as quoted by Robert Frank, in *Choosing the Right Pond: Human Behavior and the Quest for Status* (New York: Oxford University Press, 1985), p. 156. See also S. Webb and B. Webb, *Industrial Democracy* (London: Longman and Green, 1911); and H.N. Wheeler, *The Future of American Labor* (Cambridge: Cambridge University Press, 2002).

Notes to Chapter 1

1. A.R. Hochschild, *Time Bind: When Work Becomes Home and Home Becomes Work* (New York: Metropolitan Books, 1997).

2. J.S. Lublin, "Ex-CEOs get lush perks, fees for 'consulting' work," *Wall Street Journal*, September 13, 2002.

3. I thank my colleagues Jerry Greenberg and Violet Ho for helping in the development of the notion of i-deals and aspects of the theory presented in this chapter. A detailed treatment of the theory we developed together is found in D.M. Rousseau, V.T. Ho, and J. Greenberg, "Idiosyncratic deals: Some i-deal propositions," *Academy of Management Review,* forthcoming.

4. Lublin, "Ex-CEOs get lush perks."

5. D.M. Rousseau, "Under the table deals: Preferential, unauthorized, or idiosyncratic," in *The Darkside of Organizational Life: Preferential, Unauthorized or Idiosyncratic?* ed. A. O'Leary-Kelly and R. Griffin (San Francisco: Jossey-Bass, 2004), pp. 262–90.

6. K.M. Bartol and D.C. Martin, "Effects of dependence, dependence threats, and pay secrecy on managerial pay allocations," *Journal of Applied Psychology* 74 (1989): 105–13. Note that some individuals, regardless of market value, may be more willing to ask employers for arrangements that match their personal preferences. See, for example, L. Babcock and S. Laschever, *Women Don't Ask* (Princeton, NJ: Princeton University Press, 2003). The willingness of workers to ask, demand, or negotiate is the immediate psychological driver of i-deals. Possessing market power can amplify an individual's willingness to negotiate. When market power increases for a group of workers, negotiation can become normative.

7. John Mitchell, 1903, as quoted by Robert Frank, in *Choosing the Right Pond: Human Behavior and the Quest for Status* (New York: Oxford University Press, 1985), p. 156.

8. R.G. Rajan and L. Zingales, "The influence of the financial revolution on the nature of firms," *American Economic* Review 91 (2001): 206–11; C.R. Leana and D.M. Rousseau, *Relational Wealth: Advantages of Stability in a Changing Economy* (New York: Oxford University Press, 2000).

9. M. Guillen, *Models of Management: Work, Authority, and Organization in a Comparative Perspective* (Chicago: University of Chicago Press, 1994).

10. D.M. Rousseau, Z. Shperling, and C.J. Ferrante, "Ownership practices in start-up firms: An Israel-U.S. comparison." Unpublished manuscript, Carnegie Mellon University, Pittsburgh, PA, 2004.

11. D.M. Rousseau and Z. Shperling, "Pieces of the action: Ownership and the changing employment relationship," *Academy of Management Review* 28 (2003): 553–70.

12. K.J. Klein, F. Dansereau, and R.J. Hall, "Levels issues in theory development, data collection, and analysis," *Academy of Management Review* 19 (1994): 195–229.

13. D. Pink, *Free Agent Nation: The Future of Working for Yourself* (New York: Warner, 2002).

14. E.P. Hollander, "Conformity, status, and idiosyncrasy credit," *Psychological Review* 63 (1958): 117–27.

15. Jason Merante, former steel worker and Carnegie Mellon alumnus, personal communication, November 2000.

16. D.M. Rousseau, "The idiosyncratic deal: Flexibility versus fairness," *Organizational Dynamics* 24 (2000): 260–73.

17. V. Vroom, *Work and Motivation* (New York: McGraw-Hill, 1964).

18. D.M. Rousseau and T.G. Kim, "When coworkers have special deals: Within-group heterogeneity and fairness" Unpublished manuscript, Carnegie Mellon University, Pittsburgh, PA, 2005.

19. Rousseau, "Under the table deals." M.H. Lubatkin, W.S. Schulze, Y. Ling, and R.N. Dino, "A behavioral economic framing of agency at private family owner-managed firms," *Journal of Organizational Behavior* (forthcoming, 2005).

20. E.P. Lazear, "Agency, earnings profiles, productivity, and hours restrictions," *American Economic Review* 71 (1981): 606–20.

21. C.J. Ferrante and D.M. Rousseau, "Justice issues in expatriate compensation." Unpublished manuscript, Carnegie Mellon University, Pittsburgh, PA, 2003.

22. R. Frank and P. Cook, *Winner Take All: How More and More Americans Compete for Fewer and Bigger Prizes, Encouraging Economic Waste, Income Inequality, and an Impoverished Cultural Life* (New York: Free Press, 1994).

23. Smoking Gun, http://www.thesmokinggun.com (accessed October 15, 2003). To be fair, it is important to note that not all conditions celebrities bargain for are lavish. Jay Leno, the workaholic host of the *Tonight Show* on NBC, reportedly bargained for *less* vacation time—and 16 million dollars a year (M. Gunther, "The MVP of late night," *Fortune,* February 2004, pp. 102–9).

24. For example, see S. Rosen, "The economics of superstars," *American Economic Review* 71 (1981): 845–58; Frank and Cook, *Winner Take All.*

25. D.M. Rousseau, "Psychological contracts in the United States: Diversity, individualism, and associability in the marketplace," in *Psychological Contracts in Employment: Cross-national Perspectives,* ed. D.M. Rousseau and R. Schalk (Thousand Oaks, CA: Sage, 2000); Rousseau, "The idiosyncratic deal."

26. D.M. Rousseau, V.T. Ho, and T.G. Kim, "I-deals and the psychological contract." Unpublished manuscript, 2004; D.M. Rousseau and T.G. Kim, "I-deals and the employment relationship." Unpublished manuscript, 2004.

27. J. Glaser and S. Hornung, "Mitarbeiterorientierte Flexibilisierung von Arbeit im öffentlichen Dienst. Eine arbeits- und organisationspsychologische Evaluation der Telearbeit in der bayerischen Steuerverwaltung" [Employee-oriented flexibility of work in the public service. A work- and organizational psychological evaluation of telework in the Bavarian tax administration], report no. 77 (Munich: Technical University, Chair of Psychology, 2004).

28. See M.D. Lee, S.M. MacDermid, and M.L. Buck, "Organizational paradigms of reduced-load work: Accommodation, elaboration, and transformation," *Academy of Management Journal* 43 (2000): 1211–26. See also P. Cappelli, "A market-driven approach to retaining talent," *Harvard Business Review* 78 (2000): 103–111, for an array of illustrations on new workplace practices reflecting employee demand for customization. Freeman and Rogers, *What Workers Want.*

29. See, for example, D.J.B. Mitchell, *Human Resource Management: An Economic Approach* (Boston: PWS Kent, 1989); L.S. Kleiman, *Human Resource Management: A Tool for Competitive Advantage* (St. Paul, MN: West, 1997); P. Muchinsky, *Psychology Applied to Work* (Belmont, CA: Thomson/Wadsworth, 2003).

30. Rousseau and Shperling, "Pieces of the action."

31. Rousseau, "Psychological contracts in the United States." See also R.N. Block, P. Berg, and D. Belman, "The economic dimension of the employment relationship," in *The Employment Relationship: Examining Psychological and Contextual Perspectives,* ed. J.A.-M. Coyle-Shapiro, L.M. Shore, M.S. Taylor, and L.E. Tetrick, pp. 94–118 (New York: Oxford University Press, 2004).

32. Cappelli, "A market-driven approach."

33. Block, Berg, and Belman, "The economic dimension of the employment relationship."

34. N. Fondas, "Feminization at work: Career implications," in *The Boundaryless Career: A New Employment Principle for a New Organizational Era*, ed. M.B. Arthur and D.M. Rousseau, pp. 282–93 (New York: Oxford University Press, 1996).

35. J.H. Gilmore and B.J. Pine II, *Markets of One: Creating Customer-Unique Value through Mass Customization* (Boston: Harvard Business School Press, 2000).

36. Wikipedia, http://en.wikipedia.org/wiki/externality (accessed September 27, 2004).

37. R.B. McKersie, "Payment by results systems in the United States," in *International Management Seminar on Forms of Wage and Salary Payments for High Productivity* (Versailles, 1967).

38. D.M. Cowherd and D.I. Levine, "Product quality and pay equity between lower-level employees and top management: An investigation of distributive justice theory," *Administrative Science Quarterly* 37 (1992): 302–20; E.A. Lind and T.R. Tyler, *The Social Psychology of Procedural Justice* (New York: Plenum Press, 1988).

Notes to Chapter 2

1. R.B. Freeman and J. Rogers, *What Workers Want* (Ithaca, NY: ILR Press, 1999).

2. J. Dewey, http://www.Quotationspage.com (accessed June 15, 2004).

3. *Webster's Seventh New Collegiate Dictionary* (Springfield, MA: G and C Merriam, 1970).

4. See also M. Kaminsky, "If only guilt would take a holiday," *Wall Street Journal,* June 4, 2004, p. W15. This article contrasts the American anti-vacation norm with the French practice of regular and extensive vacations.

5. H.A. Simon, "A formal theory of the employment relation," *Econometrica* 19 (1951): 293–305.

6. M.A. Eisenberg, "The limits of cognition and the limits of contract," *Stanford Law Review* 47 (1995): 211–59.

7. Simon, "A formal theory of the employment relation."

8. Ibid.

9. H.A. Simon, *Administrative Behavior,* 4th ed. (New York: Free Press, 1997), p. 10.

10. Simon, *Administrative Behavior*, refers to this as the "right of the last word" (p. 182).

11. Simon, "A formal theory of the employment relation."

12. R. Folger, "Justice and employment: Moral retribution as a contra-subjugation tendency," in *The Employment Relationship: Examining Psychological and Contextual Perspectives,* ed. J.A.-M. Coyle-Shapiro, L.M. Shore, M.S. Taylor, and L.E. Tetrick, pp. 29–47 (New York: Oxford University Press, 2004).

13. J.L. Pearce, "Employability as trustworthiness," in *Relational Wealth: The Advantages of Stability in a Changing Economy,* ed. C. Leana and D.M. Rousseau, pp. 79–90 (New York: Oxford University Press, 2001).

14. A. Wrezniewski and J.E. Dutton, "Crafting a job: Revisioning employees as active crafters of their work," *Academy of Management Review* 26 (2001): 179–201.

15. M. Frese and D. Fay, "Personal initiative: An active performance concept for work in the 21st century," *Research in Organizational Behavior* 23 (2001): 133–87.

16. G.E. Dabos and D.M. Rousseau, "Social interaction patterns shaping employee psychological contracts: Network-wide and local effects," in *Proceedings of the Academy of Management Meetings,* ed. M.K. Weaver (Briarcliff Manor, NY: Academy of Management, 2004).

17. B. Groysberg, A. Nanda, and N. Nohria, "The risky business of hiring stars," *Harvard Business Review* 82, no. 5 (2004): 92–101. Note: Groysberg et al. report only that long-standing stars are more likely to remain with the firm than are newer stars. The attribution that this is due to i-deals is mine.

18. M.R. Pergamit and J.R. Veum, "What is a promotion?" *Industrial and Labor Relations Review* 52 (1999): 581–601.

19. J.E. Rosenbaum, "Tournament mobility: Career patterns in a corporation," *Administrative Science Quarterly* 24 (1979): 220–41.

20. Pergamit and Veum, "What is a promotion?"

21. S. Gael, *Job Analysis: A Guide to Assessing Work Activities* (San Francisco: Jossey-Bass, 1983), p. 115.

22. Freeman and Rogers, *What Workers Want.*

23. *Oxford English Dictionary* (Oxford: Oxford University Press, 1971).

24. C.I. Barnard, *Functions of the Executive* (Cambridge, MA: Harvard University Press, 1938); Simon, *Administrative Behavior.* For a discussion of the ideologies associated with social constructs of management and authority, see M. Guillen, *Models of Management* (Chicago: University of Chicago Press, 1994). Guillen describes models of management that function as ideologies intended to create legitimacy and reinforce credibility of powerful actors. Ideology, Guillen maintains, not only justifies authority but also functions as a cognitive tool to help organization members frame problems so that they can be interpreted, inviting legitimate action and helping managers and workers to make sense of their organizational experiences. The long process of rationalization of work in terms of specified authority relations, according to Guillen, began in the nineteenth century with wage dependency and factory bureaucracy, creating what has been termed *Homo hierarchicus.*

25. Simon, *Administrative Behavior,* p. 201.

26. Simon, *Administrative Behavior,* p. 183. Note that Simon's zone of acceptance is akin to Chester Barnard's notion of zone of indifference; Barnard, *Functions of the Executive,* p. 169.

27. Simon, *Administrative Behavior,* p. 201.

28. *Oxford English Dictionary.*

29. Wrezniewski and Dutton, "Crafting a job."

30. Simon, *Administrative Behavior;* Folger, "Justice and employment."

31. P. Cappelli, *The Changing Nature of Work* (Boston: Harvard Business School Press, 1997).

32. L. Van Dyne and J.B. Ellis, "Job creep: A reactance theory perspective on organizational citizenship behavior as overfulfillment of obligations," in Coyle-Shapiro, Shore, Taylor, and Tetrick, *The Employment Relationship,* pp. 181–205.

33. C.L. Hulin, M. Roznowski, and D. Hachiya, "Alternative opportunities and withdrawal decisions: Empirical and theoretical discrepancies," *Psychological Bulletin* 97 (1985): 233–50.

34. S. Parker, "Enhancing role breadth self-efficacy: The roles of job enrichment and other organizational interventions," *Journal of Applied Psychology* 83 (1998): 835–52; D.M. Rousseau and S.A. Tijoriwala, "What's a good reason to change? Motivated reasoning and social accounts in promoting organizational change," *Journal of Applied Psychology* 84 (1999): 514–28.

35. D.M. Rousseau, "Changing the deal while keeping the people," *Academy of Management Executive* 10, no. 1 (1996): 50–61.

36. See the classic *Harvard Business Review* article by R.H. Schaeffer, "Demand better results and get them" (March–April 1991): 142–49.

37. Rousseau, "Changing the deal while keeping the people."

38. See, for example, A.M. Mohrman, S.A. Mohrman, G.E. Ledford, T.G. Cummings, and E. Lawler and Associates, *Large-Scale Organizational Change* (San Francisco: Jossey-Bass, 1989); C. Hendry, "Understanding and creating whole organizational change through learning theory," *Human Relations* 49 (1996): 621–41.

39. See Parker, "Enhancing role breadth self-efficacy"; Rousseau and Tijorwala, "What's a good reason to change?"

40. D.A. Lax and J.K. Sebenius, *The Manager as Negotiator: Bargaining for Cooperation and Competitive Gain* (New York: Free Press, 1986).

41. P.M. Blau, *Exchange and Power in Social Life* (New York: John Wiley and Sons, 1964); G.E. Dabos and D.M. Rousseau, "Mutuality and reciprocity in the psychological contracts of employees and employers," *Journal of Applied Psychology* 89 (2004): 52–72.

42. Lax and Sebenius, *The Manager as Negotiator,* p. 21.

43. R.L. Florida, *The Rise of the Creative Class: And How It Is Transforming Work, Leisure, Community, and Everyday Life* (New York: Basic Books, 2002).

44. As quoted by J. de Leede, J. Kees Looise, and M. van Riemdsijk, "Balancing between collectivism and individualism: The effects of decentralization and industrialization on Dutch employment relations." (Paper presented at the Thirteenth World Congress of International Industrial Relations Association, Berlin, September 2003.)

45. M. Minkler and R.P. Biller, "Role shock: A tool for conceptualizing stresses accompanying disruptive role transitions," *Human Relations* 32 (1979): 327–51; L.L. Levesque, "Role creation processes in start-up firms" (Ph.D. diss., Carnegie Mellon University, 2001).

46. Levesque, "Role creation processes in start-up firms," p. 89.

47. J. Cashman, F. Dansereau, G. Graen, and W.J. Haga, "Organizational understructure and leadership: A longitudinal investigation of managerial role-making process," *Organizational Behavior and Human Performance* 15 (1976): 278–96; G. Graen and J.F. Cashman, "A role-making model of leadership in formal organizations: A developmental approach," in *Leadership Frontiers,* ed. J.G. Hunt and L.L. Larson, pp. 143–65 (Carbondale: Southern Illinois University Press, 1975).

48. Max Weber, *The Protestant Ethic and the Spirit of Capitalism* (London: Harper Collins Academic, 1930); *Economy and society: An outline of interpretive sociology.* 2 vols. Edited by G. Roth and C. Wittich (Berkeley: University of California Press, 1978). The issue in highly bureaucratic organizations is that idiosyncratic arrangements are often kept secret to avoid challenging the rule-driven focus of such firms. The process can entail indirectly feeling out the boss, and monitoring to see what special treatment others get. The slippery slope of i-deals in highly bureaucratic firms is that it is often difficult to differentiate idiosyncratic arrangements from their dysfunctional counterparts, preferential treatment and rule breaking (see Chapter 3). Workers with specialized roles that are difficult to alter and whose jobs cannot be done by anyone else are often allowed to alter their roles to maintain their satisfaction.

49. Rule breaking is a form of flexibility if the employer does not sanction (or catch) this deviance. It can constitute a form of unauthorized employment arrangement (addressed more fully in Chapter 3). Violating formal rules without offsetting conditions (such as framing the changes as experimental) is a form of deviance and does not constitute an i-deal.

Notes to Chapter 3

1. T. Gray, "Ode on the death of a favorite cat," in *Macmillan Dictionary of Quotation* (Edison, NJ: Chartwell, 2000).

2. J. Racine, "Phedre" (1677), act 4, scene 2, in *Bartlett's Familiar Quotations,* 15th ed. (Boston: Little, Brown, 1980).

3. M. Lewis, *The Exposed Self* (1992), chap. 11, cited in *Columbia World of Quotations* (1996), www.bartleby.com.66/18/35918.html.

4. D.M. Rousseau, "Under the table deals: Idiosyncratic, preferential or unauthorized?" in *Darkside of Organizational Behavior,* ed. R. Griffin and A. O'Leary-Kelly, pp. 262–90 (San Francisco: Jossey-Bass, 2004).

5. P. Friedlander, *The Emergence of a UAW Local 1936–1939* (Pittsburgh, PA: University of Pittsburgh Press, 1975), p. 33.

6. J.L. Pearce, *Organization and Management in the Embrace of Government* (Mahwah, NJ: Erlbaum, 2001); J.P. Wright, *On a Clear Day You Can See General Motors: John Z. DeLorean's Look Inside the Automotive Giant* (Grosse Point, MI: Wright Enterprises, 1979).

7. N. Khatri, E.W.K. Tsang, and T.M. Begley, "Croneyism: The downside of social networking," in *Proceedings of the Academy of Management Meetings,* ed. D. Nagao (Briarcliff Manor, NY: Academy of Management, 2003).

8. J.L. Pearce, I. Branyicki, and G. Bigley, "Person-based reward systems," *Journal of Organizational Behavior* 15 (1994): 261–82.

9. In the case of union busting, buying support to throw an election, while ostensibly serving the employer's interest, undermines due process, which arguably is not in the firm's long-term interest where resolving labor conflict is concerned. See Friedlander, *The Emergence of a UAW Local 1936–1939.* Also see M. Williams and J.E. Dutton, "Corrosive political climates: The heavy toll of negative political behavior in organizations," in *The Pressing Problems of Modern Organizations: Transforming the Agenda for Research and Practice,* ed. R.E. Quinn, R.M. O'Neill, and L. St. Clair, pp. 3–30 (New York: American Management Association, 1999); J. Clarke, "Just when you thought it was safe—Dare you swim in the shark infested waters of office politics," *The Guardian,* April 24, 1999, p. 3.

10. D.M. Rousseau and T.G. Kim, "I-deals and the employment relationship." Unpublished manuscript, Carnegie Mellon University, Pittsburgh, PA, 2004.

11. R.B. Freeman and J. Rogers, *What Workers Want* (Ithaca, NY: ILR Press, 1999), p. 19. Note, however, that gender and race may still be important, particularly in terms of perceived opportunities for and appropriateness of negotiation. See, for example, L. Babcock and S. Laschever, *Women Don't Ask* (Princeton, NJ: Princeton University Press, 2003).

12. G.R. Ferris and K.M. Kacmar, "Perceptions of organizational politics," *Journal of Management* 18 (1992): 93–116; G.R. Ferris, J.F. Brand, S. Brand, K.M. Rowland, D.C. Gilmore, T.R. King, K.M. Kacmar, and C.A. Burton, "Politics and control in organizations," *Advances in Group Process* 10 (1993): 83–111; Rousseau, "Under the table deals."

13. D.M. Rousseau, *Managing Diversity for High Performance* (New York: Business Week/Advance, 1996).

14. L.M. Shore, L.E. Tetrick, S. Taylor, J.A.-M. Coyle-Shapiro, R. Liden, J. McLean Parks, E. Wolfe Morrison, et al., "The employee-organization relationship: A timely concept in a period of transition," in *Research in Personnel and Human Resource Management,* vol. 23, ed. J. Martucchio, pp. 291–370 (San Diego, CA: Elsevier, 2004).

15. http://www.att.com/hr/life/culture.html (accessed May 15, 2004).

16. J.N. Cleveland, J.L. Barnes-Farrell, and J.M. Ratz, "Accommodation in the workplace," *Human Resource Management Review* 7 (1997): 77–107; A. Colella, "Coworker distributive fairness judgments of the workplace accommodation of employees with disabilities," *Academy of Management Review* 26 (2001): 100–116.

17. R.C. Hollinger and J.P. Clark, *Theft by Employees* (Lexington, MA: Lexington Books, 1983); J. Greenberg and K.S. Scott, "Why do workers bite the hand that feeds them? Employee theft as a social exchange process," in *Research in Organizational Behavior,* vol. 18, ed. B.M. Staw and L.L. Cummings, pp. 111–56 (Greenwich, CT: JAI Press, 1996).

18. Greenberg and Scott, "Why do workers bite the hand that feeds them?"

19. J. Ditton, "Perks, pilferage, and the fiddle: The historical structure of invisible wages," *Theory and Society* 4 (1997): 39–71.

20. J. Ditton, *Part-Time Crime: An Ethnography, of Fiddling and Pilferage* (London: Macmillan, 1997).

21. D.M. Rousseau, *Psychological Contracts in Organizations: Understanding Written and Unwritten Agreements* (Newbury Park, CA: Sage, 1994).

22. B. Gerhart and G.T. Milkovich, "Employee compensation: Research and practice," in *Handbook of Industrial and Organizational Psychology,* 2nd ed., ed. M.D. Dunnette and L.M. Hough, pp. 481–569 (Palo Alto, CA: Consulting Psychologists Press, 1991).

23. R.H. Frank, *Choosing the Right Pond: Human Behavior and the Quest for Status* (New York: Oxford University Press, 1985).

24. Ibid., p. 8.

25. Ibid.

26. Frank Thomas as quoted in I. Berkow, "'The big hurt': Feeling pained by his contract," *New York Times,* February 26, 2001, p. D2.

27. D. Pink, *Free Agent Nation: The Future of Working for Yourself* (New York: Warner Business Books, 2001).

28. J.W. Thibaut and L. Walker, *Procedural Justice: A Psychological Analysis* (Hillsdale, NJ: Erlbaum, 1975); S.S. Masterson, K. Lewis, B.M. Goldman, and M.S. Taylor, "Integrating justice and social exchange: The differing effects of fair procedures and treatment on work relationships," *Academy of Management Journal* 43 (2000): 738–48.

29. E.A. Lind and T.R. Tyler, *The Social Psychology of Procedural Justice* (New York: Plenum Press, 1988); J. Greenberg, *The Quest for Justice* (Thousand Oaks, CA: Sage, 1996).

30. Freeman and Rogers, *What Workers Want,* p. 100.

31. G.S. Leventhal, "The distribution of rewards and resources in groups and organizations," in *Advances in Experimental Social Psychology,* vol. 9, ed. L. Berkowitz and E. Walster, pp. 91–131 (New York: Academic Press, 1976).

32. Greenberg, *The Quest for Justice.*

33. J.L. Pearce, I. Branyiczki, and G. Bigley, "Insufficient bureaucracy: Trust and commitment in particularistic organizations," *Organizational Science* 11 (2000): 148–62.

34. M.D. Lee, S.M. MacDermid, and M.L. Buck, "Organizational paradigms of reduced-load work: Accommodation, elaboration, and transformation," *Academy of Management Journal* 43 (2000): 1211–26.

35. M. Hammers, "A 'family-friendly' backlash," *Workplace Management* (August 2003): 77–79.

36. M.W. Barringer and G.T. Milkovich, "A theoretical exploration of the adoption and design of flexible benefit plans: A case of human resource innovation," *Academy of Management Review* 23 (1997): 305–24.

37. P.S. Goodman, "An examination of the referents used in the evaluation of pay," *Organizational Behavior and Human Performance* 12 (1974): 170–95.

38. G.T. Milkovich and P.H. Anderson, "Management compensation and secrecy policies" *Personnel Psychology*, 25 (1972): 293–302; C.M. Futrell and O.C. Jenkins "Pay secrecy versus pay disclosure for salesman: A longitudinal study," *Journal of Marketing Research*, 15 (1978): 214–219; D. Farnham "Pay, conditions, and pay determination for heads and professors in the new universities," *Higher Education Review*, 28 (Fall 1995): 20–33. See also J.N. Baron and D.M. Kreps, *Strategic Human Resources: Frameworks for General Managers* (New York: John Wiley and Sons, 1999) for a discussion of some unresolved issues surrounding pay secrecy.

39. D.M. Rousseau, S.L. Robinson, and M.S. Kraatz, "Renegotiating the psychological contract" (Paper presented at the Society for Industrial/Organizational Psychology meetings, Montreal, 1992).

40. D.M. Rousseau, V.T. Ho, and T.G. Kim, "I-deals and the psychological contract." Unpublished manuscript, 2004; D.M. Rousseau and T.G. Kim, "I-deals and the employment relationship." Unpublished manuscript, Carnegie Mellon University, Pittsburgh, PA, 2004.

41. R.J. Bies and J. Moag, "Interactional justice: Communication criteria of fairness," in *Research on Negotiation in Organizations*, vol. 1, ed. R.J. Lewicki, B.H. Sheppard, and M.H. Bazerman, pp. 43–55 (Greenwich, CT: JAI Press, 1986).

42. Masterson, Lewis, Goldman, and Taylor, "Integrating justice and social exchange."

43. S.B. Sitkin and R.J. Bies, "Social accounts in conflict situations: Using explanations to manage conflict," *Human Relations* 46 (1993): 349–70.

44. Bies and Moag, "Interactional justice."

45. See K.A. Hegtvedt and C. Johnson, "Justice beyond the individual: A future with legitimation," *Social Psychology Quarterly* 63 (2000): 298–311, esp. p. 303. Also see M. Zelditch and H.A. Walker, "Legitimacy and the stability of authority," *Advances in Group Process* 1 (1984): 1–25; and S.M. Dornbush and W.R. Scott, *Evaluation and Exercise of Authority* (San Francisco: Jossey-Bass, 1975).

46. H.A. Simon, *Administrative Behavior,* 4th ed. (New York: Free Press, 1997).

Notes to Chapter 4

1. R. Shaw as quoted in J. Gleick, *Chaos: The Making of a New Science* (New York: Viking, 1987), p. 262.

2. A. Russell Hochschild, *Time Bind: When Work Becomes Home and Home Becomes Work* (New York: Metropolitan, 1997). "Amerco" is the fictitious name given to Corning Incorporated in *Time Bind.*

3. Ibid., p. 79.

4. L.A. Perlow, *Finding Time: How Corporations, Individuals and Families Can Benefit from New Work Practices* (Ithaca: ILR Press, 1997).

5. Ibid., pp. 41–42.

6. I am not above borrowing a catchy phrase and must acknowledge that the inspiration for this statement is C.A. Thompson, L. Beauvais, and H.K. Carter, "Work-family programs: Only slow-trackers need apply? An investigation of the impact of work-family culture" (Paper presented at Academy of Management meetings, Boston, 1997).

7. S.J. Behson, "Informal work accommodations to family: A potential coping strategy for reducing the work stress associated with work-family conflict among professional employees" (Paper presented at Academy of Management meetings, 1997).

8. J.O. Berry and J.M. Rao, "Balancing employment and fatherhood: A systems perspective," *Journal of Family Issues* 18 (1997): 386–402.

9. P.M. Christensen, "Toward a comprehensive work/life strategy," in *Integrating Work and Family: Challenges and Choices for a Changing World,* ed. S. Parasuraman and J.H. Greenhaus, pp. 25–37 (Westport, CT: Quorum Books, 1997); S. Miller, "The role of a juggler," in Parasuraman and Greenhaus, *Integrating Work and Family,* pp. 38–47.

10. Behson, "Informal work accommodations to family."

11. S.I. Grover, "Predicting the perceived fairness of parental leave policies," *Journal of Applied Psychology* 76 (1991): 247–55; D. Harris, "The fairness furor," *Working Mother,* September 1997, pp. 28–32.

12. A.M. Hayashi, "Mommy-track backlash: HBR case study," *Harvard Business Review,* March 2001, pp. 33–42.

13. S.L. Grover and K.J. Crooker, "Who appreciates family-responsiveness human resource policies," *Journal of Applied Psychology* 48 (1995): 271–88.

14. T.D. Allen, "Family-supportive work environments: The role of organizational perceptions," *Journal of Vocational Behavior* 58 (2001): 414–35.

15. Grover and Crooker, "Who appreciates family-responsiveness human resource policies"; E.E. Kossek and C. Ozeki, "Bridging the work-family policy and productivity gap: A literature review," *Community Work and Family* 2, no. 1 (1999): 7–32.

16. Grover and Crooker, "Who appreciates family-responsiveness human resource policies."

17. A.S. Miner, "Idiosyncratic jobs in formalized organizations," *Administrative Science Quarterly* 32 (1987): 327–51.

18. M. Granovetter, *Getting a Job: A Study of Contacts and Careers,* 2nd ed. (Chicago: University of Chicago Press, 1995).

19. Miner, "Idiosyncratic jobs in formalized organizations."

20. Laurie Levesque, "Role creation processes in start-up firms" (PhD diss., Graduate School of Industrial Administration, Carnegie Mellon University, 2001).

21. Laurie Levesque, personal communication, 2001.

22. K.H. Weick, "Enactment and the boundaryless career: Organizing as we work," in *The Boundaryless Career: A New Employment Principle for a New Organizational Era,* ed. M.B. Arthur and D.M. Rousseau, pp. 40–57 (New York: Oxford University Press, 1996). For early discussion of how weak versus strong situations amplify or suppress the impact of individual differences, see W. Mischel, *Personality and Assessment* (New York: John Wiley and Sons, 1968).

23. D. Katz and R.H. Kahn, *Social Psychology of Organizations,* 2nd ed. (New York: McGraw Hill, 1978); R.L. Kahn, D.M. Wolfe, R.P. Quinn, J.D. Snoek, and R.A.Rosenthal, *Organizational Stress: Studies of Role Conflict and Ambiguity* (New York: John Wiley and Sons, 1964); B. Biddle, *Role Theory: Expectations, Identities, and Behaviors* (New York: Academic Press, 1979); Levesque, "Role creation processes in start-up firms."

24. M. Abrahamson, *Interpersonal Accommodation* (Princeton, NJ: Van Nostrand, 1966).

25. D. Feldman, "A contingency theory of socialization," *Administrative Science Quarterly* 2 (1976): 433–51, esp. p. 446.

26. Ibid.

27. A. Wrzesniewski and J.E. Dutton, "Crafting a job: Revisioning employees as active crafters of their work," *Academy of Management Review* 26 (2001): 179–201.

28. J. Cashman, F. Dansereau, G. Graen, and W.J. Haga, "Organizational understructure and leadership: A longitudinal investigation of managerial role-making process," *Organizational Behavior and Human Performance* 15 (1976): 278–96; G. Graen and J.F. Cashman, "A role-making model of leadership in formal organizations: A developmental approach," in *Leadership Frontiers,* ed. J.G. Hunt and L.L. Larson, pp. 143–165 (Carbondale: Southern Illinois University, 1975).

29. D.M. Rousseau, "LMX meets the psychological contract: Looking inside the black box of leader-member exchange," in *Leadership: The Multiple-Level Approaches,* ed. F. Dansereau and F. Yammarino (Vol. 23, 149–54) (Greenwich, CT: JAI Press, 2000).

30. Arthur and Rousseau, *The Boundaryless Career;* D.M. Rousseau and Z. Shperling, "Pieces of the action: Ownership and the changing employment relationship," *Academy of Management Review* 28 (2003): 115–34; D.M. Rousseau and Z. Shperling, "Ownership and the changing employment relationship: Why stylized notions of labor no longer generally apply. Reply to Zardkoohi and Paetzgold," *Academy of Management Review,* 29 (2004): 562–569.

31. M. Fugate and B. Ashford, "Employability: The construct, its dimensions, and applications," in *Proceedings of the Academy of Management* meetings, ed. D. Nagao (Briarcliff Manor, NY: Academy of Management, 2003).

32. Arthur and Rousseau, *The Boundaryless Career.*

33. P.H. Mirvis and D.T. Hall, "Psychological success and the boundaryless career," in Arthur and Rousseau, *The Boundaryless Career,* pp. 237–55.

34. D.T. Hall, *Careers in Organizations* (Glenview, IL: Scott Foresman, 1976), p. 201.

35. D.M. Rousseau, *Psychological Contracts in Organizations: Understanding Written and Unwritten Agreements* (Newbury Park, CA: Sage, 1995).

36. G.E. Dabos and D.M. Rousseau, "Mutuality and reciprocity in the psychological contracts of employee and employer," *Journal of Applied Psychology* 89 (2004): 52–72.

37. S.L. Robinson, "Trust and breach of the psychological contract," *Administrative Science Quarterly* 41 (1996): 574–99; W.H. Turnley and D.C. Feldman, "The impact of psychological contract violations on exit, voice, loyalty, and neglect," *Human Relations* 52 (1999): 895–922.

38. D.M. Rousseau and S. Tijoriwala, "What's a good reason to change? Motivated reasoning and social accounts in promoting organizational change," *Journal of Applied Psychology* 84 (1999): 514–28.

39. D.M. Rousseau and T.G. Kim, "I-deals and the Employment Relationship." Unpublished manuscript, Carnegie Mellon University, Pittsburgh, PA, 2004.

40. In support of this assertion, Dabos and Rousseau, "Mutuality and reciprocity in the psychological contracts of employer and employer," found transactional psychological contracts on the part of both employer and employee to be negatively related to worker contributions, whether subjectively or objectively measured, and work-related attitudes. In contrast are the findings of C. Hui, C. Lee, and D.M. Rousseau, "Psychological contract and organizational citizenship behaviors in China: Exploring generalizability and instrumentality," *Journal of Applied Psychology* 89 (2004): 311–21, which reports that in mainland Chinese workers, transactional psychological contracts were associated with roughly comparable levels of contributions (in this case, of citizenship behavior) to relational or balanced contracts. The difference between these was attributed to the broader role definition characteristic of traditional Chinese authority relations.

41. G.E. Dabos and D.M. Rousseau, "Social interaction patterns shaping employee psychological contracts: Network-wide and local effects," in *Academy of Management Best Paper Proceedings,* ed, K.M. Weaver (Briarcliff Manor, NY: Academy of Management, 2004).

42. D.M. Rousseau, *Psychological Contracts in Organization: Understanding Written and Unwritten Agreements* (Newbury Park, CA: Sage, 1995); Dabos and Rousseau, "Social interaction patterns shaping employee psychological contracts."

43. Dabos and Rousseau, "Social interaction patterns shaping employee psychological contracts."

44. Rousseau, *Psychological Contracts in Organization*; N. Nicholson and G. Johns, "The Absence of Culture and the Psychological Contract: Who's in Charge of Absence?" *Academy of Management Review* 10 (1985): 397–407.

45. D.M. Rousseau, "Surprises in psychological contract research." Paper presented at British Psychological Society's Division of Occupational Psychology meeting, Stratford-upon-Avon, January 2004.

46. Jason Merante, personal communication, 2000.

47. Rousseau, "Surprises in psychological contract research."

48. Rousseau, *Psychological Contracts in Organization.*

49. MBA students participating in study described in Rousseau, Ho, and Kim, "I-deals and the psychological contract."

50. There is recognition of idiosyncratic or individual employment contracting in economics. See O.E. Williamson, M.L. Wachter, and J.E Harris, "Understanding the employment relation: The analysis of idiosyncratic exchange," *Bell Journal of Economics,* 6 (1975): 250–78. However, I have not found further development of this concept in the context of employment.

Notes to Chapter 5

1. L. Babcock and S. Laschever, *Women Don't Ask* (Princeton, NJ: Princeton University Press, 2003), p. 59.

2. M.B. Arthur and D.M. Rousseau, *The Boundaryless Career: A New Employment Principle for a New Organizational Era* (New York: Oxford University Press, 1996).

3. C.J. Ferrante and D.M. Rousseau, "Expatriate compensation." Unpublished manuscript, Carnegie Mellon University, Pittsburgh, PA, 2003.

4. D.M. Rousseau and R. Schalk, *Psychological Contracts in Employment: Cross-National Perspectives* (Newbury Park, CA: Sage, 2000).

5. J.M. Schlesinger, "Operational serenade: Laying groundwork for Reagan's funeral," *Wall Street Journal,* June 10, 2004, pp. A1, A4.

6. J. Gionfriddo and L. Dhingra, "Making allowances: NIIT retains top talent," *Human Resource Management International Digest* 8, no. 4 (2000): 9–11; P. Gwynne, "Desperately seeking scientists at US technology firms," *Research Technology Management* 41, no. 1 (1998): 4–6.

7. D.M. Rousseau, V.T. Ho, and T.G. Kim, "I-deals and the psychological contract." Unpublished manuscript, Carnegie Mellon University, Pittsburgh, PA, 2004.

8. G.B. Graen and T.A. Scandura, "Toward a psychology of dynamic organizing," in *Research in Organizational Behavior,* vol. 9, ed. L.L. Cummings and B.M. Staw, pp. 175–208 (Greenwich, CT: JAI Press, 1987).

9. D.M. Rousseau and T.G. Kim, "I-deals and the employment relationship. Unpublished manuscript, Carnegie Mellon University, Pittsburgh, PA, 2004.

10. Ibid.; Rousseau, Ho, and Kim, "Ideals and the psychological contract."

11. D.M. Rousseau, S.L. Robinson and M.S. Kraatz, "Renegotiating the psychological contract" (Paper presented at Society for Industrial/Organizational Psychology meetings, Montreal, 1992).

12. J.B. Olson-Buchanan and W.R. Boswell, "The role of loyalty and formality in voicing discontent," *Journal of Applied Psychology* 87 (2002): 1167–74.

13. L. Thompson, *The Heart and Mind of the Negotiator*, 2nd ed. (Upper Saddle River, NJ: Prentice-Hall, 2001), p. 25.

14. Individual negotiators differ in terms of the situations in which they believe it is appropriate to bargain; Babcock and Laschever, *Women Don't Ask.* However, though we might expect wide variation in the circumstances in which individual employees

proactively bargain, employees are likely to show greater similarity in their attempts to negotiate reactively. Reactive i-deals are more commonly triggered by situations where it is in the employer's interest to grant employee requests.

15. Rousseau and Kim, "I-deals and the employment relationship"; Rousseau, Kim and Ho, "Ideals and the psychological contract."

16. Rousseau and Kim, "I-deals and the employment relationship."

17. Ibid.

18. Rousseau, Ho, and Kim, " I-deals and the psychological contract"; Rousseau and Kim, "I-deals and the employment relationship."

19. Rousseau, Robinson, and Kraatz, "Renegotiating the psychological contract."

20. R.C. Huseman, J.D. Hatfield, and E.W. Miles, "A new perspective on equity theory: The equity sensitivity construct," *Academy of Management Review* 12 (1987): 222–34.

21. R. M. Dawes, *House of Cards: Psychology and Psychotherapy Built on Myth* (New York: Free Press, 1994) p. 288.

22. Huseman, Hatfield, and Miles, "A new perspective on equity theory."

23. L. Baxter and W. Wilmot, "Secret tests: Social strategies for acquiring information about the state of relationships," *Human Communication Research* 11 (1984): 171–201; D.M. Rousseau, *Psychological Contracts in Organizations: Understanding Written and Unwritten Agreements*, pp. 119–20 (Newbury Park, CA: Sage, 1995).

24. L. Suein Hwang, "For some employees, great parking spaces fulfill a primal need." *Wall Street Journal,* June 26, 2002, p. B1.

25. G.R. Ferris, F.R. Blass, C. Douglas, R.W. Kolodinsky, and D.C. Treadway, "Personal reputation in organizations," in *Organizational Behavior: The State of the Science,* 2nd ed., ed. J. Greenberg (Mahwah, NJ: Lawrence Erlbaum Associates, 2003).

Notes to Chapter 6

1. T. Draxe, 1663, as quoted in H.L. Mencken, *A New Dictionary of Quotations on Historical Principles from Ancient and Modern Sources* (New York: Knopf, 1991), p. 65.

2. V.S. Clark, "Making sense of part-time professional work arrangements" (PhD diss., University of British Columbia, 1998).

3. Ibid.

4. L. Thompson, *The Heart and Mind of the Negotiator,* 2nd ed. (Upper Saddle River, NJ: Prentice-Hall, 2001).

5. Ibid.

6. L. Babcock and S. Laschever, *Women Don't Ask* (Princeton, NJ: Princeton University Press, 2003).

7. In some cases the existence of precedent can mean that the arrangement is not an i-deal, depending on whether the precedent is in the same setting, in a closely related area or department of the same firm, or in a more distant location, for which employment practices and policies are not comparable.

8. Babcock and Laschever, *Women Don't Ask.*

9. Ibid.

10. Ibid., p. 146.

11. D.M. Rousseau and T.G. Kim, "I-deals and the employment relationship." Unpublished manuscript, Carnegie Mellon University, Pittsburgh, PA, 2004.

12. M. Freese and D. Fay, "Personal initiative: An active performance concept for work in the 21st century," *Research in Organizational Behavior* 23 (2003): 133–87.

13. A. Rafaeli, "Employment advertising and employment socialization" (manuscript, Technion Institute, Haifa, Israel, 2003).

14. Peter Cappelli, personal communication, Harvard Business School Conference on Careers Evolution, London, June 2002.

15. A. Russell Hochshild, *Time Bind: When Work Becomes Home and Home Becomes Work* (New York: Metropolitan, 1997).

16. M. Wheatley, *Leadership and the New Science: Discovering Order in the Chaotic World* (San Francisco: Berrett Koehler, 1999); R. Marion, *The Edge of Organization: Chaos and Complexity Theories of Formal Social Systems* (Thousand Oaks, CA: Sage, 1999), p. 221.

17. C. Argyris and D.A. Schoen, *Organizational Learning II* (Reading, MA: Addison-Wesley, 1996).

18. Wheatley, *Leadership and the New Science,* pp. 99–100.

19. Marion, *The Edge of Organization.*

20. H.A. Simon, *Administrative Behavior,* 4th ed. (New York: Free Press, 1997).

21. Babcock and Laschever, *Women Don't Ask,* p. 151.

22. D. Thomas and M. Higgins, "Mentoring and the boundaryless career: Lessons from the minority experience," in *The Boundaryless Career: A New Employment Principal for a New Organizational Era,* ed. M.B. Arthur and D.M. Rousseau, pp. 268–81 (New York: Oxford University Press, 1996).

23. C.J. Ferrante and D.M. Rousseau, "Expatriate compensation and fairness." Unpublished manuscript, Carnegie Mellon University, 2003.

24. V.T. Ho, "Evaluations of psychological contract fulfillment: The social network perspective" (PhD diss., Graduate School of Industrial Administration, Carnegie Mellon University, 2002).

25. See, for example, S. Nollen and H. Axel, *Managing Contingent Workers: How to Reap Benefits and Reduce the Risks* (New York: AMACOM, 1996), which advises the downplaying of social contact between workers with different deals.

26. Thompson, *The Heart and Mind of the Negotiator.*

27. L. Baxter and W. Wilmot, "Secret tests: Social strategies for acquiring information about the state of relationships," *Human Communications Research* 11 (1984): 171–201.

28. R.C. Huseman, J.D. Hatfield, and E.W. Miles, "A new perspective on equity theory: The equity sensitivity construct," *Academy of Management Review* 12 (1987): 222–34.

29. Clark, "Making sense of part-time professional work arrangements."

30. Ibid., p. 68.

31. Ibid.

32. Ibid., p. 64.

33. Ibid., p. 82.

34. Thompson, *The Heart and Mind of the Negotiator.*

35. Ibid.

36. *Oxford English Dictionary* (Oxford: Oxford University Press, 1971).

37. Politeness theory developed from the work of P. Brown and S.C. Levinson, *Politeness: Some Universals in Language Usage* (New York: Cambridge University Press, 1987). It specifies the dynamics by which individuals communicate with others to obtain their cooperation.

38. Ibid.

39. Song Mei Lee-Wong, *Politeness and Face in Chinese Culture* (Frankfurt: Peter Lang, 2000); D.A. Morand, "Language and power: An empirical analysis of linguistic strategies used in superior-subordinate communication," *Journal of Organizational Behavior* 21 (2000): 235–48; N. Ambady, J. Koo, F. Lee, and R. Rosenthal, "More than words: Linguistic and nonlinguistic politeness in two cultures," *Journal of Personality*

and Social Psychology 70 (1996): 996–1011. Politeness theory has been found to generalize across cultures, with its rules applying in the different cultural contexts that shape the nature of relative power, social distance, and imposition. We note that Ambady and her colleagues found that Americans' strategies were influenced more by the content of the message, while those of Koreans were influenced more by relational cues.

40. Brown and Levinson, *Politeness*.

41. L.M. Shore, personal communication, September 2003 regarding research findings on employee requests.

42. Thompson, *The Heart and Mind of the Negotiator,* p. 67.

43. Ibid.

44. Babcock and Laschever, *Women Don't Ask.*

45. Thompson, *The Heart and Mind of the Negotiator*, p. 15.

46. R. Fisher, W. Ury, and B. Patton, *Getting to Yes,* 2nd ed. (New York: Penguin, 1991).

47. Thompson, *The Heart and Mind of the Negotiator*, pp. 40–42. Similarly, temp workers commonly use multiple placement agencies to get themselves the best deal. J. Krasas Rogers, *Temps: The Many Faces of the Changing Workplace* (Ithaca, NY: ILR Press, 2000), p. 109.

48. Clark, "Making sense of part-time professional work arrangements," pp. 71, 76, 78.

49. Ibid.

50. Babcock and Laschever, *Women Don't Ask.*

51. Thompson, *The Heart and Mind of the Negotiator.*

52. Levesque, "Role creation processes in start-up firms" (PhD diss., Graduate School of Industrial Administration, Carnegie Mellon University, 2001), p. 40.

53. Clark, "Making sense of part-time professional work arrangements," p. 71.

54. In termination-related i-deals, threat is implied if not explicit. Some workers may indeed use hard tactics in this case since it is uncertain whether the relationship will continue.

55. M. Fichman, "Straining toward trust: Some constraints on studying trust in organizations," *Journal of Organizational Behavior* 23 (2003): 133–58.

56. D.H. Pink, *Free Agent Nation: The Future of Working for Yourself* (New York: Warner, 2001), p. 177, citing Deal and Kennedy, *The New Corporate Cultures: Revitalizing the American Workplace after Downsizing, Mergers, and Reengineering* (New York: Perseus, 1999).

57. Babcock and Laschever, *Women Don't Ask.*

58. Wilkie Collins, *Woman in White* (London: E.P. Dutton, 1924), p. 133.

59. Clark, "Making sense of part-time professional work arrangements," reports that part-time professionals had relatively elaborate ways of managing expectations, consistent with the practices of contract making. See also D.M. Rousseau, *Psychological Contracts in Organizations: Understanding Written and Unwritten Agreements* (Newbury Park, CA: Sage, 1995).

60. P.D. Sherer and L.A. Coakley, "Developing your part time employee practices," *Workforce Management,* p. 5. http://www.workforce.com/archive/feature/22/24/48 (accessed February 6, 2004).

61. Clark, "Making sense of part-time professional work arrangements."

62. Ibid., pp. 103–7.

63. Rousseau, *Psychological Contracts in Organizations.*

64. S. Shellenbarger, "The incredible shrinking family leave: Pressed bosses are cutting into time off," *Wall Street Journal,* October 17, 2002, p. D1.

65. Sue Vinncombe, Personal communication at Career Evolution Conference sponsored by Harvard Business School, London, June 2002.

66. P.S. Goodman, *Missing Organizational Linkages* (Newbury Park, CA: Sage,

2001); P.S. Goodman and D.M. Rousseau, "Organizational change that produces results: The linkage approach," *Academy of Management Executive* 18 (2004), 7–21.
67. Clark, "Making sense of part-time professional work arrangements."

Notes to Chapter 7

1. *Bartlett's Familiar Quotations* 15th ed. (Boston: Little, Brown, 1980), p. 508.
2. Other third parties can include prospective job applicants and future workers for whom i-deals create legacy effects by setting new standards or altering beliefs about what is expected or negotiable; stockholders who witness large outlays of company resources to attract, motivate, and retain key individuals; and the general public, whose attitudes toward a firm, or firms in general, can be impacted by i-deals that appear excessive, outlandish, or in otherwise in breach of shared beliefs and norms.
3. J.R. Meindl, "Managing to be fair: An exploration of values, motives, and leadership," *Administrative Science Quarterly* 34 (1989): 252–76.
4. R.M. Landes, J.B. Rebitzer, and L.J Taylor, "Rat race redux: Adverse selection in the determination of work hours in law firms," *American Economic Review* 86 (1996): 329–48.
5. "Dual-career ladders: Keeping technical talent on track," *HR Focus* 69, no. 12 (1992): 24.
6. V. Corwin, T.B. Lawrence, and P.J. Frost, "Five strategies of successful part-time work," *Harvard Business Review* (July–August 2001): 121–27; T.B. Lawrence and V. Corwin, "Being there: The acceptance and marginalization of part-time professional employees," *Journal of Organizational Behavior* 24 (2003): 923–43.
7. S. Nollen and H. Axel, *Managing Contingent Workers: How to Reap the Benefits and Reduce the Risks* (New York: AMACOM, 1996).
8. J. Greenberg, M.-E. Roberge, V.T. Ho, and D.M. Rousseau, "Fairness in idiosyncratic work arrangements: Justice as an 'i-deal,'" in *Research in Personnel and Human Resources Management,* vol. 23, ed. J. Martocchio, pp. 1–34 (San Diego, CA: Elsevier, 2004).
9. D.M. Rousseau, *Psychological Contracts in Organizations: Understanding Written and Unwritten Agreements* (Newbury Park, CA: Sage, 1995).
10. Ibid.
11. K.A. Wade-Benzoni, H. Sondak, and A. Galinsky, "Leaving a legacy: Intergenerational allocations of benefits and burdens." Unpublished manuscript, Fuqua School, Duke University, Durham, North Carolina, 2004.
12. D.M. Rousseau and M.B. Arthur, "The boundaryless human resource function: Building agency and community in the new economic era," *Organizational Dynamics* (1999): 7–18; Rousseau, *Psychological Contracts in Organizations.*
13. D.M. Rousseau, V.T. Ho, and J. Greenberg, "Idiosyncratic deals: Theoretical implications of workers bargaining as individuals," *Academy of Management Review* (forthcoming).
14. J. Aselage and R. Eisenberger, "Perceived organizational support and psychological contracts: A theoretical integration," *Journal of Organizational Behavior* 24 (2003): 491–509. Also see, R. Eisenberger, S. Armeli, B. Rexwinkel, P.D. Lynch, and L. Rhoades, "Reciprocation of perceived organizational support," *Journal of Applied Psychology* 86 (2001): 42–51.
15. Eisenberger, Armeli, Rexwinkel, Lynch, and Rhoades, "Reciprocation of perceived organizational support."

16. Aselage and Eisenberger, "Perceived organizational support and psychological contracts."

17. M.S. Clark and R.T. Reis, "Interpersonal processes in close relationships," *Annual Review of Psychology* 39 (1988): 609–72.

18. Ibid.

19. Ibid.

20. M.A. Cronin, "The effect of respect on interdependent work" (PhD diss., Tepper School of Business, Carnegie Mellon University, 2003).

21. F.J. Flynn, "How much should I give and how often? The effects of generosity and frequency of favor exchange on social status and productivity," *Academy of Management Review* 46 (2003): 539–53.

22. Ibid.

23. E.P. Hollander, "Conformity, status, and idiosyncrasy credit," *Psychological Review* 65 (1958): 117–27.

24. See, for example, A. Abele, "Thinking about thinking: Causal, evaluative, and finalistic cognitions about social situations," *European Journal of Social Psychology* 15 (1985): 315–32; G. Peeters and J. Czapinsky, "Positive-negative asymmetry in evaluations: The distinction between affective and informational negativity effects," *European Journal of Social Psychology,* 20 (1990): 3–60.

25. See Rousseau, *Psychological Contracts in Organizations,* for a discussion of how workers compensate for incomplete information regarding the employment relationship by using social cues and other information.

26. G.S. Leventhal, "The distribution of rewards and resources in groups and organizations," in *Advances in Experimental Social Psychology,* vol. 9, ed. L. Berkowitz and E. Walster, pp. 91–131 (New York: Academic Press, 1976).

27. Robert E. Kelly, personal communication, February 2004. R.E. Kelly, *How to Be a Star at Work: Nine Breakthrough Strategies You Need to Succeed* (New York: Times Business, 1998).

28. This is a composite case. It is inspired by the Karen Leary case of an office manager facing a similar situation (L.A. Hill and J. Elias, *Karen Leary (A)* (Cambridge, MA: Harvard Business School Press, 1986). During an in-class discussion of this case, one of my students provided virtually the same example from his experience and relayed the solution his own managing partner used. I have grafted the Karen Leary case onto the events the student reported.

29. Leventhal, "The distribution of rewards and resources in groups and organizations."

30. Greenberg, Roberge, Ho, and Rousseau, "Fairness in idiosyncratic work arrangements." In 2001, when the Democrats became the majority party in the U.S. Senate, they had second thoughts about whether to move their Tuesday lunches from the Lyndon B. Johnson Room, where the minority party has always met, to the Mike Mansfield Room down the hall, where the majority part has had its lunches. The Johnson Room is bright, with giant windows and a gorgeous view, while the Mansfield Room is interior space, dark, and windowless. "I told Tom Daschle we'd be crazy to move," said Senator Charles E. Schumer of New York (p. A26 D.E. Rosenbaum, "Lunch? Sure. Where?" *New York Times,* June 7, 2001). Moving to the majority party's room was less important to the Democrats than knowing they could have moved if they had wanted to.

31. M.B. Arthur and D.M. Rousseau. *The Boundaryless Career: A New Employment Principle for a New Organizational Era* (New York: Oxford University Press, 1996).

32. D. Kahneman and A. Tversky, "Prospect theory: An analysis of decision under risk," *Econometrica* 47 (1979): 263–91.

33. R.J. Bies and J.S. Moag, "Interactional justice: Communication criteria of fairness," in *Research on Negotiation in Organizations,* vol. 1, ed. B. Sheppard, pp. 43–55 (Greenwich, CT: JAI Press, 1986).

34. Wade-Benzoni, Sondak, and Galinsky, "Leaving a legacy"; Greenberg, Roberge, Ho, and Rousseau, "Fairness in idiosyncratic work arrangements."

35. P.E. Tetlock, L. Skitka, and R. Boettger, "Social and cognitive strategies for coping with accountability: Conformity, complexity, and bolstering," *Journal of Personality and Social Psychology* 57 (1989): 632–640; Wade-Benzoni, Sondak, and Galinsky, "Leaving a legacy."

36. A.G.F. Wagstaff, "Equity, equality, and need: Three principles of justice or one? An analysis of 'equity as desert,'" *Current Psychology: Developmental, Learning, Personality, Social* (Summer1994): 138–52, discusses how politeness rules impact allocations, with a focus on how those who allocate downplay the difference between themselves and others. I-deals can lead to inequality, and politeness can convey equality of status or signal the status of the coworker relative to the i-dealer, a means of adding resources back into the relationship. Adding resources back into a situation to promote trust and reduce injury to parties treated less well than others is evident in the practical advice provided to workers who burden their social networks with too many demands, see J.S. Lublin, "Overused contacts respond to apologies, rewards, updates," *Wall Street Journal,* January 4, 2005, B1. For research on rebuilding trust via adding resources back into relationships see and M.A. Korsgaard, E.M. Whitener, and S.E. Brodt, "Trust in the face of conflict: Role of managerial trustworthy behavior and organizational context," *Journal of Applied Psychology* 87 (2002): 312–19.

37. R. Ford and J. Newstrom. "Dues-paying: Managing the costs of recognition," *Business Horizons,* 42 (July–August 1999): 14–20.

38. V. Clark, "Making sense of part-time professional work arrangements" (PhD diss., University of British Columbia, 1998).

39. Ibid.

40. S. Schellenger, "Push for flexibility puts special pressure on factory managers," *Wall Street Journal,* May 9, 2001, p. B1.

41. R.H. Frank, *Choosing the Right Pond: Human Behavior and the Quest for Status* (New York: Oxford University Press, 1985).

42. Thomas Shadwell, *The Virtuoso, II,* 1676.

43. Bies and Moag, "Interactional justice."

44. V.S. Mouly and J.K. Sanharan, "The enactment of envy within organizations: Insights from a New Zealand academic department," *Human Relations* 38 (2002): 36–56 (quotes from p. 46).

45. E.B. Foa and U.G. Foa, *Societal Structures of the Mind* (Springfield, IL: Charles C. Thomas, 1974).

46. J.R. Hackman and G.R. Oldham, *Work Design* (Reading, MA: Addison-Wesley, 1980).

47. One condition we don't treat here is when the initial i-deal is acceptable to coworkers but positions the i-dealer to access subsequent resources that coworkers do value.

48. M.A. Andrew and K.M. Kacmar, "Discriminating among organizational politics, justice and support," *Journal of Organizational Behavior* 22 (2001): 347–66; M. Williams and J.E. Dutton, "Corrosive political climates: The heavy toll of negative political behavior in organizations," in *The Pressing Problems of Modern Organizations: Transforming the Agenda for Research and Practice,* ed. R.E. Quinn, R.M. O'Neill, and L. St. Clair, pp. 3–30 (New York: American Management Association, 1999).

49. V. Gerson, "Pinning down the value of premier benefits," *Business and Health* 15, no. 2 (1997): 31–34.

50. P.S. Goodman, "An examination of referents used in the evaluation of pay," *Organizational Behavior and Human Performance* 12 (1974): 170–95.

51. Ford and Newstrom, "Dues-paying."

52. Ibid., p. 14.

53. Ibid.

54. B.W. Brown and S.A. Woodbury, "Seniority, external labor markets, and faculty pay," *Quarterly Review of Economics and Finance* 38 (1998): 771–98.

55. A phenomenon termed "selective rational exploitation" by Rusbelt and her colleagues; C.E. Rusbelt, M.A. Campbell, and M.E. Price, "Rational selective exploitation and distress: Employee reactions to performance-based and mobility-based reward allocations," *Journal of Personality and Social Psychology* 59 (1990): 487–500; C.E. Rusbelt, D. Lowery, M.L. Hubbarb, and O.J. Maravankin, "Impact of employee mobility and employee performance on the allocation of rewards under conditions of constraint," *Journal of Personality and Social Psychology* 54 (1988): 605–15.

56. D.M. Rousseau and V.T. Ho, "Psychological contract issues in compensation," in *Compensation in Organizations: Current Research and Practice,* ed. S.L. Rynes and B. Gerhart, pp. 273–310 (San Francisco: Jossey-Bass, 2000).

57. Ibid.; Clark and Reis, "Interpersonal processes in close relationships." I also note that social motives and socialization experiences can impact beliefs regarding allocation rules. There is little research on such individual differences in response to personnel decisions, let alone i-deals. This would seem to be a fruitful area of study and a future direction for i-deal research as posed in chapter 10.

58. A. Colella, "Coworker distributive fairness judgments of the workplace accommodations of employees with disabilities," *Academy of Management Review* 26 (2001): 100–116. In effect, the norm of being kind to colleagues in need seems to disappear in many competitive situations where coworkers fear their standing is diminished by another's i-deal. See also R. Paetzold, A. Colella, E. Simnons, and M.F. Garcia, "Peer perceptions of accommodation fairness: The effects of disability, accommodation, and outcome in competitive task situations" (Unpublished manuscript, Texas A&M University, College Station, 2003). D.L. Stone and C. Michaels, "Effects of nature of the disability and competitiveness of reward systems on selection of disabled team members" (Paper presented at the Academy of Management meetings, Dallas, Texas, 1994).

Notes to Chapter 8

1. P. Cappelli, "A market-driven approach to retaining talent," *Harvard Business Review,* January–February 2000, pp. 103–11 (quote from p. 108).

2. J.A. Ritter and L.J. Taylor, "Are employees stakeholders? Corporate finance meets the agency problem," in *Relational Wealth: The Advantages of Stability in a Changing Economy,* ed. C.R. Leana and D.M. Rousseau, pp. 49–61 (New York: Oxford University Press, 2000). Quote from p. 56.

3. D.M. Rousseau, "Changing the deal while keeping the people," *Academy of Management Executive* 10, no. 1 (1996): 50–61.

4. C.E. Rusbelt, D. Lowery, M.L. Hubbarb, and O.J. Maravankin, "Impact of employee mobility and employee performance on the allocation of rewards under conditions of constraint," *Journal of Personality and Social Psychology* 54 (1988): 605–15; C.E. Rusbelt, M.A. Campbell, and M.E. Price, "Rational selective exploitation and distress: Employee reactions to performance-based and mobility-based reward allocations," *Journal of Personality and Social Psychology* 59 (1990): 487–500.

5. R. Ford and J. Newstrom. "Dues-paying: Managing the costs of recognition,"

Business Horizons 42 (July–August 1999): 14–20.

6. D.M. Rousseau, V.T. Ho, and J. Greenberg, "Idiosyncratic deals: Some I-deal propositions," *Academy of Management Review* (forthcoming).

7. D.M. Rousseau and S.A. Tijoriwala, "What's a good reason to change? Motivated reasoning and social accounts in promoting organizational change," *Journal of Applied Psychology* 84 (1999): 514–28.

8. E.H. Schein, "Career anchors revisited: implications for career development in the 21st century," *Academy of Management Executive* 10, no. 4 (1996): 80–88.

9. D.M. Rousseau and Ho, "Psychological contract issues in compensation," in *Compensation in Organizations: Current Research and Practice,* ed. S.L. Rynes and B. Gerhart, pp. 273–310 (San Francisco: Jossey-Bass, 2000).

10. F.C. Ashby and A.R. Pell, *Embracing Excellence: How to Become the Employer of Choice to Attract and Keep the Best Talent* (Paramus, NJ: Prentice-Hall, 2001).

11. J. Pfeffer, "Six dangerous myths about pay," *Harvard Business Review* (May–June 1998) 108-119.

12. R.E. Miles and C.C. Snow, "Designing strategic human resource systems," *Organizational Dynamics* (Summer 1984): 36–52; D.M. Rousseau, *Psychological Contracts in Organizations: Understanding Written and Unwritten Agreements* (Newbury Park, CA: Sage, 1995). Note that Jeff Pfeffer has questioned how close HR practices and business strategy need to be aligned, arguing that firms that use "best practices" such as high-involvement workforces, skill building, and retention are likely to perform well regardless; J. Pfeffer, *Competitive Advantage Through People: Unleashing the Power of the Work Force* (Boston: Harvard Business School Press, 1994). I-deals, particularly recruiting and retention-based ones, are used in response to market forces more on a case-by-case basis. See, for example, C.A. Olson, D.P. Schwab, and B. Rau, "The effects of local market conditions on two pay-setting systems in the federal sector," *Industrial and Labor Relations Review* 53 (2000): 272–89; C. DeBaise, "Something extra: Companies are turning to 'special' options to keep valued employees," *Wall Street Journal,* April 6, 2000, p. R7.

13. E.P. Lazear, "Agency, earnings profiles, productivity, and hours restrictions," *American Economic Review* 71 (1981): 606–20; P. Milgrom and J. Roberts, "An economic approach to influence activities in organizations," *American Journal of Sociology* 94 (1988): S154–S179; M. Waldman, "Ex ante versus ex post optimal promotion rules: The case of internal promotion," *Economic Inquiry* 41 (2003): 27–41; A.S. Tsui, J.L. Pearce, L.W. Porter, and A.M. Tripoli, "Alternative approaches to the employee-organization relationship: Does investment pay off?" *Academy of Management Journal* 40 (1997): 1089–1121. For contemporary examples of the expansion of standardized rewards when large numbers of skilled workers are needed, see J. Pereira, "Back in the game: After big cutbacks, employer 401(k) contributions appear to be on the rise again," *Wall Street Journal,* July 19, 2004, p. R3.

14. S.L. Gaertner, J.F. Dovidio, and B.A. Bachman, "Revisiting the contact hypothesis: The induction of common group identity," *International Journal of International Relations* 20 (1996): 271–90; D.M. Rousseau, "Why workers still identify with their organization," *Journal of Organizational Behavior* 19 (1998): 217–33.

15. P.D. Sherer, "Bringing organization and labor relationships into psychological research on compensation," in Rynes and Gerhart, *Compensation in Organizations,* pp. 241–72.

16. P.D. Sweeney and D.B. MacFarlin, "Social comparisons and income satisfaction," *Journal of Occupational and Organizational Psychology* 77 (2004): 149–54.

17. D. Cowherd and D. Levine, "Product quality and pay equity between lower-level

employees and top management: An investigation of distributive justice theory," *Administrative Science Quarterly* 37 (1992): 302–20.

18. See J. Martin, *Organizational Culture: Mapping the Terrain* (Thousand Oaks, CA: Sage, 2002), for a discussion of differentiation effects associated with positions. I note that positional differences can make across-the-board flexibility difficult to achieve due to bona fide job requirements. One hospital's dress code specified that clinical caregivers could not have multiple pierced ears (though managers had no dress code). This difference irked some employees, who saw it as a double standard. Only when a nurse was assigned to a management task force did she learn that the reason for the rule was to manage relations with the hospital's elderly clientele. When distinctive roles and titles coincide with legitimate differences in treatment, the reasons can be understood as appropriate—but only if those reasons are effectively communicated and reiterated as newcomers join the organization.

19. Rousseau and Ho, "Psychological contract issues in compensation."

20. R. Eisenberger, J. Cummings, S. Armeli, and P. Lynch, "Perceived organizational support, discretionary treatment, and job satisfaction," *Journal of Applied Psychology* 82 (1997): 812–20.

21. M.C. Bloom and G.T. Milkovich, "Issues in managerial compensation research," *Trends in Organizational Behavior,* vol. 3 (Chichester, UK: John Wiley and Sons, 1966), pp. 23–47.

22. J.E. Rosenbaum, "Tournament mobility: Career patterns in a corporation," *Administrative Science Quarterly* 24 (1979): 220–41.

23. On the dysfunctional aspects of competition, see for example, T.R. Mitchell and W.S. Silver, "Individual and group goals when workers are interdependent: Effects on task strategies and performance," *Journal of Applied Psychology* 75 (1990): 185–93.

24. J.P. Macduffie, "Human resource bundles and manufacturing performance: Organizational logic and flexible production systems in the world auto industry," *Industrial and Labor Relations Review* 48 (1995): 197–221.

25. Eisenberger, Cummings, Armeli, and Lynch, "Perceived organizational support, discretionary treatment, and job satisfaction."

26. Miles and Snow, "Designing strategic human resource systems"; L.R. Gomez-Mejia and D. Balkin, *Compensation, Organizational Strategy, and Firm Performance,* (Cincinnati: South-Western, 1992).

27. Rousseau, *Psychological Contracts in Organizations.*

28. Rousseau and Tijoriwala, "What's a good reason to change?"; C.J. Ferrante and D.M. Rousseau, "Bringing open book management into the academic line of sight," in *Employee Versus Owner Issues,* ed. C.L. Cooper and D.M. Rousseau, Trends in Organizational Behavior series, vol. 8 (Chichester, UK: John Wiley and Sons, 2001).

29. For information on flexibility for individual workers in professional service organizations such as accounting firms, see the following articles, which describe practices in these firms over time: "Accountant consult thyself," *Economist* 308 (September 10, 1988): 89–90; "Accounting women," *Insight,* http://www.insight-mag.com/insight/03/11–12/col-4-pt2-Understudy.asp (accessed July 12, 2004); L. Uchitelle, "Job or 'mommy track'? Some do both, in phases," *New York Times,* July 5, 2002, pp. C1, C5.

30. As quoted in M. Hammers, "A 'family friendly' backlash," *Workforce Management,* August 2003, pp. 77–79.

31. On the role of market power in incentive systems, see M.M. Elvira, "Pay me now or pay me later: Analyzing the relationship between bonus and promotion incentives," *Work and Occupations* 28 (2001): 346–70. For the role of interdependence on the preference for standardized or equal rewards, see D. Bagarozzi, "The effects of cohesiveness on distributive justice," *Journal of Psychology* 100 (1982): 267–73; and T. Schwinger,

"Just allocations of goods: Decisions among three principles," in *Justice and Social Interaction: Experimental and Theoretical Contributions from Psychological Research,* ed. G. Mikula, pp. 95–125 (New York: Springer-Verlag, 1980).

32. Lazear, "Agency, earnings profiles, productivity, and hours restrictions"; C.R. Leana and D.M. Rousseau, *Relational Wealth: The Advantages of Stability in a Changing Economy* (New York: Oxford, 2000).

33. D.M. Cable and T.A. Judge, "Pay preferences and job search decisions: A person-organization fit perspective," *Personnel Psychology* 47 (1994): 317–48; H.G. Heneman and T.A. Judge, "Compensation attitudes," in Rynes and Gerhart, *Compensation in Organizations,* pp. 61–103.

34. P.D. Sherer, "Bringing organization and labor relationships into psychological research on compensation," in Rynes and Gerhart, *Compensation in Organizations,* pp. 241–72.

35. Ritter and Taylor, "Are employees stakeholders?"

36. G.T. Milkovich and C. Milkovich, "Strengthening the pay-performance relationship: The research," *Compensation and Benefits Review* 24, no. 6 (1992): 53–62. R.M. Wiseman, L.R. Gomez-Mejia, and M. Fugate, "Rethinking compensation risk," in Rynes and Gerhart, *Compensation in Organizations,* pp. 311–47.

37. R.L. Heneman, G.E. Ledford, and M.T. Gresham, "The changing nature of work and its effects on compensation design and delivery," in Rynes and Gerhart, *Compensation in Organizations,* pp. 195–240.

38. Jean de la Bruyere from *Les Caractères*, as quoted on p. 492 in *The Macmillan Dictionary of Quotations* (Edison, NJ: Chartwell Books, 2000).

39. R.H. Frank, "Are workers paid their marginal product?" *American Economic Review* 74 (1984): 549–71; R.H. Frank, *Choosing the Right Pond: Human Behavior and the Quest for Status* (New York: Oxford University Press, 1985).

40. Frank, "Are workers paid their marginal product?"; Frank, *Choosing the Right Pond*. Nonstars, and established stars with higher tenure, tend to quit at much lower rates than newly ranked stars; B. Groysberg and A. Nanda, "Does stardom affect job mobility? Evidence from analyst turnover in investment banks" (Unpublished manuscript, Harvard Business School, 2001). While the latter authors attribute this lower turnover among stars to firm-specific capital, I am not convinced that such an explanation applies in an industry with the level of standardization characteristic of investment banking. The argument downplaying firm-specific capital in favor of industry-specific capital is summarized in D.M. Rousseau and Z. Shperling, "Ownership and the changing employment relationship: Why stylized notions of labor no longer generally apply. A reply to Zardkoohi and Paetzgold." *Academy of Management Review* 29 (2004): 562–69. I think it is more likely that established stars are advantaged by the particular idiosyncratic rewards they access via their long-standing roles as high contributors in the firms that employ them.

41. Frank, *Choosing the Right Pond,* p. 56.

42. Ibid. Participants in a work group are rarely compensated solely for their current performance, although rewards are more often allocated based on merit and market value in today's workforce due to expanded access to information and performance metrics.

43. Managers in highly decentralized units can also act as employers for all intents and purposes, see for example, G.E. Dabos and D.M. Rousseau, "Mutuality and reciprocity in the psychological contracts of employee and employer," *Journal of Applied Psychology* 89 (2004): 52–72.

44. See, for example, V.S. Clark, *Making Sense of Part-Time Professional Work Arrangements* (PhD diss., University of British Columbia, 1998); and A.R. Hochschild, *Time Bind: When Work Becomes Home and Home Becomes Work* (New York: Metropolitan Books, 1997).

45. L.M. Shore, L.W. Porter, and S.A. Zahra, "Employer-oriented strategic approaches to the employee-organization relationship," in *The Employment Relationship: Examining Psychological and Contextual Perspectives,* ed. J.A.-M. Coyle-Shapiro, L.M. Shore, M.S. Taylor, and L.E. Tetrick, pp. 135–60 (New York: Oxford University Press, 2004). The agency perspective argues that managers in the same firm should have little variation in the way they implement employment relations (p. 146).

46. See, for example, Y. Fried, R.B. Tiegs, and A.R. Bellamy, "Personal and interpersonal predictors of supervisors' avoidance of evaluating subordinates," *Journal of Applied Psychology* 77 (1992): 462–68.

47. Clark, *Making Sense of Part-Time Professional Work Arrangements*; Hochschild, *Time Bind.*

48. V.D. Miller, J.R. Johnson, Z. Hart, and D.L. Peterson, "A test of antecedents and outcomes of employee role negotiation ability," *Journal of Applied Communication Research* (1999): 24–48. Self-rated high-status work-group members had more negotiability. Other items on this list include:

- I have considerable "say-so" in shaping and adjusting my work role.
- I am able to negotiate the nature and content of my work role.

49. M.S. Feldman and B.T. Pentland, "Reconceptualizing organizational routines as a source of flexibility and change," *Administrative Science Quarterly* 48 (2003): 94–120.

50. L.L. Levesque, "Role creation processes in start-up firms" (PhD diss., Graduate School of Industrial Administration, Carnegie Mellon University, 2001), p. 77.

51. R.T. Mowday, "The exercise of upward influence in organizations," *Administrative Science Quarterly* 23 (1978): 137–56; E.P. Hollander, "Conformity, status, and idiosyncrasy credit," *Psychological Review* 63 (1958): 117–27.

52. Decentralization gives lower and mid-level managers freedom; K.J. Krone, "Structuring constraints on perceptions of upward influence and supervisory relationships," *Southern Communication Journal* 59 (1994): 215–26.

53. G. Yukl and D.D. Van Fleet, "Theory and research on leadership in organizations," in *Handbook of Industrial Organizational Psychology,* 2nd ed., ed. M.D. Dunnette and L. Hough (Palo Alto, CA: Consulting Psychologists Press, 1992) vol. 3, pp. 147–97.

54. T.R. Hinkin and C.A. Schriesheim, "An examination of subordinate-perceived relationships between leader reward and punishment behavior and leader bases of power," *Human Relations* 47 (1994): 779–800.

55. Krone, "Structuring constraints on perceptions of upward influence and supervisory relationships"; G. Graen and J.F. Cashman, "A role-making model of leadership in formal organizations: A developmental approach," in *Leadership Frontiers,* ed. J.G. Hunt and L.L. Larson (Carbondale: Southern Illinois University, 1975), pp. 143–65.

56. F.J. Flynn and J. Brockner, "It's different to give than to receive: Predictors of giver's and receiver's reactions to favor exchange," *Journal of Applied Psychology* 88 (2003): 1034–45.

57. H. Tajfel, "Social psychology of intergroup relations," *Annual Review of Psychology* 33 (1982): 1–39.

58. L. Thompson, *The Heart and Mind of the Negotiator,* 2nd ed. (Upper Saddle River, NJ: Prentice-Hall, 2001).

59. Ibid.

60. For a discussion of the process of learning via modeling, see A. Bandura, *Social Foundations of Thought and Action: A Social Cognitive View* (Upper Saddle River, NJ: Prentice Hall, 1985).

61. Ibid.

62. S.D. Friedman, P. Cristensen, and J. DeGroot, "Work and life: The end of the zero-sum game," *Harvard Business Review* (November–December 1998): 119–29.

63. R.P. Castanias and C.E. Helfat, "Managerial resources and rents," *Journal of Management*, 17 (1991): 155–72. Individual managers have been known to take pains to make it clear that acts of support they provide are on behalf of the employer and not themselves personally. A plant manager, Paul Sweet of Parker Hannifin Corporation, was celebrated in the *Wall Street Journal* for saving his 130 factory workers their jobs through creative improvisation. He moved people from parts of the plant where work was slow into busier areas, shifting them from assembly lines to sales or new product development, and bringing work in-house that was once outsourced. When one worker approached him and said that he was going to do the manager a favor by taking more blocks of unpaid leave, Paul Sweet was irked. Telling the man that he appreciated it, Sweet reminded him that this was not a personal favor but something that needed to be done for the factory; T. Aeppel, "A factory manager improvises to save jobs in a downturn," *Wall Street Journal,* December 27, 2001, pp. A1, A14.

64. Clark, *Making Sense of Part-Time Professional Work Arrangements*; G. Acklerlof, "Gift exchange and efficiency wages: Four views," *American Economic Review* 74 (1984): 79–83.

65. Clark, *Making Sense of Part-Time Professional Work Arrangements,* p. 71.

66. G. Graen and J.F. Cashman, "A role-making model of leadership in formal organizations: A developmental approach," in Hunt and Larson, *Leadership Frontiers.*

67. Ibid. Managers who act as principals as well as agents may promise more to workers than their own superiors might be willing to authorize. This difference in what local managers and senior executives are willing to commit to the workforce may account in part for the gap between worker perceptions of inducements their employer offers and what executives report having promised; L.W. Porter, J.L. Pearce, A.M. Tripoli, and K.M. Lewis, "Differential perceptions of employers' inducements: Implications for psychological contracts," *Journal of Organizational Behavior* 19 (1998): 769–82. Such behaviors on the part of managers suggest that it might be useful to examine the idiosyncrasies managers themselves introduce both into their own and their employee's employment relationship.

68. M.H. Bazerman, *Judgment in Managerial Decision Making,* 5th ed. (New York: Wiley, 2001).

69. D.M. Rousseau, "Assessing organizational culture: The case for multiple methods," in *Frontiers of Industrial and Organizational Psychology* ed. B. Schneider (San Francisco: Jossey-Bass, 1990), vol. 3, pp. 153–92.

70. J. Martin, *Cultures in Organizations* (New York: Oxford, 1992).

71. Hochschild, *Time Bind,* p. 139. To downplay the effects of status and create a more integrated culture, firms have been known to remove positional differences in perks and privileges; see, for example, E. Tahmincioglu, "Equality in offices: Some companies have moved managers from corners to the cubicles, saving cash and dissolving barriers," *Star Tribune* (Minneapolis), December 15, 2000, p. 1D.

72. J.S. Adams, "Toward an understanding of equity," *Journal of Abnormal and Social Psychology* 67 (1963): 422–36.

73. K.J. Klein, L. Berman, and M. Dickson, "May I work part time? An exploration of predicted employer responses to employee requests for part time work," *Journal of Vocational Behavior* 57 (2000): 85–101. E.A. Mannix, M.A. Neale, and G.B. Northcraft, "Equity, equality or need? The effects of organizational culture on the allocation of benefits and burden," *Organizational Behavior and Human Decision Processes* 63 (1995): 276–86. The notion that organizational legitimacy rests in procedures and incentives that allow realization of deeply held values is a hallmark of institutional theory; A.

Stinchcombe, "Social structure and organizations," in *Handbook of Organizations,* ed. J.G. March, pp. 142–93 (Chicago: Rand McNally, 1975); A. Stinchcombe, "On the virtues of the old institutionalism," *Annual Review of Sociology* 23 (1997): 1–18.

74. C.E. Rusbelt, D. Lowery, M.L. Hubbarb, and O.J. Maravankin, "Impact of employee mobility and employee performance on the allocation of rewards under conditions of constraint," *Journal of Personality and Social Psychology* 54 (1988): 605–15; C.E. Rusbelt, M.A. Campbell, and M.E. Price, "Rational selective exploitation and distress: Employee reactions to performance-based and mobility based reward allocations," *Journal of Personality and Social Psychology* 59 (1990): 487–500.

75. L.M. Shore, L.E. Tetrick, S. Taylor, J.A.-M. Coyle-Shapiro, R. Liden, J. McLean Parks, E. Wolfe Morrison, et al., "The employee-organization relationship: A timely concept in a period of transition," in *Research in Personnel and Human Resource Management,* ed. J. Martucchio, vol. 23, pp. 291–370 (San Diego, CA: Elsevier, 2004). If everything is subject to a bargaining process, it signals that the employment relationship is more of a transaction, suitable to organizations where workers do their jobs independently. Nonetheless, it can be frustrating when the only way to get a raise, a new computer, or time off—or any other really attractive feature of employment —is to bargain with the boss. Ensuring that important inducements and supports, from flexibility to training, are automatically provided by the firm operates as both a means of attracting and retaining quality people and a way of signaling the quality of the employment relationship. In transactional employment, this might mean providing a minimally safe and functional work setting; in more relational employment where workers are interdependent, more elaborate personal supports and benefits might be the basic minimum.

76. M.S. Viteles, *Industrial Psychology* (New York: Norton, 1932).

77. D.M. Rousseau and R. Schalk, *Psychological Contracts in Employment: Cross-National Perspectives* (Newbury Park, CA: Sage, 2000).

Notes to Chapter 9

1. J.N. Baron and D.M. Kreps, *Strategic Human Resources: Frameworks for General Managers* (New York: John Wiley and Sons, 1999).

2. D.M. Rousseau and R. Schalk, *Psychological Contracts in Employment: Cross-National Perspectives* (Newbury Park, CA: Sage, 2000).

3. Ibid.

4. See E. Zerubavel, *Hidden Rhythms: Schedule and Calendars in Social Life* (Berkeley: University of California Press, 1981) for a general discussion of cultural conflicts regarding personal and work time.

5. R.B. Freeman and J. Rogers, *What Workers Want* (Ithaca, NY: ILR Press, 1999).

6. Ibid.; D.M. Rousseau, "Psychological contracts in the United States: Diversity, individualism, and associability in the marketplace," in Rousseau and Schalk, *Psychological Contracts in Employment.*

7. L. Cadin, "Does psychological contract theory work in France?" in Rousseau and Schalk, *Psychological Contracts in Employment,* pp. 67–86; L. Sels, M. Janssens, I. Van der Brande, and B. Overlaet, "Belgium: A culture of compromise," in Rousseau and Schalk, *Psychological Contracts in Employment,* pp. 47–66.

8. Nonetheless, these conditions warrant further consideration by employment scholars.

9. J.L. Pearce, *Organization and Management in the Embrace of Government* (Mahwah, NJ: Erlbaum, 2001).

10. Cadin, "Does psychological contract theory work in France?"

11. S. Ang, M.L. Tan, and K.Y. Ng, "Psychological contracts in Singapore," in Rousseau and Schalk, *Psychological Contracts in Employment*, pp. 213–30.

12. Rousseau and Schalk, *Psychological Contracts in Employment*.

13. R. Westwood, P. Sparrow, and A. Leung, "Challenges to the psychological contract in Hong Kong," *International Journal of Human Resource Management* 12 (2001): 621–51.

14. P. Herriot and C. Pemberton, *New Deals: The Revolution in Managerial Careers* (Chichester, UK: John Wiley and Sons, 1998); M.B. Arthur, K. Inkson, and J. Pringle, *The New Careers: Individual Action and Economic Change* (Newbury Park, CA: Sage, 1999).

15. Rousseau, "Psychological contracts in the United States."

16. S. Peel and K. Inkson, "Economic deregulation and psychological contracts: The New Zealand experience," in Rousseau and Schalk, *Psychological Contracts in Employment*, pp. 195–212; Arthur, Inkson, and Pringle, *The New Careers*; K. Inkson, A. Heising, and D.M. Rousseau, "The interim manager: Prototype of the 21st century worker," *Human Relations* 54 (2001): 259–84. I note however that legal changes in 2004 have increased regulation in some aspects of the New Zealand labor market; see "The Employment Relations Amendment passed," www.psa.org.nz/era.asp accessed, January 5, 2005.

17. Arthur, Inkson, and Pringle, *The New Careers*; Rousseau, "Psychological contracts in the United States."

18. Ang, Tan, and Ng, "Psychological contracts in Singapore."

19. Ng and Ang, "Human resource management in Asia"; Z.X. Chen, A.S.Tsui, and J.L. Farh, "Loyalty to supervisor versus organizational commitment: Relationships to employee performance in China," *Journal of Occupational and Organizational Psychology* 75 (2002): 339–56; C. Hui, C. Lee, and D.M. Rousseau, "Employment relationships in China: Do workers relate to the organization or to people?" *Organization Science* 15 (2004): 232–40.

20. Ng and Ang, "Human resource management in Asia."

21. Ibid.

22. *Managing in China,* videocassette, P.S. Goodman, producer and director (Glenshaw, PA: Changing Nature of Work Series, 1996).

23. C.C. Chen, Y.-R. Chen, and K. Xin, "Guanxi practices and trust in management: A procedural justice perspective," *Organization Science* 15 (2003): 200–209.

24. K.Y. Ng and S. Ang, "Human resource management in Asia: Understanding variations in human resource practices using a resource exchange perspective," in *Handbook of Asian Management,* ed. K. Leung and S. White (London: Kluwer, 2003).

25. R. Florida, *The Rise of the Creative Class: And How It's Transforming Work, Leisure, Community, and Everyday Life* (New York: Basic Books, 2002).

26. K.J. Klein, L. Berman, and M. Dickson, "May I work part time? An exploration of predicted employer responses to employee requests for part time work," *Journal of Vocational Behavior* 57 (2000): 85–101.

27. It is unclear whether either weak or strong situations are more prone to politicking and self-serving behavior. M. Williams and J.E. Dutton, "Corrosive political climates: The heavy toll of negative political behavior in organizations," in *The Pressing Problems of Modern Organizations: Transforming the Agenda for Research and Practice,* ed. R.E. Quinn, R.M. O'Neill, and L. St. Clair, pp. 3–30 (New York: American Management Association, 1999), report in their review that politicking is more likely to occur when power is concentrated at the top of the hierarchy (a strong-situation characteristic), formalization is low, the performance appraisal system is weak (weak situational features), advancement is restricted, and manager-subordinate relations are of low quality.

28. K. Weick, "Enactment and the boundaryless career," in *The Boundaryless Career: A New Employment Principle for a New Organizational Era,* ed. M.B. Arthur and D.M. Rousseau, pp. 40–57 (New York: Oxford University Press, 1996). The expression "people make the place" describes how organizations are shaped by the individuals whom they recruit and retain; B. Schneider, "The people make the place," *Personnel Psychology* 40 (1987) 437–53.

29. R.H. Frank, *Choosing the Right Pond: Human Behavior and the Quest for Status* (New York: Oxford University Press, 1985).

30. Rousseau and Schalk, *Psychological Contracts in Employment.*

31. Cadin, "Does psychological contract theory work in France?" p. 74.

32. The MBA quote is from a study conducted by Rousseau, Ho, and Kim. See D.M. Rousseau, V.T. Ho, and T.G. Kim, "I-deals and the psychological contract" (Unpublished mansucript, Carnegie Mellon University, Pittsburgh, PA, 2004). The veteran worker quote is from an employee at Fel-Pro in Skokie, Illinois, in 1991.

33. A. Colella, "Coworker distributive fairness judgments of the workplace accommodation of employees with disabilities," *Academy of Management Review* 26 (2001): 100–116; A. Colella, R. Paetzgold, and M. Belliveau, "Coworkers' procedural justice judgements of the workplace accommodation of employees with disabilities" (Unpublished manuscript, Texas A&M University, Department of Management, College Station, TX, 2002).

34. D.L. Stone and C. Michaels, "Effects of nature of the disability and competitiveness of reward systems on selection of disabled team members" (Paper presented at the annual meeting of the Academy of Management, Dallas, TX, 1994); R.L. Paetzgold, A. Colella, E. Simmons, and M. Fernanda Garcia, "Peer perceptions of accommodation fairness: The effects of disability, accommodation and outcome in competitive task situations" (Unpublished manuscript, Texas A&M University, Department of Management, College Station, TX, 2002).

35. Quote from S. Encel, *Equality and Authority: A Study of Class, Status and Power in Australia* (Melbourne: Longman Cheshire, 1970). B. Kabanoff, N.L. Jimmieson, and M.J. Lewis, "Psychological contracts in Australia: A 'fair go' or a 'not so happy' transition?" in Rousseau and Schalk, *Psychological Contracts in Employment,* pp. 19–46.

36. Ng and Ang, "Human resource management in Asia"; M. Morishima, "Embedding HRM in a social context," *British Journal of Industrial Relations* 33 (1995): 617–40.

37. R. Schalk and C. Freese, "Psychological contracts in the Netherlands: Dualism, flexibility, and security," in Rousseau and Schalk, *Psychological Contracts in Employment,* pp. 176–93.

38. Ng and Ang, "Human resource management in Asia."

39. H. Diaz-Saenz and P.D. Witherspoon, "Psychological contracts in Mexico: Reflections of historical, familial, and contemporary forces on work relationships," in Rousseau and Schalk, *Psychological Contracts in Employment.*

40. P. d'Iribarne, "Motivating workers in emerging countries: Universal tools and local adaptations," *Journal of Organizational Behavior* 23 (2002): 243–56.

41. R.H. Frank and P.J. Cook, *Winner Take All: How More and More Americans Compete for Fewer and Bigger Prizes, Encouraging Economic Waste, Income Inequality, and an Impoverished Cultural Life* (New York: Free Press, 1995); Rousseau, "Psychological contracts in the United States."

42. D.M. Rousseau and R.J. Anton, "Fairness and implied contract obligations in termination: A policy capturing study," *Human Performance* 1 (1988): 273–89; D.M. Rousseau and R.J. Anton, "Fairness and implied contract obligations in termination: The role of contributions, promises, and performance," *Journal of Organizational Be-*

havior 12 (1991): 287–99; D.M. Rousseau and K. Aquino, "Fairness and implied contract obligations in termination: The role of remedies, social accounts, and procedural justice," *Human Performance* 6 (1993): 135–49.

43. Florida, *The Rise of the Creative Class.*

44. Ng and Ang, "Human resource management in Asia."

45. Euromonitor Pic, *European Business Planning Factors: Key Issues for Corporate Strategy in the 1990s* (London: Euromonitor Pic, 1992).

46. The quote is from Ursula Goodenough, *The Sacred Depths of Nature* (New York: Oxford University Press, 1998), p. 67.

47. The repeal of labor regulation and welfare protections may also create greater pressure on workers who can negotiate to do so if employers provide fewer standard benefits. See for example, G. T. Sims, "Germany under a microscope: Its labor-market experiment will offer lessons for rest of Europe." *Wall Street Journal,* December 31, 2004, p. A6.

48. Ng and Ang, "Human resource management in Asia."

Notes to Chapter 10

1. Ralph Waldo Emerson, in *Bartlett's Familiar Quotations.* 15th ed. (Boston: Little, Brown, 1980), p. 500.

2. R. Marion, *The Edge of Organization: Chaos and Complexity Theories of Formal Social Systems* (Thousand Oaks: Sage, 1999), p. xiii.

3. P. Milgrom and J. Roberts, *Economics, Organization, and Management* (Englewood Cliffs, NJ: Prentice-Hall, 1992).

4. Leo Troy as referenced in H.N. Wheeler, *The Future of the American Labor Movement* (New York: Cambridge University Press, 2002), pp. 4–6.

5. J. Rawls, *A Theory of Justice* (Cambridge, MA: Belknap of Harvard University Press, 1971), p. 62.

6. S.J. Brams and A.D. Taylor, *Fair Division: From Cake Cutting to Dispute Resolution* (Cambridge: Cambridge University Press, 1996).

7. L. Thompson, *The Heart and Mind of the Negotiator,* 2nd ed. (Upper Saddle River, NJ: Prentice-Hall, 2001).

8. M.S. Feldman and B.T. Pentland, "Reconceptualizing organizational routines as a source of flexibility and change," *Administrative Science Quarterly* 48 (2003): 94–120.

9. Ibid.

10. For a discussion of cafeteria plans, see M.W. Barringer and G.T. Milkovich, "A theoretical exploration of the adoption and design of flexible benefit plans: A case of human resource innovation," *Academy of Management Review* 23 (1997): 305–24. It is important to reiterate that some degree of standardization or good bureaucracy is necessary for effective organizational functioning. We who have grown up in North America or in western Europe often take for granted the institutional infrastructure of job descriptions and position requirements. When people must work interdependently and cooperatively to get work done, consistency in treatment and transparency in reward allocations promote a climate of trust. Despite the bad rap that bureaucracy receives as "red tape," impeding individual action and choice, Jone Pearce and her colleagues persuasively argue that "insufficient bureaucracy" can erode trust and commitment. The point is that too little bureaucracy has negative consequences. This is to say that standardized procedures and policies are necessary and appropriate for recurring circumstances such as the allocation of essential inducements for job retention and hard work, such as pay and promotion. Nonetheless, just as one can have too little bureaucracy, one can have too much, in particular when flexibility is required in the face of changing

circumstances and new demands. We need to carefully craft the boundaries between insufficient bureaucracy and rigidity. Understanding when it is legitimate and necessary to promote idiosyncrasy in employment relationships is a means to accomplish this. See J.L. Pearce, I. Branyicki, and G. Bakacski, "Person-based reward systems: A theory of organizational reward practices in reform-communist organizations," *Journal of Organizational Behavior* 15 (1994): 261–82; and J.L Pearce, I. Branyiucczki, and G.A. Bigley, "Insufficient bureaucracy: Trust and commitment in particularistic organizations," *Organizational Science* 11 (2000): 148–62.

11. *Paid Time Off Banks* (Scottsdale, AZ: World at Work, 2000).

12. S. Iyengar and M. Lepper, "When choice is too much of a good thing," *Journal of Personality and Social Psychology*, 79 (2000): 995–1006.

13. J. Galbraith, *Designing Complex Organizations* (Reading, MA: Addison-Wesley, 1973).

14. For the complex individual and organization-based learning required to make matrix organizations effective see "The Matrix Organization," www.gantthead.com/presentation (accessed October 5, 2004). T. Chi and P. Nystrom, "An Economic Analysis of Matrix Structure, Using Multinational Corporations as an Illustration," *Managerial and Decision Economics*, 19 (1998): 141–56.

15. Thompson, *The Heart and Mind of the Negotiator*.

16. Ibid.; L. Babcock and S. Laschever, *Women Don't Ask* (Princeton, NJ: Princeton University Press, 2003).

17. Babcock and Laschever, *Women Don't Ask*.

18. Allocation rules have been found to vary by resource type. See J. McLean Parks, D.E. Conlon, S. Ang, and R. Bontempo, "The manager giveth, the manager taketh away: Variation in distribution/recovery rules due to resource type and cultural orientation," *Journal of Management* 25 (1999): 723–57. In particular, status and love/affiliation/ friendship resources have been found to generate wide disagreement on how to allocate them. The impact of the nature of resources exchanged in employment has received relatively little attention, not only from the perspective of allocation fairness but also in terms of the meanings workers and employers attribute to them.

19. Rawls, *A Theory of Justice*, p. 62.

Index

About the Author

Denise M. Rousseau is the H.J. Heinz II Professor of Organizational Behavior and Public Policy at Carnegie Mellon University and served as president of the Academy of Management in 2004–2005. A graduate of the University of California at Berkeley (AB, MA, PhD), she has been elected Fellow of the American Psychological Association, the Society for Industrial/ Organizational Psychology, the Academy of Management, and the British Academy of Management, and currently is editor-in-chief of the *Journal of Organizational Behavior*. Her book *Psychological Contracts in Organizations* won the Academy of Management's Terry Award in 1996. Her research examines employment relations and change in start-ups, high-technology firms, hospitals, high-reliability organizations, and nonprofits in many countries.